Essential Microeconomics for Public Policy Analysis

JOHN M. LEVY

Westport, Connecticut
London

Library of Congress Cataloging-in-Publication Data

Levy, John M.
  Essential microeconomics for public policy analysis / John M.
  Levy.
      p.   cm.
  Includes bibliographical references and index.
  ISBN 0–275–94362–3 (alk. paper).—ISBN 0–275–94363–1 (pbk. :
  alk. paper)
    1. Microeconomics. 2. Neoclassical school of economics.
  3. Economic policy. I. Title.
  HB172.L48   1995
  338.5—dc20   95–7990

British Library Cataloguing in Publication Data is available.

Library of Congress Catalog Card Number: 95–7990
ISBN: 0–275–94362–3 (hardcover)
      0–275–94363–1 (paperback)

First published in 1995

Praeger Publishers, 88 Post Road West, Westport, CT 06881
An imprint of Greenwood Publishing Group, Inc.

Printed in the United States of America

The paper used in this book complies with the
Permanent Paper Standard issued by the National
Information Standards Organization (Z39.48–1984).

10 9 8 7 6

To Lucie, Rachel, Bernie, and Kara

Contents

Figures and Tables

FIGURES

TABLES

Acknowledgments

I wish to express thanks to my former teaching assistant, Jaixun Dong, for preparing all of the artwork for this book and to my former student, Bradley K. Townsend, for contributing the chapter on "The Economics of Health Risk Analysis."

Introduction

The purpose of this book is to provide a background in microeconomics for the study of public policy. The emphasis is on basic economic concepts and their implications for policy.

WHAT IS MICROECONOMICS?

Because this book is about microeconomics, we begin by distinguishing between microeconomics and macroeconomics. Macroeconomics deals with the workings of the economy taken as a whole. The macroeconomist will thus be concerned with matters such as the level of employment, changes in the money supply and interest rates, the rate of growth of the GNP, the rate of inflation, and the like. The microeconomist takes these magnitudes and trends as given and then looks at particular parts of the economy. He or she might look at the market for a particular good, to see how the burden of a particular tax is distributed, or to view the effect of a particular regulation or law on a certain industry or market. Benefit-cost analysis, which is performed for virtually every major state or federal project, is essentially applied microeconomics.

Though the distinction is clear in principle, the two realms do intersect. For example, the rate of inflation is generally considered to be a macroeconomic question, affected by such matters as the rate of growth in the money supply. But a myriad of laws and regulations affect the cost structure of firms, the mobility of labor, and the like. Thus, these micro matters will have an effect upon how suppliers respond to increases in demand—do they respond primarily with increases in output or primarily with increases in prices? Similarly, the rate at which an economy grows is considered to be a macroeconomic matter related to such factors as the rate of change in the size of the capital stock and the labor force of the country. But clearly, the rate of growth is also affected by the efficiency with which particular firms, industries, and markets operate. That takes us back into the realm of microeconomics.

Toward the end of the Carter administration there began a movement toward deregulation. We have subsequently seen major deregulation in trucking, the airlines, and banking, among other industries. The effect of deregulation within the trucking industry is a microeconomic matter. But the larger argument for deregulation was that it would increase the efficiency of a variety of industries and accelerate the rate of growth of the U.S. economy—clearly a macroeconomic effect.

The average newspaper reader is probably more familiar with the work of the macroeconomists than the microeconomists. This work might include data on or prognostications of inflation rates, interest rates, or unemployment rates, or it might include advice on national economic policy— for example, how to deal with the federal deficit. Most of the economists whose names are well-known among non-economists (for example, Nobel Prize winners such as Milton Friedman, Lawrence Klein, Paul Samuelson, and Robert Solow) are known primarily for work they did in macroeconomics.

Curiously, however, it is microeconomics that is often on much more solid ground than the better-known and in some ways more prestigious field of macroeconomics. The predictive power of macroeconomics is limited, in part because the field with which it deals is so complex. And there is basic disagreement about theory down to the very core of the subject. There is, for example, fundamental disagreement between monetarists and Keynesians about the relative efficacy of monetary versus fiscal policy. Rational-expectations theorists will maintain that neither is very efficacious.

Perhaps because it has a somewhat more restricted purview, microeconomics is much less troubled. There is a great deal of theory that is very well established and almost universally accepted. Steven E. Rhoades, a political scientist well versed in economics, states: "Economists feel misunderstood. People notice only their showy, disheveled, and presumptuous half, macroeconomics, while their solid, elegant, better half, microeconomics, remains unseen."[1] Regarding the practice of economics, he states:

In academia there are more micro- than macroeconomists, and in government there are far more. Microeconomists and those associated with fields that have spun off from microeconomics, such as welfare and benefit-cost economics, public finance, and public choice, have never been more influential. In the universities economic concepts and models appear often in the work of psychologists and sociologists. Economists have been so influential in political science that one of their number, Gordon Tullock, was elected to the governing council of the American Political

Science Association. . . . In the interdisciplinary public policy programs that have grown enormously at our best universities, microeconomics is acknowledged to be the most influential specialty. Almost all the better law schools now have at least one economist on their faculties.[2]

THE MEANING OF NEOCLASSICAL

The microeconomics in this text is part of the larger body of neoclassical economics. The adjective "neoclassical" refers to a major change, a paradigm shift, that swept through economics in the period around 1870, and it separates the economics that followed from the earlier or "classical" period. Adam Smith, David Ricardo, John Stuart Mill, and that greatest of all economic heretics, Karl Marx, are all part of the classical tradition. The names associated with the transition from classical to neoclassical economics include Alfred Marshall, Leon Walras, Stanley Jevons, and Vilfredo Pareto.

This paradigm shift is sometimes referred to as the "marginalist revolution," as it introduced marginal analysis into economics. As the reader will see in subsequent chapters, the concept of events at the margin pervades the microeconomics. The introduction of marginal analysis in economics was as much of a paradigm shift as was the introduction of quantum mechanics in physics or plate tectonics in geology.

The term "neoclassical" is sometimes used, particularly on the political Left, as a synonym for "conventional" or "orthodox." Neoclassical economics is mainstream economics and thus is conventional or orthodox, hence the confounding of the term "neoclassical" with these other meanings. But, used correctly, the term simply refers to marginal economics— the mode of analysis that came to dominate the profession after the marginalist revolution. (The term "marginal" is left undefined here but is discussed in the next chapter.)

Microeconomics is useful for public policy because it is a powerful analytic tool for looking at "what happens when" with regard to questions of taxation, subsidy, regulation, and the like. It helps to clarify the true costs of public actions and expenditures and the effects of those actions upon individuals and groups. To a very great extent, the functions of government are economic, and it is hard to think of any government program of significance that does not have important economic consequences. Much of the daily political combat in a democratic society is about what is to be done for whom and who will pay for it. Microeconomics is the most powerful instrument available for examining these matters.

One advantage of applying economic theory to matters of public policy is that it can often move the debate away from the purely normative (right or wrong) and toward the positive (how do things work and what will happen if), thus decreasing the amount of heat while increasing the amount of light. Admittedly, no major public issue is ever decided on purely rational grounds. But microeconomic analysis can move the debate in that direction.

We might briefly note a few examples. Most municipalities in the United States maintain a system of zoning and other land use controls. Microeconomics provides a set of concepts for analyzing the effects of these controls on land prices and housing prices. Microeconomics will not tell you what should be done, but it will help you to think through the consequences of various policy alternatives. Similarly, it will help you to think through the likely effects of a new sales tax, of tariff policy, of farm price supports, and so on. It will help clarify the effects on prices and quantities and it will shed some light on who may be the winners and losers.

There was much concern in 1993 and 1994 over the question of how to finance health care. In part the problem is bedeviled by the fact that a substantial market for medical care is very far from a "perfect market" in a number of major ways. Designing a system of rules and procedures that assures the entire population of access to adequate (however we define that term) medical care without producing massive inflation of medical costs is not a simple matter. The microeconomist, with an understanding of markets, can make a serious contribution to the debate.

Microeconomic theory will not tell you whether or not the United States should adopt a comparable worth policy for the determination of wages, but it will help you think through the likely effects on wages, prices, and the distribution of income. And that should help you decide whether, on balance, you think comparable worth is a good idea or a bad idea. A little microeconomic theory will enable you to at least ask the right questions on policy issues. Will interdicting the supply of drugs raise or lower the incomes of drug dealers? A key issue here is whether the demand for drugs is elastic or inelastic (terms discussed in a subsequent chapter).

Recently, the Environmental Protection Agency has permitted firms to buy and sell "offsets," meaning that one firm may emit more pollution than the standard permits, provided it purchases an offset from another firm that has more than met its emission requirements. This notion of being able to "buy the right to pollute" is intuitively offensive to many, but in terms of efficiently achieving environmental goals there is considerable logic behind it. To understand that logic one must have some grip on basic microeconomic principles.

THE INCREASING INFLUENCE OF NEOCLASSICAL ECONOMICS

In recent years the influence of the neoclassical economics discussed in this book has increased. There are several loosely related reasons for this. In the United States the political shift to the right exemplified by the Reagan and Bush administrations placed an increased emphasis on market mechanisms. Beyond that, the growth of productivity in the United States has slowed considerably in the last two decades or so. The older, liberal assumption that government could focus on matters of equity while simply taking increases in total and per capita wealth for granted has given way to a viewpoint that sees questions of efficiency as, if not paramount, at least highly important.

There have also been important changes internationally. It was not that long ago that many thought the socialist model offered a real competitor to the market. For example, older texts on microeconomics discussed Langian (after the economist Oskar Lange) socialism under which capital would be allocated not by the market but by the decisions of a Central Planning Board operating under rules designed to produce optimum resource allocation. The theoretical arguments for Langian socialism are no weaker than they used to be, but there are few in the Western world, and probably not many in the former Soviet Union, who would take them as serious prescriptions for how the economy ought to be organized.

Even before the collapse of communism in Eastern Europe and the former Soviet Union, there was considerable disillusion with socialism in Western Europe. The Mitterrand government came into power in France in 1981 on a socialist platform, but a brief experience with the inflationary effects of raising wages while cutting working hours quickly turned it to the right. In May 1995 Mitterrand was succeeded by the Conservative candidate Jacques Chirac. The very conservative Margaret Thatcher remained prime minister in England for the longest term of any prime minister in the twentieth century. When she was forced out of office she was replaced by another conservative, John Major, who, despite poor performance by the British economy at the time, won reelection in 1992. In Scandinavia there was, in general, movement toward the right during the 1980s.

The socialist model, from Brezhnevian rigidity to Langian reasonableness, has lost credibility in recent years. If, as the political saying goes, "you can't fight something with nothing," then it is not hard to understand why the star of the market, and with it neoclassical economics, has been rising.

NOTES

1. Steven E. Rhoades, *The Economist's View of the World: Governments, Markets and Public Policy* (New York: Cambridge University Press, 1985), pp. 1–2.
2. Ibid.

PART I

BASIC PRINCIPLES OF MICROECONOMICS

CHAPTER 1

Who Is Economic Man and Where Does He Come from?

Economic man is the behavioral model for economics and thus the central figure in economic theory. In fact, economics is the only social science that has a single, easily articulated behavioral model used throughout the discipline. Textbooks state that economic man has two defining characteristics: He is rational and he acts in his own self-interest. Beyond that, many writers will add one qualification. Because we know that much consumption is joint consumption by multiperson households, rather than by isolated individuals, they will also state that we can think of the household as a single entity and treat its behavior as we treat the behavior of economic man. (No gender bias is intended by the term "economic man." The term "economic person" would have exactly the same meaning. This text simply adheres to a standard usuage that is over a century old.)

To understand the arguments, the diagrams, and the equations of microeconomics, the above is all one really needs to know of economic man. But there is a good deal more to be said about him if one wants to take a philosophical view of modern economics. The term "economic man" was coined by the great English economist, Alfred Marshall about a century ago, but the idea goes back much further. Adam Smith (1723–1790), in one of the most quoted passages in economics, stated:

It is not from the benevolence of the butcher, the brewer or the baker, that we expect our dinner, but from their regard to their own self interest. We address ourselves, not to their humanity but to their self love, and never talk to them of our necessities but of their advantages.[1]

That, in a nutshell, describes a society in which people's economic relationships are structured as voluntary agreements (you are not obligated to buy from the butcher nor is he obligated to sell or give to you) based on the self-interest of the contracting parties.

Smith not only described the world of economic man but he looked upon it and concluded that it was good. He propounded the idea of the "invisible hand," which stated that the net effect of self-interested behavior was to promote the general prosperity. "He [the worker or entrepreneur] intends only his own gain, and he is in this, as in many other cases, led by an invisible hand to promote an end which was no part of his intention."[2]

That idea apparently was not entirely original with him. De Mandeville, several decades earlier in "The Fable of the Bees," had suggested that "private vices" do, in the workings of the hive, produce "public virtues." The private vice is self-interest—greed, acquisitiveness, the desire for wealth.[3] The public virtue is general prosperity. A certain stamp of approval was thus placed on what generally had been referred to as the "sin of avarice."

Before De Mandeville it can be argued that the intellectual roots of the concept of economic man might be traced back to the seventeenth-century political philosophers Thomas Hobbes (1588–1679) and John Locke (1623–1704). Both argued in somewhat different ways that society was, in principle, formed by voluntary contract among individual men because they saw that it served their self-interest to do so. Hobbes argued that men voluntarily ceded their freedom to a ruler who would establish and maintain order and rescue them from the original state of nature in which life was "solitary, poore, nasty, brutish and short." It was so because men acting in unrestrained self-interest would make it that way. We thus have the beginnings of the idea that man's relationship to society is contractual and that the contract is entered into because it suits the interest of the individual. In Hobbes's view men acted only out of self-interest and he claimed that this accorded with what was then known as natural law or natural reason. On the subject of gratitude he stated: "For no man giveth, but with intention of good to himself; because gift is voluntary; and of all voluntary acts, the object is to every man his own good; of which if men see they will be frustrated, there will be no beginning of benevolence, or trust; nor consequently of mutual help."[4]

This is economic man. He is motivated by self-interest and if he helps another it is only in the expectation of reciprocity. The Hobbesian view is very different from the medieval view in which the structure of society is ordained by God and in which people play out the roles into which they have been born, obedient to the will of God as best they can discern it. By the standards of pre-Reformation Christianity, economic man is a despicable fellow. He does not labor, or buy or sell, on the basis of faith, custom, moral obligation, community loyalty, or kindness. He does not seek a fair price for his goods or services, but rather the maximum price. He lends money not to help someone in need, but only to receive interest, that is, to commit the sin of usury.[5]

The extent to which building a discipline on the basis of this sinful fellow is a departure from the world view of an earlier age is clearly expressed by the economic historian R. H. Tawney.

When the age of the reformation begins, economics is still a branch of ethics, and ethics of theology; all human activities are treated as falling within a single scheme, whose character is determined by the spiritual destiny of mankind; the appeal of theorists is to natural law, not to utility; the legitimacy of economic transactions is tried by reference, less to the movements of the market, than to moral standards derived from the traditional teaching of the Christian Church; the Church itself is regarded as a society wielding theoretical, and sometimes, practical authority in social affairs.[6]

Economic man became thinkable only in a society vastly more secular than that which existed in Europe at the time of the Reformation. As Tawney puts it, the world in which economic man becomes thinkable is one whose "essence is a dualism which regards the secular and the religious aspects of life not as successive stages in a larger unity, but as parallel and independent provinces, governed by different laws, judged by different standards, and amenable to different authorities."[7]

Thus, the Reformation made the concept of economic man acceptable. In the classic, *The Protestant Ethic and the Spirit of Capitalism,* Max Weber argues that the Calvinistic worldview that emerged in the century after the Reformation provided the soil in which modern capitalism emerged and flourished. It diverted the energy of Christian asceticism from the monastic life into the marketplace and the workshop, it legitimized the pursuit of wealth, and it made hard work into a religious duty. It made the self-interested behavior of economic man socially and morally acceptable.[8]

The point of the above digression is simply to say that economic man is a particular vision of human behavior but it is far from a universal one. It emerged at a particular point in history when Western society was ripe for its emergence.

IMPLICATIONS AND ARGUMENTS

The idea of economic man is at the root of a viewpoint that sees society as the creation of individuals rather than individuals as a creation of society. It gives primacy to the individual and places society in a subordinate position. The nation and its institutions exist to serve the citizen and not the other way round. In that sense, the concept of economic man is consistent with a secular, representative democracy. The idea of economic man evolved in a period when mercantilism was yielding to the free market and autocracy of one sort or another was yielding to representative government. The idea of economic man was a liberating one.

If one sees the individual and not society as primary it is only a small step to the position that the public interest consists of nothing other than the sum of private interests. Indeed, many economists take exactly this view.

The concept of economic man is also at the root of the concept of "consumer sovereignty." This is the idea that it is the preferences of the consumer that should determine the output of the economy. If one takes the position that there is no public interest apart from private interests, then the idea of consumer sovereignty follows naturally, for what other basis can there be for deciding what is to be produced? If it is individual preferences which count then a large measure of decision-making power must be left in individual hands, since it is the individual who knows his or her own preferences best. Clearly, then, accepting the concept of economic man pulls us to the political Right, as it suggests that the economic role of government should be sharply limited.

In a very general way, the notion of a society peopled by economic man presents an atomistic picture. Just as we picture the gas in a container as being composed of molecules colliding and rebounding, so we might picture a society of individuals in the social equivalent of Brownian motion. Thus, the picture conjured up by the concept of economic man is one that tends to emphasize the individual and deemphasize the role of groups and organizations. Economic man is, in Amitai Etzioni's usage "undersocialized."[9] This is in contrast to, say, medieval man who was so wrapped up in the bonds of faith and community that he had little autonomy and might be said to be "oversocialized."

How is economic man regarded today? Views vary widely. Most economists would assert that economic man is a useful abstraction. The concept is simple and supports, with the aid of a very small number of other axioms, the building of powerful and elegant theory. A number of economists go much further than that. They argue that because economic man has proved a powerful construct in economics, it is appropriate that this construct be employed in other areas. They argue, in effect, that if people behave on the basis of rational self-interest in the marketplace, it is reasonable to believe that they act on the same basis in their roles as voters, as legislators, and as bureaucrats. Public Choice, a field which is generally considered to have begun with the publication of Anthony Down's *An Economic Theory of Democracy,* is the application of economic reasoning and the paradigm of economic man to the subject matter of political science.[10] The leading figure in Public Choice today, James Buchanan, received the Nobel Prize in Economics in 1986 for his work in Public Choice. Gordon Tullock, another leading figure in the field and a frequent collaborator with Buchanan, was elected to the board of governors of the American Political Science Association in recognition of the importance of Public Choice in political science.

The economists' view, centered on economic man, has also surfaced in the law schools in what is generally termed the "law and economics" movement. Richard Posner, who is both an economist and a lawyer, argues that a great deal of the common law can be explained in terms of rational economic criteria, that is, that it is wealth maximizing. Beyond that he argues that the criteria of wealth maximization can form the basis of an efficient and, in his view, morally acceptable legal system.[11] The law and economics movement was a major force in legal education in the late 1970s and 1980s and one of its devotees, Antonin Scalia, now sits on the U.S. Supreme Court.

Economic man also has his detractors. Two related arguments are raised. The first is that the concept of economic man is so inaccurate as a depiction of human nature that it cannot serve as an adequate foundation for any discipline which purports to describe and predict human behavior. The second argument is that the concept of economic man, even though the economist treats it as no more than a useful fiction, has pernicious moral implications for society. Though the two arguments are analytically separable they are often voiced together.

Let us turn first to accuracy argument. We know from the experience of everyday life that a large part of human behavior is not motivated by self-interest. People do not give to charity out of self-interest. They do not volunteer to fight in wars out of self-interest. In fact, it is very difficult to explain why people vote if one posits only self-interest. If there is only one chance in ten million that your vote will be decisive in a presidential election, then there is no way that the "value of the expectation" of being able to swing the election is worth to you the half hour of your time required to vote. Therefore, there must be some reason, other than self-interest, that explains why you vote. It is argued that building a discipline on economic man throws out all of the insight into the nature of human personality that literature, psychology, anthropology, and direct experience give us and replaces it with a caricature.

At this point we come to an argument which has a bit of a history. A number of economists take the view that the concept of economic man can easily be rescued from this attack by means of a simple maneuver. The pattern of preferences or wants that each individual is assumed to carry in his or her head is sometimes referred to as the individual's "utility function." They argue that the problem is resolved simply by saying that economic man's utility function can include part of someone else's utility function.[12] Then when economic man gives to charity he is still acting as economic man.

The sociologist Amitai Etzioni retorts that this inclusion does not rescue the concept of economic man, but rather gives us an "empty" concept.[13] To pursue just a part of Etzioni's argument we can say that if we accept this maneuver then the saint is simply a specimen of economic man whose utility function happens to be composed exclusively of other people's interests. The sociopath, on the other hand, is also a specimen of economic man. His utility function, however, excludes the interests of other people. The mystic who abandons this world for a life of poverty and meditation is also a species of economic man. His or her utility function just happens to include a large amount of concern for his or her soul in the next world. This is all fine, except that the point of a definition is to make distinctions. If all people (or, at least, all sane people, since the definition of economic man specifies rationality) fit the definition then the definition is useless. If we can say that both Ivan Boesky and Mother Teresa act out of self-interest then how much analytical meaning can "self-interest" have? Thus, Etzioni argues that we can rescue the concept of self-interest only by expanding it to the point of meaninglessness.

Etzioni argues that the proper model of human nature would have in addition to the dimension of self-interest a dimension of morality (hence the title of his book *The Moral Dimension*). He suggests that people regularly act on both bases and that units along one dimension are not convertible into units along the other dimension in the sense that francs are convertible into dollars.

Moral acts are a source of value other than pleasure. *Indeed, many are explicitly based on the denial of pleasure in the name of principle(s) invoked.* Doing penance, abstention from premarital sex, and Ramadan fasting are not what most people consider sources of pleasure. (italics in original)[14]

But many economists will argue that, caricature or not, the economic man model is the right model to use. Geoffrey Brennan and James Buchanan make the following argument:

The butcher [referring to the earlier quote from Adam Smith] may or may not be benevolent to his customers. The crucial point is that such benevolence *need* not be present, and hence whether or not it is present is essentially irrelevant . . . if we want to examine the extent to which a particular set of rules, such as that of market order, succeeds in transforming the self-oriented interests of human agents into actions that further the interests of others, it is but natural for us to assume that such agents are entirely self-oriented, even if, empirically, they may not be. . . . Homo economicus is a uniquely appropriate caricature of human behaviour, not because it is empirically valid but because it is analytically germane.[15] (italics in original)

One might make the analogy that the law, both civil and criminal, deals largely with matters of deviant behavior, although we know that deviant behavior constitutes only a miniscule fraction of total behavior. But there is no problem with this imbalance, for it is the deviant behavior and not the normal behavior which is "analytically germane."

Brennan and Buchanan also make another point in the same work. They suggest that it is not the content of "self-interest" which is central, but rather the psychic locus of that self-interest.

the person who recognizes the social relationship of the exchange relationship may be allowed to incorporate the interests of the party on the other side of the potential exchange, and such incorporation may be allowed to modify choice behavior. . . . Nonetheless, even in this construction, the value to be maximized by the individual remains *internal* to his own psyche.[16] (italics in original)

The argument over whether or not economic man is a suitable assumption brings us to a fundamental conundrum of social science which one writer has expressed succinctly in the phrase "context is the enemy of parsimony." The real context in which the social sciences function is complex and the more complexity one acknowledges the less simple and less elegant becomes the structure that one erects. The simplicity of the caricature lends itself to parsimony and elegance in a way that the rich detail of a photograph does not. If one insists on a great deal of context one may encounter so many obstacles, exceptions, and qualifications that one cannot construct an intellectual apparatus of any power or generality. As a very simple example, if we assume the existence of economic man then many problems have a single solution. For example, the competitive firm will continue to produce until the point at which marginal cost is equal to market price, as it can be easily shown that this is the point at which profits are maximized. But if we assume some more complicated basis of behavior then the solution to the problem becomes indeterminate. Perhaps the firm will take the buyer's interest into account and sell to the buyer for less than the market price, or perhaps the buyer will take the seller's interest into account and pay more than the market price. Perhaps the firm will produce more than the profit-maximizing amount because of its view of the "need" for its product. Or perhaps it will produce less than the profit-maximizing amount so as not to put another firm out of business.

Etzioni's book illustrates the context/parsimony problem very well. He argues for a discipline based on a model of behavior which incorporates the "moral dimension." The last section of his book contains about 50 propositions and subpropositions which he offers as tentative suggestions for the building of such a system. And most of his propositions are stated in ways that are not absolutely clear and parsimonious, but rather somewhat fuzzy. For example, his proposition 11.1 states: "The price of an item reflects its costs, and the relative economic and political power of producers . . . and other parties. . . . In short, cost + power = price."[17]

The reader will note that the words are subject to many interpretations and that the equation is not really mathematics, but just notation for a very general idea. This is very much in contrast to the theoretical precision of microeconomics as it now is.

Those who make the moral argument against the use of economic man claim that economics is the only discipline built on the notion that greed is good. Given that ideas from one field of thought often spill over into other fields of thought, it is argued that the effect upon the moral fabric of society as a whole is pernicious. Kenneth Lux develops the point at some length in *Adam Smith's Mistake*.[18] The subtitle of the book, "How a Moral Philosopher Invented Economics and Ended Morality," expresses Lux's position quite clearly. Lux grounds some of his argument in history by noting that a number of the economists who followed Adam Smith, notably Thomas Malthus and David Ricardo, took quite cruel positions on questions of social policy following what they took to be the logical conclusions of the emerging discipline of economics. For example, both opposed any sort of public assistance to the poor.[19] The Social Darwinism of Herbert Spencer, a worldview that most of us today would regard as heartless, drew strength from nineteenth-century economics.

The economist who is comfortable with the concept of economic man might respond to the moral arguments by saying that if economics is to be a science then the relevant question about its assumptions is whether they permit the building of a science. The moral implications of economic man are no more relevant in economics than were the moral implications of Darwinism in biology.

I make no pretense of being able to resolve the argument over the suitability of economic man as the model but present my own view simply as "truth in packaging" about what follows. I am quite comfortable with the idea of economic man and with defining the term "self-interest" narrowly. I agree with Etzioni that defining the term very broadly renders it meaningless. I would argue that economic man dwells within the psyche of all of us except the saint, but is totally dominant only within the psyche of the sociopath. Most of us have a sense of moral balance about when to let the economic man within us roam and when to keep him caged. The most hardnosed businessperson may be quite generous with his or her time and money after business hours. On the other hand, the charity, the church, or even the monastic order, when it must go to the marketplace, may attempt to buy low and to sell high just as does the profit-maximizing firm. I would suggest, then, that economic man is the best available behavioral model for market-mediated behavior, but that the further we get from the market the less "analytically germane" he becomes.

NOTES

1. Adam Smith, *The Wealth of Nations* (New York: Random House, 1965), p. 14.

2. Ibid., p. 423.

3. Bernard De Mandeville, *The Fable of the Bees: Or Private Vices, Publick Benefits*, with commentary by F. B. Kaye (London: Oxford University Press, 1957). See "The Grumbling Hive: or, Knaves turn'd Honest."

4. Thomas Hobbes, *Leviathan: Or the Matter, Forme and Power of a Commonwealth Ecclesiastical and Civil*, edited by Michael Oakeshott (Oxford: Basil Blacksford, 1946), p. 99. There are many editions of *Leviathan* in print with different pagination. This quote is from the Fourth Law of Nature in chapter 15, "Other Laws of Nature."

5. Medieval theologians condemned the lending of money at interest (usury) and, more generally, took the view that it was wrong for one person to profit from the labor of another. For example, Thomas Aquinas took the view that a merchant should profit from trade only to the extent that profits compensated him fairly for his own labors. This view that it was not right for one person to profit from the labor of another found an echo centuries later in the Marxian notion of "exploitation." Tawney summarized this by saying, "The last of the schoolmen was Karl Marx." R. H. Tawney, *Religion and the Rise of Capitalism* (London: John Murray, 1944), p. 36.

6. Ibid., p. 278.

7. Ibid., p. 279.

8. Max Weber, *The Protestant Ethic and the Spirit of Capitalism* (New York: Scribner, 1958).

9. Amitai Etzioni, *The Moral Dimension: Toward a New Economics* (New York: The Free Press, Macmillan, 1988), p. 29.

10. Anthony Downs, *An Economic Theory of Democracy* (New York: Harper, 1957).

11. Richard Posner, *The Economics of Justice* (Cambridge, MA: Harvard University Press, 1981).

12. This argument goes back at least as far as Phillip H. Wicksteed, *The Commonsense of Political Economy*, reprinted by Augustus M. Kelly, New York, 1967. See chapter 5.

13. Etzioni, *The Moral Dimension*, p. 35.

14. Ibid., p. 46.

15. Geoffrey Brennan and James Buchanan, *The Reason of Rules* (Cambridge: Cambridge University Press, 1985), p. 53.

16. Ibid., p. 35.

17. Etzioni, *The Moral Dimension*, p. 268.

18. Kenneth Lux, *Adam Smith's Mistake: How a Moral Philosopher Invented Economics and Ended Morality* (Boston: Shambala, 1990).

19. Ibid., chapter 2.

CHAPTER 2

Definitions and Axioms

Below are set forth five definitions followed by three assumptions or axioms. Much of microeconomics, including realms of theory not covered in this book, can be built up from the three assumptions.

DEFINITIONS

1. *Ceterus paribus.* This simply means "all other things being equal." It is often abbreviated as cet. par. Many statements in economics texts are explicitly indicated as cet. par., but the reader should understand that even when the term is not used explicitly it is often understood or implied. If one says, for example, that when the price of widgets rises the quantity purchased will fall, it is assumed that other factors in the situation remain constant. We assume that the price of gizmos, which are a close substitute for widgets, has not changed, that the Congress has not just voted to ban all widget manufacturing after next Wednesday, that the Surgeon General has not just released a report stating that widget use affects the risk of cardiovascular disease, and so forth.

Ceterus paribus thinking sometimes frustrates or irritates the non-economist because in the real world it is very rare that other variables do hold constant. We obviously do not live in a ceterus paribus world. However, the fact is that one cannot build a system of thought if one cannot hold other variables constant, any more than one can erect a building on ground that is constantly shaking. But once the structure of economic thought has been developed it turns out to be very powerful in thinking about real issues in a non–ceterus paribus world.

2. *Marginal.* The marginal change is the change associated with the *last*

Table 2.1
Total and Marginal Costs

Number of Units	Total Cost	Marginal Cost
1	$50	$50
2	90	40
3	120	30
4	140	20
5	160	20
6	185	25
7	215	30
8	250	35

unit. For example, if it costs $1,000 to produce 100 units and $1,006 to produce 101 units then the marginal cost of the 101st unit is $6. The relationship between total and marginal costs is illustrated in Table 2.1.

As indicated in Table 2.1, the marginal cost of producing unit *n* is the cost of producing *n* units minus the cost of producing *n-1* units. Note, also, the sum of the marginal costs up to unit *n* is equal to the total cost of producing *n* units. This is analogous to saying that the height of a staircase is equal to the sum of the heights of the individual steps of which it is composed.

The concept of change at the margin can be applied to any two variables. We can thus have the marginal cost, marginal revenue, or marginal benefit associated with another unit of the product. We can have the marginal product associated with another unit of labor. And so on. The items in question do not have to be expressible in monetary terms. A political campaign director might think in terms of the marginal number of votes to be garnered from running one more commercial. A polling organization might think of the marginal increase in accuracy associated with increasing the size of a survey by one respondent.

The concept of change measured at the margin is perhaps the most basic concept in microeconomics, as will become apparent in this book. In fact, the transition from "classical" to "neoclassical" economics, generally dated at about 1870, is sometimes referred to as the "marginalist revolution," because the process of analyzing economic phenomena by looking at events at the margin transformed the field and made many phenomena which had been very difficult to explain very simple to explain.

3. *Market.* This is a place where buyers and sellers can come together to engage in voluntary exchange. The market may be a physical place, but in

this age of electronic communications it need not have a physical locus. The key notion is that of voluntary exchange.

4. *Utility.* This term may take on the meaning of usefulness or of satisfaction, or of pleasure, depending on context. For some purposes we may treat utility as something which can be measured in the sense that one can say how much someone would give in order to obtain the utility of a good or service. In other instances we might speak of utilities simply as being ordered in the sense that one might say only that one good or service has more or less utility than another without quantifying utility any further.

5. *Opportunity cost.* The opportunity cost of anything is that which had to be foregone in order to obtain it. Thus, the opportunity cost of your reading this book is that which you could have purchased instead of purchasing it, and that which you could have done instead with the time spent reading it.

6. *Economy of scale.* An economy of scale exists when additional increments of one or more factors of production produce more than proportionate increases in output. Economies of scale may exist because a larger scale of production permits the use of more efficient production technology. Or they may exist because a larger scale of production permits greater specialization of labor or brings underutilized resources into fuller use.

AXIOMS

1. *Economic man as the model for economic behavior.* In economic affairs people behave rationally and act on the basis of self-interest.

2. *The law of diminishing marginal utility.* After some point, the additional utility obtained from the consumption of an additional unit of any good or service begins to decline.

In principle an axiom is offered without proof and, in fact, is, by definition, beyond proof. However, one might note that this axiom seems to accord with ordinary experience as it is very difficult to think of an exception to it. If one is very hungry, the first bite of food brings great utility (satisfaction), but after a number of bites one approaches satiation and additional bites bring less and less additional satisfaction. Comparable comments can be made with regard to virtually any other good or service or experience that one can name.[1]

3. *The law of diminishing returns.* In any production process, if one holds one or more factors of production constant, then after some point the additional amount of output from an additional unit of input must begin to diminish. For example, if one holds the amount of land constant, then after some point the additional amount of crop produced by each additional farmer must fall. If the law of diminishing returns did not prevail, we would be able to grow all of the nation's food supply in a flower pot. We would simply continue to add more labor, more seed, and more fertilizer to reach

any level of output that we needed.[2] The law of diminishing returns explains why, after some point, the marginal cost of production must rise. Like axiom 2 this axiom seems to accord with common sense and ordinary experience. The economy of scale concept noted earlier might appear to contradict the law of diminishing returns, but this is not the case. The economy of scale concept pertains to the relationship between efficiency and the size of an operation. The law of diminishing returns describes what must inevitably happen to any operation, regardless of scale, if one holds one or more factors of production constant while increasing another factor(s).

NOTES

1. When I once challenged a class to think of an exception, a student finally suggested that addictive drugs might violate this principle on the grounds that the more one consumes the more intense one's craving for still another dose becomes. Perhaps so, but the point is that one has to stretch to find an exception.

2. I am indebted to Professor Ralph Kaminsky of New York University for this example.

CHAPTER 3

Supply and Demand

The concepts of demand and supply are two of the most fundamental ideas in economics. We present these very briefly here, link them to the three axioms listed in the previous chapter, and then proceed to the concepts of equilibrium and elasticity.

THE DEMAND CURVE

We assume that a market exists and that some particular good is for sale. The term "demand" is not used in its ordinary meaning of insisting upon something; rather it refers to the amount the consumer(s) will buy at various prices. Each point on the demand curve in Figure 3.1 equates a particular price to a particular quantity that will be demanded (purchased). One generally thinks of the consumer as being an individual or a household buying goods and services for private consumption. However, the ideas presented here apply equally well to firms purchasing raw materials, labor, intermediate goods, and other factors of production.

The demand curve plots the quantity that can be sold against the price that is charged. Its downward slope is an expression of the law of diminishing marginal utility.[1] The consumer, whom we assume to be rational and self-interested, (the economic man axiom) will continue to buy the item as long as the value (to the consumer) of the marginal item is greater than the price. Consumption stops when this ceases to be the case. Note that the value of the item in this usage is a subjective matter, determined entirely by the consumer. The demand curve might be that of a single consumer or might be the sum of the demand curves of many consumers. To produce a

Figure 3.1
The Demand Curve

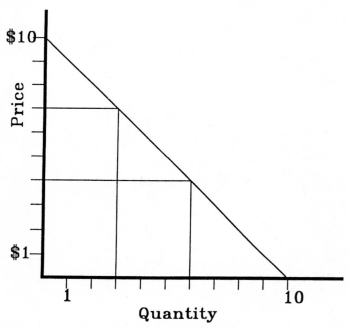

The demand curve is a plot of quantity sold against price. In this case, at a price of $4, six units will be sold. At $7, three units will be sold.

demand curve for many consumers, one simply adds the demand curves of individual consumers horizontally as shown in Figure 3.2.

The demand curves shown in this and many other books on economics are straight lines. This is just a matter of convention. The actual shape of the demand curve for a particular good or service is an empirical question. For purposes of this discussion, it is sufficient to say that the demand curve slopes downward without specifying a precise shape.

What causes the demand curve to have the particular position that it does? One factor is consumers' incomes. In general, an increase in incomes will shift the demand curve for a particular product to the right, meaning that at any given price more of it will be purchased.[2] Changes in the price of substitute goods will affect the demand curve. For example, if the price of meat goes up, the demand for chicken is likely to increase. Changes in consumer preferences, regardless of why they occur, will shift demand curves. Firms spend money on advertising to shift demand curves to the right. The American Cancer Society spends money on informing the public about the effects of smoking in order to shift the demand curve for cigarettes to the left.

Figure 3.2
Combining Demand Curves

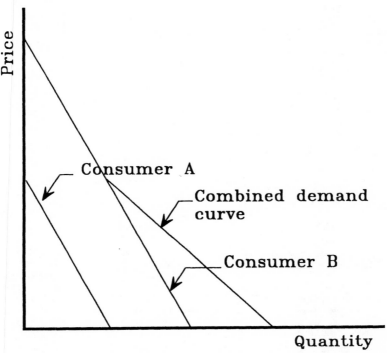

The demand curves of consumer A and consumer B are added horizontally to get the combined demand curve.

The demand curve for a particular product is where it is and is shaped the way it is by the above and other factors. The one thing it is *not* affected by is the prevailing market price.[3] The demand curve expresses the quantities of the product which would be purchased at various prices. If the seller changes the price of the product it will change the quantity sold, but it will not make the product inherently more or less desirable. Thus, it will not move the demand curve. This difference between a change or shift in demand, referring to a movement of the entire curve, and a change in the quantity demanded, meaning a movement along the curve, may sound like a fine semantic difference. But it is actually an important distinction which should be held clearly in mind.

The downward slope of the demand curve leads to the concept of consumer surplus as shown in Figure 3.3. At the point where the demand curve and the price line intersect, the marginal value of the good is the same as the price. However, for all items purchased before that point, the value of the item to the consumer is greater than the price. This difference between

Figure 3.3
Consumer Surplus

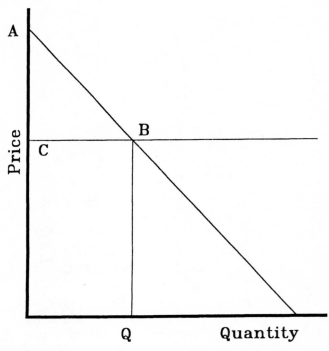

The intersection price and the demand curve determine the quantity, Q, that will be sold. The triangle ABC represents the consumer surplus.

value and the price is consumer surplus—the increase in the consumer's welfare that occurs because of the transaction. For the entire market shown in the figure, the total consumer surplus is the area of triangle ABC. The concept is important in regard to the efficiency of markets as discussed subsequently in this chapter, and in regard to benefit-cost analysis as discussed in Chapter 9.

THE SUPPLY CURVE

Just as the demand curve represents a plot of the diminishing marginal utility of the good to the consumer, the supply curve is a plot of the supplier's marginal costs. Thus, in most usages the terms supply curve and marginal cost curve are interchangeable. The supply curve may have a downward sloping portion as shown in Figure 3.4. This portion expresses the idea of economies of scale, also referred to as increasing returns to scale, noted in Chapter 2. It is the region in which additional

Figure 3.4
The Supply Curve

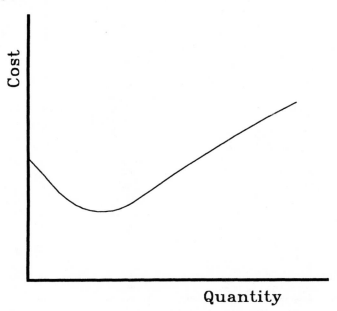

The downward slope represents the region in which economies of scale prevail, and the upward slope the region in which the law of diminishing returns predominates and causes
marginal costs to rise.

inputs produce more than proportionate increases in output. For example, if a factory has equipment or workers who are busy only part of the
time the marginal cost of additional units may fall as output is increased
to absorb this slack.

At some point, however, the law of diminishing returns, discussed in
Chapter 2, will prevail and the supply curve will slope upward. For most
purposes of this book it is the upward sloping portion of the supply
curve that is of interest and therefore, most of the diagrams in this book
will show only that portion. The upward sloping portion of the supply
curve shows the supplier's willingness to supply the good. As long as the
additional revenue received from selling another unit of the good exceeds
the marginal cost of producing another unit, it will be in the interest of
the producer to produce that unit. Note that we have invoked the economic man assumption here in that we assume the seller is capable of rational calculation and also that the seller will act in self-interest. If we are
speaking of a group of producers we can add their supply curves horizontally, as we did previously with demand curves, to produce the industry supply curve.

Figure 3.5
Shifts in Supply

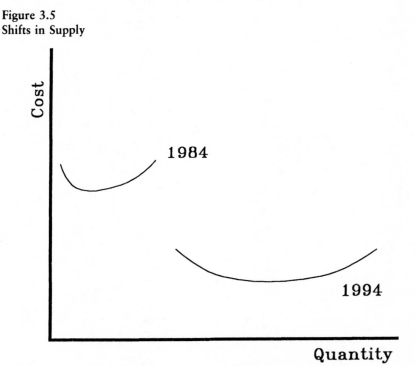

Hypothetical supply curves for personal computers in 1984 and 1994. The 1994 curve has a larger span because the industry grew greatly over the decade. It is lower because of improved production technology and greater economies of scale.

Assuming ceterus paribus conditions, the supply curve itself remains fixed. The supplier will adjust the quantity supplied on the basis of changes in the market price. Movements along the curve will occur in response to changes in the market price. For example, if demand increases, the market price will rise and production will move out along the supply curve to the new equilibrium point.

It is also possible for the curve itself to move. If, for example, the price of labor declines, then it will be possible to supply more units of the good at any given price. This increase in supply is expressed graphically as a shift of the curve to the right. An increase in the cost of labor, cet. par., would cause a decrease in supply, represented graphically as a shift to the left. Changes in supply can also be produced by changes in technology, changes in the price of raw materials or intermediate goods, changes in the cost of production equipment, of power, changes in the cost of borrowing money, changes in environmental regulations, and so on. In this litigious age many suppliers of goods and services have found that the cost of legal representation and liability insurance have shifted their supply curves quite a dis-

Figure 3.6
Producer Surplus

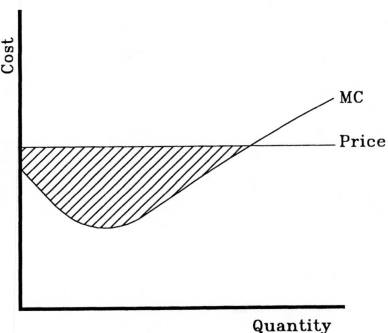

The shaded area between the price line and the supply curve (the producer's marginal cost curve) represents producer's surplus analagous to the consumer's surplus shown in Figure 3.3.

tance to the left. As with demand, one should distinguish clearly between a movement along the curve in response to a change in price and a movement of the curve itself. The movement of the curve may be caused by anything *other than* a change in price.

The position of the supply curve may change over the passage of time as the scale of the industry changes. Figure 3.5 is a hypothetical supply curve for personal computers in 1985 and 1995. The position of the new curve relative to the old curve is due both to the expansion of the industry and to improvements in technology. Note that these two factors are related. Increases in the scale of the industry may permit the use of more efficient production technologies. Conversely, improvements in technology may reduce the cost or increase the performance of the product and thus broaden its market, permitting the industry to expand to a larger scale. The drawing simplifies reality by treating all personal computers as if they were a single product class.

The shaded area in Figure 3.6 illustrates the concept of producer surplus,

Figure 3.7
Supply and Demand

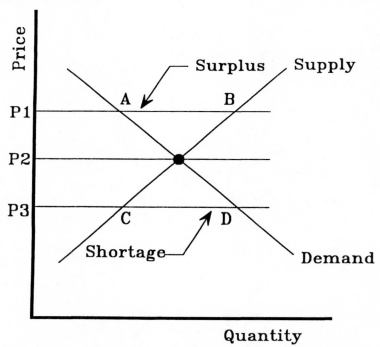

At price P1 the surplus indicated by line segment AB will exert downward pressure on prices. At price P3 the shortage represented by line segment CD will exert upward pressure on prices. The market will come to equilibrium at price P2, the market clearing price, where there is neither surplus nor shortage.

analogous to consumer surplus discussed previously. When the producer can sell the product for more than marginal cost, the difference is a gain for the producer. If the producer is making a profit, this gain adds to the producer's profit. If the producer is operating at a loss, this gain reduces the producer's total loss.

COMBINING DEMAND AND SUPPLY

Up to this point we have introduced the downward sloping demand curve and noted that its downward slope follows from the law of diminishing marginal utility. We have also introduced the upward sloping supply curve and noted that its upward slope is implied by the law of diminishing returns.

Figure 3.7 combines a supply and a demand curve and shows their intersection as the point at which the market is in equilibrium. Why will the market come to equilibrium at this point? Consider what will happen if the market begins to operate at price P1. It is evident from the diagram that suppliers will be willing to supply more units than buyers will demand. The excess of quantity supplied over quantity demanded, line segment AB, constitutes a surplus. Faced with unsold inventory, sellers will have no choice but to reduce prices. Conversely, at price P2 consumers will demand more than sellers are willing to supply. This shortage is represented by line segment CD. Sellers contemplating the long lines of customers will do the obvious and raise prices. At P there is neither surplus nor shortage and hence neither downward nor upward pressure on prices. The intersection thus represents the equilibrium position—the position the market will come to if no event comes along to shift the supply or the demand curve. The equilibrium price can also be referred to as the market clearing price, meaning that the market is cleared of surpluses and shortages. At the prevailing price, every willing buyer can find a willing seller and vice versa.

In a normally functioning market economy, market clearing is the usual situation. If you go to the hardware store to buy a screwdriver, you expect the store to have a reasonable selection from which you may choose. You will be surprised if you are told "we are out of screwdrivers this week but try us next week." You will also be surprised to be told "thank goodness you've come, we have sixteen unopened cases of them in the storeroom." Markets will from time to time be temporarily uncleared because of sudden changes in demand, miscalculations by suppliers, and the like. But they tend to clear because sellers are free to adjust the prices they charge and the quantities they offer.

Putting It to the Test

The idea that the intersection of the supply and demand curve establishes the equilibrium price can be put to a quick test in the classroom with an experiment referred to as a double oral auction.[4] The figure below shows a supply and a demand curve. Each of the 20 dots on the figure represents a person who would either like to buy or sell one unit. As drawn, the equilibrium price is $7.50 and the equilibrium quantity is 5.5 units. Since the curves are each made up of 10 discrete points, we might say that the equilibrium price should be between $7.00 and $8.00 and that the equilibrium quantity is 5 units. Will the market actually come to equilibrium near these theoretical results?

To convert the drawing into a classroom experiment the instructor does the following. He or she makes up ten cards for sellers. Each card has a number on it—$3, $4, $5, one for each of the ten points on the supply curve. He or she also makes up ten buyer cards, each with a number corresponding to one point on the demand curve. The cards are then given out randomly to 20 students. For the students who get a buyer card the instruction is that the card represents

(continued)

the maximum that they are willing to pay for the item. They should try to buy at as low a price as possible but in no event may they pay more than the figure on the card. For the ten students who get seller cards the instruction is that the card represents the minimum that they will accept. They should try to sell for as high a price as possible, but under no condition may they accept a price lower than the figure on the card. Neither buyer nor seller is to disclose to anyone else the actual figure written on the card. The instructor does not disclose anything about the values on the cards until after the auction is over.

The oral auction is conducted in any space big enough to hold 20 people, typically the front of the classroom. Both buyers and sellers are told to call out their buy and sell offers (hence the term double oral auction) and that when a deal is struck, both buyer and seller should leave the "market" area and sit down. Generally, the bargaining process goes quite quickly. After perhaps two minutes, when no more deals seem to be being struck, the instructor closes the market and students are asked to state the prices at which transactions occurred. At this point the instructor can present the supply and demand curves and compare the theoretical with the experimental results.

Generally, the experimental result comes out reasonably close to the theoretical result which is, in itself, reassuring. The experiment also demonstrates the

Figure 3.8
Data for a Classroom Experiment

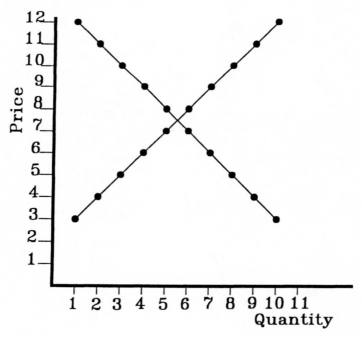

(*continued*)

ideas of consumer and producer surplus and the idea that markets are welfare-increasing devices. Suppose, for example, a buyer whose card says $10 "buys" for $7.20; then that student has realized $2.80 in consumer surplus. Or, assume a seller whose card says $6.00 sells for $7.00. That seller has realized $1.00 of producer surplus. One can easily compute the total potential consumer and producer surplus realized by the participants in the experiment. This figure can then be compared with the theoretical total consumer and producer surplus contained in the diagram (the absolute sum of the distances of all of the points to the left of the equilibrium quantity from the equilibrium price).

Note that the market rules imposed by the instructor are realistic. Buyers and sellers do normally seek to buy low and sell high and generally do not disclose the maximum they will pay or the minimum for which they will sell.

The numbers shown in this illustration are completely arbitrary and other sets of numbers will work just as well. There is no requirement that the number of buyers and sellers be equal. There is also no requirement that the demand and supply curves from which the points were taken be straight lines as shown here, or that the spacings between points be equal.

PRICE CONTROLS AND PRICE SUPPORTS

To emphasize the matter of surpluses and shortages, we briefly note the effects of public controls over market prices. Consider the matter of farm price supports. If the price for wheat is set above the market clearing price, farmers will produce more than the consumer will buy. In that case something must be done to prevent the surplus from driving the price down. Government may step in as a buyer and soon we will have storehouses filled with surplus wheat. Both the U.S. government and several governments in European Community (EC) countries do have large stockpiles of agricultural products, acquired in exactly this way. Government may try to deal with the surplus by encouraging farmers to produce less. One such effort in the United States is the Soil Bank program, which pays farmers to take land out of production; that is, to shift the supply curve of agricultural products to the left. Governments may seek to dispose of the surplus by giving it away outside the domestic market. The U.S. Food for Peace program was an example of this approach.[5]

Price controls are the reverse situation. Consider, for example, rent controls. At the controlled rents the number of appartments that would be rented exceeds the number of apartments in the city. The resulting shortage exerts upward pressure on rents but higher rents cannot legally be charged. A "black market" develops. People offer a variety of bribes and under-the-table payments to get controlled apartments. A category of economic crimes has now been created. Vacancy rates become extremely low so that one sees "rationing by inconvenience." The price of an apartment includes some

Figure 3.9
Consumer and Producer Surplus

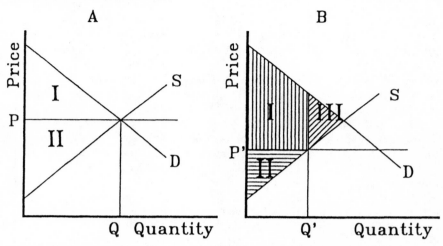

In panel A the market comes to equilibrium at price P and quantity Q. Triangles I and II represent consumer and producer surplus, respectively. In panel B the price is fixed at P' causing quantity supplied to fall to Q'. The quadrilateral I represents consumer surplus, triangle II represents producer surplus, and triangle III the net loss of surplus.

nonmonetary costs as well; many hours spent tramping the streets, rushing to the newstand to get the real estate ads the instant the paper is out, in the extreme reading obituary pages to locate soon-to-be-vacant apartments, and so on. The controls, just as do supports, produce a permanently uncleared market. That, in its turn, will produce personal behavior and perhaps special institutions to deal with the fact of permanent surplus or permanent shortage.

Note that for the economist the terms *surplus* and *shortage* simply refer to a condition in which the market is not cleared. This may be very different from the way the terms are used by others. If the politician says that there is a shortage of middle-income housing he or she is making a statement about how things ought to be. That is a normative statement and quite distinct from the economist's positive use of the term "shortage."

MARKETS AS A WELFARE-INCREASING DEVICE

Markets increase total welfare by making it possible for buyers and sellers to capture consumer and producer surplus and thus be better off than had they not engaged in exchange. In Figure 3.9 part A, triangles I and II represent consumer and producer surplus—the total increase in welfare

produced by the market. Part B of the figure shows the same market after
the imposition of price controls. In this case production stops at Q1. Areas
I and II represent the combined consumer and producer surplus. Clearly,
producer surplus is reduced. Depending upon how the figure is drawn,
consumer surplus may be larger or smaller than before. But note that the
total of consumer and producer surplus is reduced by the area of triangle
III. The fact that some producers and consumers have been blocked by the
controls from making transactions that they would have chosen to make
reduces the "gains of trade" obtainable from this market. The controls have
thus made the market suboptimal or, in terms that we will encounter in
Chapter 5, not Pareto Optimal.

One message the student of public policy might draw from the elementary economics discussed above is that market interventions have their
costs. An uncleared market, as shown above, leaves some consumer or
producer surplus unrealized and thus is necessarily suboptimal. More generally, one should recognize that market intervention, like any medication,
may cause side effects that need further medication. This is not to say that
market intervention may not be justified, but only that one should be aware
that market interventions do have costs.

SHIFTS IN SUPPLY AND DEMAND

Shifts in supply and demand and their effects on the market are easily
diagrammed. Figure 3.10 shows an increase in demand, also referred to as
a shift to the right in demand. As suggested earlier, the shift might be caused
by any number of factors such as an increase in consumers' incomes, an
increase in the price of a substitute product, a successful advertising campaign for the product, and so on. As can be seen from the figure the rightward movement of the demand curve indicates that a larger quantity will
be purchased at any given price. The result of the shift is that price increases
from P to P1 and quantity from Q to Q1. The reader can also interpret
the figure as illustrating a decrease in demand. Consider that demand was
at D1 initially and then shifted left to D. The price and quantity effects are
reversed.

Figure 3.11 shows an increase in supply, or shift to the right, as the curve
moves from S to S1. The rightward shift indicates that at any given price
a greater quantity will be supplied. The shift could have been caused by an
event which reduced the cost of one or more of the factors of production
or a change in the technology of production. As with the increase in demand, there has been an increase in the quantity sold but, in this case, there
has been a decrease in price. Note that Figure 3.11 can also be read as a
decrease in supply by taking S1 as the initial position rather than the end
position.

Figure 3.10
An Increase in Demand

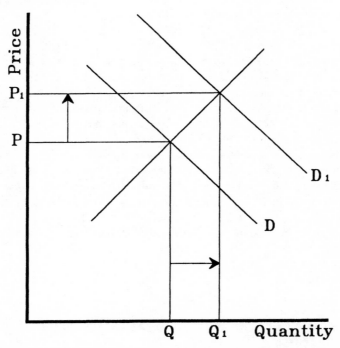

When demand increases from D to D1, prices increase from P to P1 and quantity from Q to Q1.

ELASTICITY OF DEMAND AND SUPPLY

The diagrams presented so far simply show slope. They indicate that the quantity demanded or the quantity supplied is sensitive to price but they say nothing about how great or how small is that sensitivity. Elasticity is the term used to refer to the degree of sensitivity. Specifically, elasticity is the percentage change in one quantity divided by the percentage change in another quantity. Two commonly used elasticities are spelled out below.

$$\text{elasticity of demand} = \frac{\text{percent change in quantity demanded}}{\text{percent change in price}}$$

$$\text{elasticity of supply} = \frac{\text{percent change in quantity supplied}}{\text{percent change in price}}$$

There are other elasticities as well. Income elasticity relates changes in demand to changes in income. There are also cross elasticities. These relate

Figure 3.11
An Increase in Supply

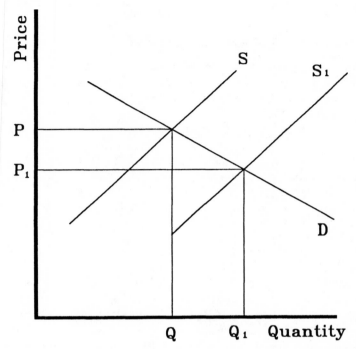

When supply increases from S to S1, price falls from P to P1 and quantity rises from Q to
Q1.

changes in the demand for one product to changes in the price of another
product. In principle, one can create an elasticity measure for any two
variables.

We use percentages rather than absolute numbers so as to make it con-
venient to compare situations in which the units or the quantities used are
very different. If the elasticity = 1 it is said to be "unitary." If the elasticity
of demand is greater than 1 we say that demand is elastic. If less than one
we say that demand is inelastic. Comparable semantics are used with regard
to elasticity of supply or any other elasticity.

As will be seen shortly, in order to think effectively about the effects on
markets of policy decisions it is essential to have some understanding of
the elasticities involved. Considerable research has been done on determining the elasticity of demand for many goods and services such as owner-
occupied housing, rental housing, public transportation, air transportation,
gasoline, alcohol, tobacco, foods of various types, and so on. Thus, for the
policy analyst looking at a specific problem, it makes sense to look into the

literature. There are, however, some general principles which are useful in doing preliminary thinking about whether demand or supply is likely to be elastic or inelastic.

Factors Influencing Elasticity of Demand

1. If there are close substitutes available the demand will tend to be more elastic than if there are not. This is because the consumer can switch to a substitute in response to small price changes. Thus, the demand for Fords is more elastic than the demand for automobiles in general.

2. Elasticities tend to be higher in the long term than the short term because the consumer has more time to make adjustments. For example, when gasoline prices went up suddenly in 1973–1974 and again in 1979–1980 the automobile commuter in the short run may have had no choice but to pay the higher price. He or she could not instantly change place of work, place of residence, or automobile. In the longer term the consumer might adapt by changing jobs, moving, trading in for a more fuel-efficient car, forming a car pool, and the like.

3. If the demand for a good is a derived demand, meaning that it is derived from the fact that said good is necessary in order for another good to be used, the elasticity of demand may be quite low. This is because the percentage change in the price of the total package will be less than the percentage change in the price of that one good alone. Assume that it costs the motorist 25 cents per mile to drive a car and that 5 of those 25 cents are the cost of gasoline. If the price of gasoline goes up by 100 percent the cost of driving a mile goes from 25 cents to 30 cents, a 20 percent increase. Thus, the elasticity of demand for gasoline is likely to be low, especially in the short term.

4. It is generally believed that elasticities tend to be lower for products or services that constitute a very small percentage of the consumer's total budget. This seems reasonable in that comparable percentage changes involve smaller sums of money.

5. It is sometimes said that the demand for luxuries is more elastic than the demand for necessities. However, one must be a bit careful with this luxury/necessity dichotomy. In the normal meaning of the word, cigarettes are not a necessity. But their demand is inelastic. Then perhaps they are a necessity. It is easy to get into a circularity in which we say that something has an inelastic demand because it is a necessity and then we decide which things are necessities on the basis of which things have inelastic demands.

Elasticity of Supply

1. In general, supply becomes more elastic with the passage of time. In the extremely short term the supply of most things is likely to be almost totally inelastic. This is because changing the level of output of a given

operation takes some time and changing the scale of the operation takes even more time. This is true whether we are discussing a factory, a university, a government bureau, and so on.

Consider, for example, the housing stock of the United States. In the very short term it is almost absolutely inelastic. From the filing of a building permit to the completion of a unit is likely to take at least a year, and for larger projects much longer. Often, the construction of new units will require that land be made ready for development. Thus, to the time required for building construction we must add time for site planning, road building, the laying of sewer and water pipes, and so on. In the very short term it is possible that changes in demand may lead to a few units that had been held off the market being put back on the market or vice versa, but basically the short-term supply is fixed. In the long term, supply may be quite elastic.

2. Supply tends to be more elastic if the factors of production are ubiquitously available and there are no impediments to or long time delays involved in creating more of those factors. As noted above, it is said that the supply curve for housing is quite elastic in the long term. Timber, bricks, and other materials used to construct it are widely available and the labor supply required to build it can be expanded fairly rapidly.[6] On the other hand, if there were to be a large increase in the demand for research in quantum physics we might find that the supply of facilities capable of doing the research was not so elastic. The work might require specialized equipment which takes a long time to design and produce. Then, too, we might find that the number of people who have the talent and taste to do the work is limited, and that the training period for new workers (say from college freshman to Ph.D. holder) was rather long.

How to Calculate Elasticities

Elasticities can be calculated at a point, if one knows the shape of the demand curve, or over a range if one has before and after data. Elasticities calculated over a range are generally referred to as arc elasticities, as in arc of a circle. Here we discuss the calculation of arc elasticities. For the mathematically more complicated matter of point elasticities the reader is referred to the literature.[7] In the notations below the symbol delta means "change in," the symbols P and Q represent price and quantity, and E represents elasticity.

Elasticity of demand is percent change in quantity over percent change in price which, expressed in symbols, is:

$$e = \frac{\dfrac{\Delta Q}{Q}}{\dfrac{\Delta P}{P}}(-1)$$

(continued)

Because price and quantity move in opposite directions, the formula above would always produce a negative number were it not for the (-1). This is added to produce a positive number, which most, but not all, authors believe to be more intuitively comfortable. For other elasticities, such as elasticity of supply, the problem does not arise because price and quantity generally move in the same direction.

Assume that when the price of widgets was $100 dollars, 100 were sold each week. When the price was raised to $125, sales dropped to 80 units a week. The elasticity calculation would be as follows:

$$e = \frac{\frac{\Delta Q}{Q}}{\frac{\Delta P}{P}}(-1) = \frac{\frac{-20}{100}}{\frac{25}{100}}(-1) = \frac{-.20}{.25}(-1) = .80$$

This method has one small flaw that is easily corrected. The results are somewhat different if one does the calculation for a price decrease than they are if one calculates for a price increase. If we use the same data items as before but assume that the price drops from $125 to $100 and that sales increase from 80 units to 100 units we get:

$$e = \frac{\frac{\Delta Q}{Q}}{\frac{\Delta P}{P}}(-1) = \frac{\frac{20}{80}}{\frac{-25}{125}}(-1) = \frac{.25}{-.20}(-1) = 1.25$$

It does not seem reasonable to get two different elasticity figures for the same set of data depending upon the arbitrary matter of which price we choose as the base price. Therefore, we can use a formula which, in effect, averages the differences and gives us the same result regardless of which price we use as the base price.

$$e = \frac{\frac{\Delta Q}{\frac{Q_1+Q_2}{2}}}{\frac{\Delta P}{\frac{P_1+P_2}{2}}} = \frac{\frac{20}{\frac{100+80}{2}}}{\frac{25}{\frac{100+125}{2}}} = \frac{\frac{20}{90}}{\frac{25}{112.5}} = 1.0$$

Graphic Representation of Elasticity

Elasticities can be represented graphically, but some cautions are necessary. If supply or demand is absolutely inelastic (no sensitivity at all to price changes), it is represented by a vertical line on the supply/demand diagram. If it is infinitely elastic (an immeasurably large change in quantity for an infinitesimal change in price) then it is represented by a horizontal line. In between these extremes, the more inelastic the demand or supply

Figure 3.12
Elasticity Along a Straight Line Demand Curve

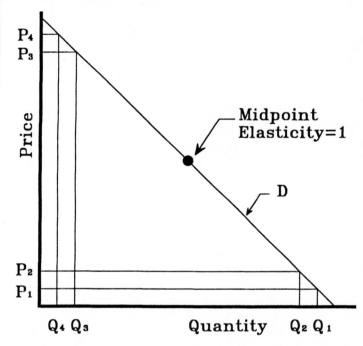

Elasticity varies from 0 at the bottom to infinity at the top. A 100 percent increase in price P1 to P2 produces only a small percentage decrease in quantity from Q1 to Q2. Conversely, a small percentage increase in price from P3 to P4 produces a large percentage decrease in quantity from Q3 to Q4.

the more nearly vertical the line, and the more elastic it is the more horizontal the line.

However, how nearly horizontal or vertical a demand or supply curve is will depend upon the way the axes of the graph are calibrated. If you use finer gradations on the quantity axis any curve will become steeper, and if you use coarser gradations it becomes more horizontal. Therefore, you cannot readily infer the actual elasticity from the slope of the curve.

Another caveat is that the straight line demand curve, the one used in most texts, does not have a constant elasticity. Rather, its elasticity varies continuously along its length. Its elasticity is 0 at the point of intersection with the quantity axis, reaches 1 at the midpoint and rises to infinity at the point of intersection with the price axis. The reason for this continuous change can be seen in Figure 3.12. Near the quantity axis the 100 percent increase in price from P1 to P2 produces only a small percentage decrease in quantity from Q1 to Q2. On the other hand, near the top of the price

axis a small percentage change in price from P3 to P4 produces a large percentage change in quantity from Q3 to Q4.[8]
For the above reasons one should not try to infer the actual elasticity from the slope. However, for purposes of explanation one can use the straight line demand curves to represent relative degrees of elasticity as is done in a number of subsequent diagrams.

Elasticities and Revenues

As suggested earlier the elasticity of demand bears upon the question of what will happen to revenues when the price changes. If the elasticity is greater than 1, then a reduction in price will cause an increase in total revenues because the increase in quantity will more than compensate for the decrease in unit price. Conversely, increasing the price will lower total revenues. If the elasticity is less than 1, lowering the price will result in a reduction in total revenues because the small increase in the number of units sold will not compensate for the lower price per unit. Conversely, increasing the price will increase total revenues.

To use a known or expected elasticity to forecast changes in revenue, you simply apply the elasticity to the proposed price change to get the change in quantity and then do the before and after revenue calculations as shown in the following example.

A commonly cited figure for the elasticity of demand for public transportation is .3. Assume that the city bus line now charges $1 per ride and sells 10,000 rides per day. Revenues are now $10,000 per day. Assume that fares are raised 10 percent to $1.10. Multiplying 10 percent by .3 and knowing that price and quantity move oppositely gives us a ridership change of −3 percent. Revenues are now $1.10 × 9,700 = $10,670 per day. If the fare is reduced by 10 percent to 90 cents we get a ridership increase of 10 percent × .3 = 3 percent. Ridership is now 10,300 and revenue is 90 cents × 10,300 = $9,270 per day.

NOTES

1. If you assume constant marginal utility instead of diminishing marginal utility then the demand curve becomes horizontal. If you assume increasing marginal utility then the demand curve will slope upward. If you assumed increasing marginal utility the consumer would spend all of his or her income on one good. The first item purchased would be whichever good offered the most utility per dollar. The fact of increasing marginal utility would mean that a second item of that good would also offer more utility per dollar than any other purchase, and so on. The consumer would continue purchasing that good until his or her funds were exhausted. In logical terms, an economics built on increasing marginal utility might

be equally valid, but it would produce results that seem bizarre and that contradict everyday experience.

2. For a few goods, an increase in incomes will reduce demand as consumers switch to purchasing higher quality goods. Such goods are referred to as "inferior goods" or "Giffen goods."

3. In reality there are some exceptions to this point. If the consumer judges the utility or quality of a product partly by its price, then an increase in price might change the consumer's opinion of the product and thus shift the entire demand curve. If a product is bought for speculative purposes then an increase in price, if it suggests further increases in price, might shift the entire demand curve.

4. The use of classroom experiments as a teaching tool is now becoming more common in economics. This writer regards it as the biggest improvement in economics pedagogy in many years. It shifts the student from a passive to an active mode and it puts flesh on concepts that may otherwise seem dry. The double oral auction described here is one of the simplest classroom experiments. Many much more complicated and sophisticated experiments have been devised. Not only are some of the more elaborate experiments useful as teaching tools in advanced classes, but they are also being used to test economic theory. For a a description of the history and state of economic experiments, see Vernon Smith, *Papers in Experimental Economics* (New York: Cambridge University Press, 1991).

5. The results of this program have been mixed. In India it prevented famine and saved many lives. In Tanzania it drove agricultural prices so low that it put farmers out of business and converted a food exporting country to a food importing country.

6. The reader might object that the supply does not seem so elastic in view of the rapid increases in housing prices during the 1970s and 1980s. The cause of the lower elasticity is not inability to build housing but a variety of other factors including land use controls, environmental constraints, lack of new streets and utilities, and so on. The problem is with the supply of sites, not with our ability to build structures.

7. The elasticity at a point is the derivative of percent change in quantity over percent change in price, and can be calculated for any point on the curve using differential calculus if the curve is described by a mathematical function that can be differentiated. Discussions of this can be found in standard intermediate or advanced microeconomics textbooks. See, for example, Walter Nicholson, *Microeconomic Theory*, 2d ed. (Hinsdale, IL: Dryden Press, 1978).

8. Demand curves with constant rather than varying elasticities have a hyperbolic shape convex to the origin of the graph and often, over some range of prices, fit empirical data better than straight lines. They are described in numerous intermediate-level microeconomics texts.

CHAPTER 4

Firms and Markets

In a standard microeconomics text the operation of the firm and the competition between firms are often discussed in considerable detail for their own sake. Here, the discussion will be much briefer. The intent here is not to discuss the firm for its own sake, but to present some models of firm behavior as a way of approaching the overall question of economic efficiency. This chapter first presents the market model of perfect competition and then its opposite, monopoly. It concludes with very brief discussions of two intermediate forms—monopolistic competition and oligopoly—that actually describe the great bulk of economic activity.

From a policy perspective the importance of the model of perfect competition is that it constitutes a model of allocative efficiency. This is the reason that this book gives it a fair amount of space despite its rarity or, if one takes all of its requirements literally, its nonexistence. If one understands the model of perfect competition and its antithesis of monopoly, then one has a useful model against which to measure reality. One can consider a real market and, at least, ask the right questions.

PERFECT COMPETITION

The model of perfect competition requires four conditions:

1. Both buyers and sellers must be numerous and, relative to the market, sufficiently small that the actions of any one buyer or seller not have a perceptible effect upon the market.
2. All producers in the market must produce the same product and those made by any producer must be indistinguishable from those made by any other producer.

3. All participants in the market must have perfect knowledge of all prices bid and asked in that market.

4. The factors of production must be able to flow freely and instantaneously into or out of the market or between one producer and another producer in the market. This implies that there be no transactions costs.[1]

If we take all of these requirements literally there can be no perfect market. Even if we interpret these requirements very loosely it is evident that the perfect market must be rare. If substantial economies of scale exist then large firms will be able to outcompete small firms and there will not be many producers in the industry. Most of the goods and services produced in our economy are not identical to competing goods. Product differentiation is one of the prevailing facts of our economy and, if anything, is increasing. It is only among commodities—coal, lumber, wheat, bauxite, and the like—that large numbers of producers may produce essentially identical products. Perfect knowledge does not exist.[2] And, of course, there is no industry in which the factors of production can be moved instantly and with no transactions costs.

To examine the model, consider a small firm producing widgets in a perfectly competitive market.[3] It is one of very many small firms and its widgets are indistinguishable from widgets produced by other firms. In this situation the market looks very different from the firm's perspective than it does when viewed by an outside observer. As shown in panel I of Figure 4.1, the market price is set by the intersection of the demand curve and a supply curve which is the sum of the supply curves of all of the widget makers. But to the individual widget maker the demand curve looks completely horizontal. If the market price of widgets is, say, $41, then the firm can sell as many widgets as it chooses to produce. But it cannot sell a single widget at $41.01 given the assumptions listed above. Nor would it make any sense at all to price its widgets at $40.99 for, as noted, it can sell all the widgets it produces for $41.00. The producer under these conditions is referred to as a "price taker" in that he or she has no choice but to accept the market price. The only market decisions for the producer are how, and how much, to produce.

Table 4.1 shows some numbers for a hypothetical producer and Figure 4.2 shows those data plotted out. Note that maximum profit occurs where the marginal cost curve and the price intersect. To construct the table we assume a fixed cost of $100 and the schedule of marginal costs as shown. The average fixed cost (AFC) is the fixed cost divided by the number of units. Total variable costs (TVC) at each level of production are the sum of the marginal costs to that point, as noted in the previous chapter. Average variable cost (AVC) is the total variable cost divided by the number of units. Average total cost (ATC) is the sum of AFC and AVC.

The firm will achieve maximum profit (or minimum loss) at that level of

Figure 4.1
The Demand Curve as Seen by the Competitive Firm

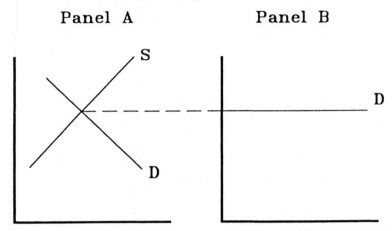

The market price is set by the intersection of the supply and demand curves as shown in panel A. But to the competitive firm, which is so small that its own actions have no perceptible effect upon the market, the price appears to be infinitely elastic as shown in panel B.

production for which *marginal cost is equal to price.* (In the case of an example like that above where the supply curve is a series of discrete points, it is more accurate to say that profit is maximized if the firm produces, as long as price exceeds marginal cost. Whether or not the firm produces that unit whose marginal cost is exactly the same as the price has no effect on profit.) For example, if the market price is $41.00, the largest profit (total revenues–total costs) will be made at an output of 16 units. Here total revenues will be $41 × 16 = $656. Total costs will be the fixed cost of $100 plus the total variable cost for 16 units which is $463. Thus $656– ($100 + 463) = $93. At an output of either 15 or 17 units the profit is lower. For example, if you do the calculations for profit at 17 units you will observe that profit falls to $90. This difference corresponds to the $3 difference between the market price of $41 and marginal cost of $44 for the 17th unit. If you do the calculations for 15 units you will observe that profits are $92 rather than the $93 for 16 units. This difference corresponds to the loss of the $1 of additional profit that would have been made on the 16th unit. From the standpoint of efficiency, one of the major concerns of microeconomic theory, this equalization of price and marginal cost is the most important point to take from the discussion of the competitive firm.

Fixed costs have no effect upon the optimal level of production. If you redo the table leaving the marginal costs unchanged but assuming a differ- ent fixed cost you will see that for any given market price the profit-

Table 4.1
The Economics of the Firm

Number of units	Average fixed cost (AFC)	Marginal cost (MC)	Average variable cost (AVC)	Average total cost (ATC)	Total variable cost (TVC)	Total cost (TC)
1	$100.00	$50.00	$50.00	$150.00	$50.00	$150.00
2	50.00	43.00	46.50	96.50	93.00	193.00
3	33.33	38.00	43.67	77.00	131.00	231.00
4	25.00	32.00	40.75	65.75	163.00	263.00
5	20.00	28.00	38.20	58.20	191.00	292.00
6	16.67	24.00	35.83	52.50	215.00	315.00
7	14.29	21.00	33.71	48.00	236.00	336.00
8	12.50	19.00	31.88	44.38	255.00	355.00
9	11.11	18.00	30.33	41.44	273.00	373.00
10	10.00	18.00	29.10	39.10	291.00	391.00
11	9.09	19.00	28.18	37.27	310.00	410.00
12	8.33	22.00	27.67	36.00	332.00	432.00
13	7.69	26.00	27.54	35.23	358.00	458.00
14	7.14	30.00	27.71	34.86	388.00	488.00
15	6.67	35.00	28.20	34.87	423.00	523.00
16	6.25	40.00	28.94	35.19	463.00	563.00
17	5.88	44.00	29.82	35.71	507.00	607.00
18	5.56	48.00	30.83	36.39	555.00	655.00

maximizing (or loss-minimizing) quantity is unaffected by the fixed costs. Fixed costs, sometimes referred to as sunk costs, thus have no bearing upon the production decision to be made now. This is analogous to saying that if you have completed part of a journey, the path that you took to get to where you are has no bearing upon the path you should take to finish your trip. The only relevant question is which is the best path from your present location to your destination.

As a small but significant point of geometry, in Figure 4.2 note that the marginal cost curve cuts both the average variable cost (AVC) and average total cost (ATC) curves at their lowest points. This makes sense in that if the marginal cost is above the average cost then it is pulling the average up. If it is below the average then it is pulling the average down. If the marginal cost curve intersects the average cost curve at its low point then the marginal cost curve pulls the average cost curve in neither direction. That point, where a tangent to the average cost curve is horizontal, is the curve's low point.

Given the costs and the $41.00 market price shown on Figure 4.2, the

Figure 4.2
The Economics of the Competitive Firm (Data from Table 4.1)

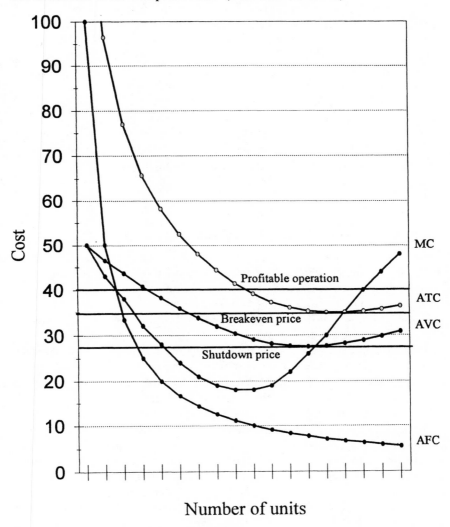

The curves are plotted from the data in Table 4.1.

hypothetical firm is operating at a profit as previously noted. The break-even price would be $34.86, the low point on the average total cost (ATC) curve. Here the firm would sell 14 units and receive 14 × $34.86, receiving $488 in revenues which just matches its total costs at 14 units. Recall that the marginal cost curve intersects the ATC curve at its low point. The break-even situation is pictured in Figure 4.2.

The minimum price at which the firm will remain in business is $27.88, the low point on the average variable cost (AVC) curve. This price is sometimes referred to as the shutdown price. Here, the firm would just cover its variable costs but none of its fixed costs. At any price between the shutdown price and the break-even price the firm would operate at a loss, covering all of its variable costs but only some of its fixed costs. As long as the firm can recoup its variable costs and any part of its fixed costs it makes sense to remain in operation. As noted above, fixed or sunk costs should not affect present decisions. The entrepreneur may regret having expended the fixed costs necessary to go into business, but those expenditures are gone in any case. Note that we are neglecting the possibility of going into bankruptcy and thus shifting some of the loss on fixed costs to one's creditors. In 1992 there were about 72,650 business bankruptcy petitions filed or pending in the United States.[4] Thus, in the real world this is not a trivial consideration.

The Theoretical Advantages of Perfect Competition

An economy composed entirely of firms competing in perfect markets would be, in theory, perfectly efficient. It would also be very peculiar. One unusual characteristic of such an economy would be an absence of profits. To understand this point one needs to know how the economist's definition of profits differs from that of the accountant. In the economy there is what is generally termed a normal return to capital. This is the rate of interest one can obtain on an essentially risk-free investment such as a government bond or, perhaps, a AAA-rated corporate bond. Profit, in the economist's meaning of the term *profit,* is that return *beyond* the normal return to capital. This is different from the accountant's view, which is that profit is whatever is left after all expenses have been covered.

Perfect knowledge and the unimpeded flow of resources would mean that as soon as the smallest differences in rate of return appeared among different sectors of the economy, capital would flow out of the low-return sectors and into the high-return sectors. This would shift supply curves so as to lower equilibrium prices in the higher rate of return sectors and raise them in the lower rate of return sectors. The process would continue until the same rate of return prevailed everywhere. That rate of return would be the normal rate of return to capital. There would thus be no profits. Given perfect knowledge and instantaneous mobility this process would, in theory, happen with infinite speed. Thus, the zero profit situation would be perpetual. The firm in zero profit operation is shown in Figure 4.3. The zero profit condition is theoretically optimal, because if no dollar of capital can be more profitably invested elsewhere than where it now is, then no further improvement in the pattern of investment can be had.

The elimination of profit in perfect competition could be said to be an

Figure 4.3
The Firm in Perfect Competition

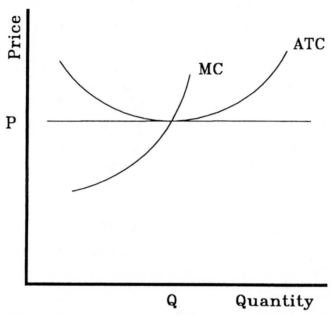

The mobility of firms and factors of production into and out of the field have brought the market price to a level such that the typical firm makes neither a profit nor a loss, but just earns a normal return on investment. This means that the ATC curve is at its low point just tangent to the line representing the market price. For reasons explained in text, the MC curve intersects to ATC curve at its low point.

example of Adam Smith's "invisible hand." The individual entrepreneur does not like the no-profit condition of perfect competition so he or she shifts resources into an area where profits are being made. But that very act decreases profit in the area by shifting the supply curve to the right and thus lowering prices. In the end, the pursuit of profit eliminates profit.

Perfect competition is also a model of efficiency in that all prices are set equal to marginal cost, a necessary condition for efficiency. Recall that under the assumption of consumer sovereignty discussed previously, the market is the arbiter of value. Thus, if a good sells for $10 then the market is telling us that at the margin it is worth $10. If the firm were to stop production when marginal costs were equal to $9, we could say that an opportunity had been lost. Here are resources worth no more than $9 in any other use but they could have been combined into a product worth $10 if only the entrepreneur had not stopped production prematurely. Clearly, we have $1 worth of lost opportunity here. One might ask how we know that these resources are worth only $9 in whatever was the next highest use. The answer is that if they were worth more than $9 in other uses the firm would not have been able to buy them for $9. Someone else would have been willing to pay more for them. Note, again, we are assuming that the market is the sole arbiter of value.

Suppose the firm produces past the $10 price to the point at which marginal costs are $11. We know that the resources that went into the last unit were worth $11 because the firm had to pay that much for them. Yet, when combined into the product, they are worth only $10. Clearly, by making that last unit the firm has, in effect, destroyed $1 of resources. Another way to say it would be that the economy has experienced an opportunity cost loss of $1. Only if the firm stops production at precisely the point at which marginal cost is equal to price has it placed exactly the right amount of resources in that use.[5] Note that according to the above reasoning, the same behavior, adjusting production so that marginal cost is equal to price, is both profit-maximizing for the firm and efficiency-maximizing for the economy in the aggregate. This brings us back to Adam Smith's notion that self-interested economic behavior can benefit society as a whole. As will be shown subsequently, it is only in perfect competition that setting MC precisely equal to price is profit-maximizing.

If, as shown above, capital is allocated in the optimal way and if each firm is producing the optimal amount of product then, necessarily the economy is operating with maximum efficiency. In terminology that we will encounter in Chapter 5, the situation is Pareto Optimal.

A Few Realities

For reasons noted before, perfect competition in even one market is just an abstraction. An economy in which all markets are perfect is even more of an abstraction. Despite its theoretical efficiency, such an economy would have a few faults. In the ordinary meaning of economic competition, namely, an intense struggle among firms for markets and profits, much of the competition takes the form of product innovation and product differentiation. This form of competition is absent from the model of perfect competition. Most of us would quickly tire of a world of homogeneous products and services. The opportunity for choice, by itself, is an important value. Advertising and salesmanship would be absent from the world of perfect competition because they could communicate nothing new in a world of perfect knowledge. The entrepreneurial drive in such an economy would be very weak because of the absence of profit. We can discuss how firms would behave in perfect competition, but it is more difficult to say why they would come into existence in the first place. Why would anyone invest money or start a business knowing that any profits (in the economist's meaning of the term) would instantly be competed away?

The economy composed of perfect competitors in perfect markets would deploy its resources with perfect efficiency at some given level of technology. But without accumulations of capital from profits, how would it make the leap to higher levels of technology? Consider the invention of the transistor at Bell Laboratories in 1948. The laboratory was supported by American Telephone and Telegraph (AT&T), a regulated monopoly that accounted for about 85 percent of U.S. telephone service. In its profitable, "fat and happy" condition, AT&T supported Bell Labs, at which top scientists and engineers worked with a great deal of freedom. The transistor was one fruit of this research, for which three Bell Labs scientists received a Nobel Prize. Subsequently, the foundations of radio astronomy, which has reshaped many of our notions of the universe, and for which two more Bell Labs scientists received a Nobel Prize, were laid at Bell Labs. There would be no Bell Labs in a world of perfect competition.

The point of these last digressions is to say that perfect competition is a powerful and useful abstraction. But that is all it is. One should also be aware that no economist thinks that it exists, any more than any physicist thinks that the frictionless plane, another useful abstraction, really exists.

MONOPOLY

In perfect competition the firm is so small that nothing it does can, by itself, measurably affect the market. In monopoly we have the other extreme. Here there is only one producer. The industry demand curve and firm's demand curve are exactly the same because the industry and the firm are one and the same. Similarly, the firm and the industry supply curves are one and the same. Whereas the perfect competitor looks at a horizontal demand curve, the monopolist looks at a downward sloping demand curve. Rather than having to accept the price determined by the marketplace, as does the competitive firm, the monopoly can, in principle, choose any point on the demand curve, each of which represents a different price–quantity combination. The result, as shown in Table 4.2, is that for the monopolist marginal revenue is always less than price. This is because to sell more units the monopolist must sell all units at a lower price. Thus, from the revenue obtained on the last unit must be subtracted the slight reduction in the price of all the other units that was necessary to move out one more unit on the demand curve. Note that this is very different from the situation of the firm in perfect competition, for which price and marginal revenue are always the same.

The rational (profit-maximizing) behavior for the monopolist would be to produce up to the point at which marginal cost equals marginal revenue. This is point A on Figure 4.4. The price will then be set as indicated by point C. Note that at this point the price is higher than the marginal cost, indicating that for an efficient allocation of resources production has

Table 4.2
Marginal Revenue under Monopoly

Number of Units	Price	Total Revenue	Marginal Revenue
1	10	10	10
2	9	18	8
3	8	24	6
4	7	28	4
5	6	30	2
6	5	30	0
7	4	28	2
8	3	24	-4
9	2	18	-6
10	1	10	-8

stopped too soon. The efficient point is B, where the marginal cost curve intersects the demand curve. At that point the marginal cost is equal to the value that the consumer places on the last unit consumed. But the monopolist will not continue out to point B because it is past the point of profit maximization. Herein, according to the economist, lies the inherent inefficiency of monopoly: the monopolist produces too little and charges too much for an efficient allocation of resources.

If only the monopoly could magically be broken up into a large number of competitors without any loss of efficiency, production would be at point B where the industry marginal cost curve intersects the demand curve. The net gain to society would be the triangle ABC in Figure 4.3. But, of course, monopolies generally cannot be broken up into a large number of competitors because one reason for the existence of monopoly is the existence of large economies of scale.

The above constitutes the very bare bones of the formal argument against monopoly. It is a simple argument but it has had and continues to have important public policy consequences. It lies at the heart of federal antitrust policy. At the turn of the century, the U.S. oil industry was restructured when the Standard Oil Company was broken up as a result of antitrust litigation by the Justice Department.[6] More recently, the Bell system was broken up into NYNEX, Bell Atlantic, and the other of the seven so called "Baby Bells," as a result of a consent decree.[7] Bell consented to be broken up in return for being allowed to expand into new areas involving data transmission. Were it not for the existence of antitrust legislation, Bell would not have needed consent and the issue of its breakup would not have arisen. The fact that you can receive your local telephone service from one of the "Baby Bells" but purchase your long distance service from U.S.

Figure 4.4
Profit Maximization under Monopoly

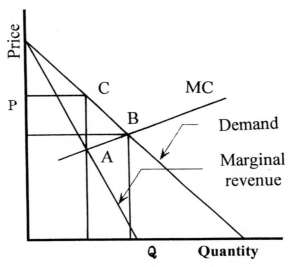

Setting P = MC, point B, would provide the efficient level of production. However, the profit maximizing monopolist will set MC = MR, point A, thus producing a smaller quantity and charging the price indicated by point C.

Sprint or MCI is also a result of antitrust legislation. Were there no such legislation there would be no reason why one of the Baby Bells like NY-NEX would allow a competitor access to its transmission lines. More recently, Microsoft Corp., in negotiations with Justice Department lawyers, agreed to change licensing practices that the Justice Department claimed were monopolistic.[8] Generally, economists tend to think that policy which moves markets away from monopoly is generally good policy and policy that moves markets toward monopoly is bad policy. This general orientation tends to pervade policy making in the United States.[9]

One might ask how common is monopoly in our system. We all have some contact with it in that most utility services are provided by monopolies. In any one area there is usually only one provider of electric power, natural gas service, water, or sewer service. This is logical in that it would be wasteful to have duplicate power lines or duplicate gas mains running down the same street. Where the physical logic of supply makes it sensible to have only a single supplier we have what is termed a "natural monopoly." Generally speaking, the monopolist in this case is not free to set price at any point on the demand curve but rather is regulated, typically by a state commission. The utility provider is allowed a price structure which permits what the regulating agency considers to be a reasonable rate of return. The monopolist's costs are set in the marketplace but the monopolist's prices are set in combined regulatory, legal, and political process. Other than the regulated natural monopoly, true monopoly is rare. One can readily test this statement by trying to think of a major industry in which there is only a single producer.

A patent might be considered to be a federally granted monopoly situation in that for the term of the patent the patent holder has a monopoly on the production of the item, unless he or she chooses to license another party to produce it. But this is a rather minor exception for which there exists the justifiable public purpose of encouraging invention. Comparable statements might be made with regard to copyrights. But these exceptions aside, true monopoly outside of the area noted above is rare.

Note that a monopoly position does not by itself guarantee high profits. There may well be no point on the demand curve at which profitable operation is possible. It is sometimes said that a monopoly can charge any price that it wants. But, even aside from the matter of regulation, this is not true. The monopoly can, in principle, choose any point on the demand curve. But it cannot choose a point to the right of the demand curve because that would be specifying a price higher than the market will bear if the monopoly is to sell that number of units. And, of course, picking a combination to the left of the demand curve would make no sense, as that would be deciding to take a lower price for that quantity than the market will bear.

OLIGOPOLY AND MONOPOLISTIC COMPETITION

In between the extremes of perfect competition and monopoly lies the great bulk of the U.S. economy. Oligopoly refers to the situation in which there are relatively few producers of a given type of product. If there are large economies of scale in product development, production, or distribution it is to be expected that there will be few producers. One sees oligopoly in many areas of manufacturing for this reason. For example, in the United States there are only two major producers of airliners (Boeing and McDonnell Douglas), in large measure because of the huge research and design costs that must be incurred before the first unit can be built.

One should note, however, that in this age of massive world trade many markets have been becoming less oligopolistic. At one time the "big three" (Ford, Chrysler, and General Motors) dominated the U.S. market. In fact, it was widely believed that General Motors, as the largest of the three, could have effectively driven the other two out of business and achieved something very close to a monopoly position had it not been restrained by fear of antitrust prosecution. That is clearly not the case now. The U.S. automobile market is intensely competitive due to imports, and many automobiles are made here in plants owned and run by overseas producers.

The largest share of the U.S. economy is characterized by what has been termed "monopolistic competition."[10] In monopolistic competition we have a large number of producers who supply substitutable but not identical products. Rather than facing the horizontal demand curve of the pure competitor, the firm in monopolistic competition faces a demand curve with some downward slope. The reason it has some downward slope is that the product is not quite identical with competing products. A small increase in price will somewhat reduce the quantity demanded. But it is not the same situation facing firms in perfect competition, where an attempt to raise the price even slightly above the prevailing price will make it impossible to sell any of the product at all. On the other hand, the fact that there are similar products on the market may make the demand for the product quite elastic. Many areas of manufacturing, for example, clothing, are characterized by monopolistic competition. The size distribution of manufacturing firms is shown in Table 4.3.

Monopolistic Competition in Manufacturing

Manufacturing is probably the most concentrated sector of the economy, but even here, the data on firm size presented in Table 4.3 suggest that monopolistic competition rather than oligopoly is the dominant form.

Table 4.3
Manufacturing Establishments by Number of Employees
(Figures in 000's)

Number of employees	1963	1987
Under 20	207	238
20 to 99	70	86
100 to 249	18	22
250 to 999	10	11
1,000 and over	3	2
Total	312	369

Source: Statistical Abstract of the United States, 1993, table 1255. The 1987 figures are the latest available at this writing.

Whether concentration increased or decreased from 1963 to 1987 is arguable. The figures in the table suggest some deconcentration. On the other hand, the percentage of all establishments that are part of multiunit firms increased from 15.0 to 21.9 percent.

We might note that the less substitutable other products are for a product, the less elastic is its demand likely to be. Much money is spent on advertising, packaging, and design modifications in order to achieve a greater degree of "product differentiation." By thus making demand for the product less elastic (giving the demand curve more downward slope) the firm gives itself a bit more of a monopoly position.

If we take having some choice of price quantity combinations as that which defines the difference between pure competition and monopoly, then we can say that most firms have some element of monopoly position because most products and services are to some degree, however small, different from their competitors. Then, too, geography gives most firms some element of monopoly position simply because of the time and money costs of shipping goods or transporting the consumer to the point at which the good or service will be consumed. If Joe's barbershop is the only one in town, or the only one in the neighborhood, it may have more of a monopoly position than does General Motors. The distance to its nearest competitor (which may or may not provide an essentially identical service) gives it a fair amount of choice of price–quantity combinations.

NOTES

1. See, for example, Miltiades Chacholiades, *Microeconomics* (New York: Macmillan Publishing Co., 1986), pp. 12–13; Edgar K. Browning and Jacquelene M. Browning, *Microeconomic Theory and Applications* (Boston: Little, Brown & Co., 1983), pp. 237–39; or many other standard texts. For the competitive market to allocate resources with perfect efficiency it is also necessary that there be no externalities. But since most texts do not list this as a characteristic of the perfect market, I have postponed a discussion of externalities to a subsequent chapter.

2. In an exchange such as a stock or commodity exchange participants may have complete information on all prices bid and offered, so in this limited sense perfect knowledge may exist.

3. In many texts the example used is an agricultural one such as the wheat farmer, because there are many producers and the product of one farm cannot be distinguished from that of another farm. I have eschewed the agricultural example because, given the overwhelming importance in agricultural markets of subsidies, price supports, manipulation of supply by the Soil Bank program, and the like, agriculture is now very far from a perfect market, although it may well have approached it at one time. Rather, I have used the economist's "widgets," whatever they are.

4. U.S. Department of Commerce, Bureau of the Census, *Statistical Abstract of the United States, 113th ed.* (Washington, DC: U.S. Government Printing Office, 1993), table 864.

5. It can be argued that if competition is not perfect in some sectors of the economy, say, because of monopoly, then there may be instances in which marginal cost pricing in the other sectors is not necessarily optimal. For example, if the competitive firm buys factors that are priced above marginal cost (say, the output of a monopoly) then it would be more efficient from an aggregate point of view for the competitive firm to use these factors somewhat past the point at which their cost to the competitive firm exceeds their marginal revenue product for the competitive firm. This general line of argument can be pursued in many intermediate and advanced microeconomics textbooks under the "theory of the second best."

6. For a brief account of the breakup of Standard Oil, see Peter Asch, *Industrial Organization and Antitrust Policy* (New York: John Wiley & Sons, 1983), pp. 236–38. The book also contains a good general account of the economic reasoning behind antitrust policy.

7. See Alan Stewart, "How Judge Greene's Recent Decision Changes Business Telecommunications," *Communications News* (November 1991), p. 42.

8. Edith Corcoran, "Anatomy of a Deal: Microsoft's Settlement," *Washington Post,* July 18, 1994.

9. The U.S. view is not universal. What might be considered a fine, healthy degree of competition in a U.S. market might be referred to as a "disorderly market" by the Japanese. The Europeans have traditionally been more tolerant of agreements that restrain competition (cartels) than has the United States.

10. The term "monopolistic competition" comes from Edward H. Chamberlin, *The Theory of Monopolistic Competition* (Cambridge, MA: Harvard University Press, 1933). Monopolistic competition, oligopoly, and monopoly are sometimes lumped together under the general term "imperfect competition."

CHAPTER 5

Welfare Economics

Welfare economics refers not to the "welfare system" that politicians argue about, but to how the net economic welfare of society can be improved or maximized. It is an outgrowth of the marginalist revolution mentioned in the introduction and is associated particularly with Francis Y. Edgeworth, Vilfredo Pareto, and Arthur C. Pigou.

In this chapter we examine some of the basic concepts and geometry of welfare economics. These are widely used in discussion and analysis of public policy. We begin with the concept of the indifference curve and a very closely related concept, that of the isoquant. We then proceed to a description of Pareto optimality, perhaps the best-known concept in the realm of welfare economics, followed by its geometrical representation, the Edgeworth box. After that we turn to the policy implications of these concepts and a few cautions for the user. At first the discussion may seem a bit abstract or stylized, but have faith. We will very shortly surface in the real world.

THE INDIFFERENCE CURVE

Consider a simple piece of geometry, the indifference curve shown in Figure 5.1. The consumer is restricted to purchasing only two types of goods, A and B. The axes of Figure 5.1 are marked off in units of good A and B. We assume that the consumer has a fixed sum (herein after referred to as the "budget") to spend. Assume that good A and good B cost $10 each and that the consumer has $100 to spend. He or she can then purchase 10 units of A and no units of B. This is the point at which budget line I intersects the A axis. Similarly, the consumer can purchase 10 units of B

Figure 5.1
The Budget Line

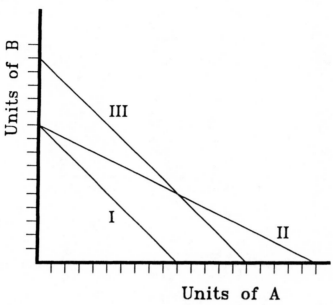

The axes are marked in physical units. If good A and good B were each priced at $10 per unit and the consumer had $100, the budget line would be line I. If the consumer's budget was increased to $150 and prices remained the same the budget line would be line III, parallel to the position of line I. If the budget was held to $100, the price of good A was reduced to $5, but the price of good B remained the same, the budget line would rotate outward to position II.

and no units of A. This is the point that line I intersects the B axis. Or, the consumer can purchase a combination of A and B represented by a point on line I, for example, 2 units of A and 8 units of B, 3 units of A and 7 units of B, and so forth. All points to the right of the budget line exceed the consumer's budget and thus cannot be reached. Conversely, any combination of A and B represented by a point that falls inside the triangle formed by the axes and the budget line will leave the consumer with some part of the budget unspent. Note, also, that the slope of the budget line reflects the relative prices of A and B. If the price of A were reduced to $5, then the budget line would extend twice as far along the horizontal axis as shown by line II. If the consumer's budget were increased by 50 percent but prices left unchanged the budget line would be shifted from position I to position III. Because the prices remain the same, its slope would be unchanged and it would simply move out parallel to its original position. Note that, so far, we have represented only the market realities by showing a system of prices and the consumer's budget.

Figure 5.2
The Indifference Curve

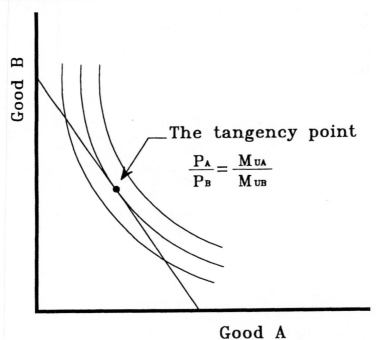

The tangency point

$$\frac{P_A}{P_B} = \frac{M_{UA}}{M_{UB}}$$

We have added the indifference curves to the budget line pictured in Figure 5.1. The curves owe their convex-to-the-origin shape to the law of diminishing maginal utility. At the tangency point the consumer is on the highest indifference curve that he or she can reach for that budget and system of prices. At the tangency point the budget line and indifference curve necessarily have the same slope and thus, at that unique point, the ratio of prices is the same as the ratio of marginal utilities.

The curved lines, added to the diagram in Figure 5.2, are referred to as indifference curves. They represent the consumer's system of preferences. Each curve, by itself, represents a set of combinations of goods A and B that would be equally satisfying to the consumer. Because any point on the curve is as satisfying to the consumer as any other point on the curve, he or she is indifferent among them and hence the name of the curve. The shape of the curve represents one of the three axioms stated in Chapter 2, namely, the law of diminishing marginal utility.[1] At a point high up on the indifference curve, where the curve is nearly vertical, the consumer has a large amount of good B relative to good A. Thus, the marginal utility of B relative to A is small and the consumer would be willing to give up a large amount of B to obtain a small amount of A. Conversely, where the curve is nearly horizontal the reverse is true. Here, the consumer would be willing to give up a large amount of A to obtain a small amount of B.

In Figure 5.2 there are a number of indifference curves. Although the consumer is indifferent as to where he is on any particular curve, he would always prefer a higher curve to a lower curve, since on a higher curve he can consume more of both A and B. Note that as a matter of geometry, for any point you pick on a lower curve, it is always possible to pick a point on a higher curve that is further out on both the vertical and horizontal axes, thus indicating greater consumption of both goods on the higher curve.

The tangency point in Figure 5.2 represents the optimal position for the consumer. It places him or her on the highest possible indifference curve that can be reached given that budget and that system of prices. It is the point at which the market reality of prices and budget meets the psychological reality of the consumer's preferences. As a matter of geometry the budget line and the indifference must have the same slope at the tangency point. The slope budget line represents relative prices and the slope of the indifference curve represents relative marginal utilities. Therefore, at the point of tangency the ratios of prices and marginal utilities must be the same. Algebraically:

$$\frac{Pa}{Pb} = \frac{MUa}{MUb}$$

where Pa and Pb are the prices of goods A and B and MUa and MUb are the marginal utilities of goods A and B. One can say that achieving the optimal balance of good A and good B is a matter of adjusting the amount of each consumed so that the ratio of their marginal utilities is the same as the ratio of their prices. If one moves the consumer along the budget line away from the tangency point, the equality between the ratios of the prices on one hand and the marginal utilities on the other hand is lost. The consumer, as shown in Figure 5.3, is pushed down to a lower indifference curve and thus experiences a welfare loss. Yet his or her expenditures remain the same because he or she is still on the same budget line.

The figure with its fixed budget and world of only two goods may seem a bit stylized and limited, but it is actually more flexible than it at first seems. One can consider one axis to represent one good and the other axis to represent all other goods. As a variation on that theme we can use one axis to represent a good and the other to represent money.[2] If we were discussing the effect of taxes on work effort we might draw the indifference curve apparatus with one axis representing income and the other representing leisure time. The curves can be drawn for three individuals and three goods. In this case the indifference curve and budget line become surfaces rather than lines. The concept can be extended to any number of goods and individuals. It is just that we cannot draw it. If we expand the

Figure 5.3
The Effects of Constraining Consumer Choice

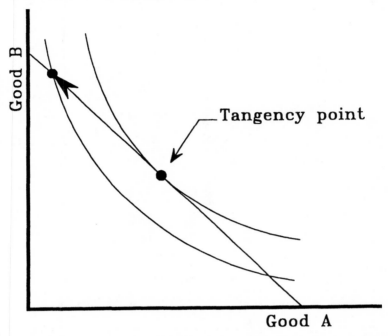

Constraining the consumer's choice while leaving his or her income unaffected (same budget line) and the system of prices unchanged pushes the consumer down to a lower indifference curve and thus reduces the consumer's welfare.

system from two consumers to n consumers then the formula presented above is generalized to:

$$\frac{MUa}{Pa} = \frac{MUb}{Pb} = \frac{MUc}{Pc} = \cdots \frac{MUn}{Pn}$$

THE ISOQUANT

The indifference curve apparatus is a statement about consumption, but with only semantic modification it becomes a statement about production. Figure 5.4 shows an isoquant. The axes are now labelled in terms of factors of production, say, labor and capital. The curved lines on the figure are isoquants. Each isoquant shows various combinations of factors that will all produce the same quantity of output. Isoquants further from the origin represent higher levels of output than do those closer to the origin. The curvature of the isoquant comes from the law of diminishing returns, one

Figure 5.4
The Isoquant

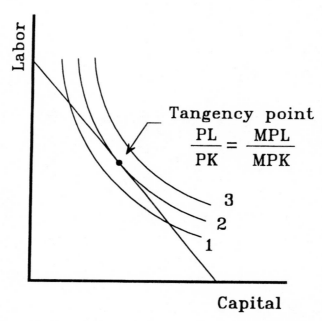

The axes of the graph are marked off in units of labor and capital. The straight diagonal line is the firm's budget line given its supply of funds and the prevailing wage of labor and price of capital. Each curved line or isoquant represents different combinations of labor and capital that will produce the same output. The further the isoquant is from the origin the greater quantity of output it represents. The notation is: PL = price of labor, PK = price of capital, MPL = marginal product of labor, and MPK = marginal product of capital. Only at the tangency point is the ratio of the price of the factors of production equated to the marginal product of the factors. This point places the firm on the highest isoquant given its budget and that system of factor prices.

of the three axioms listed in Chapter 2. If the firm has a large number of workers but very little capital then perhaps a small increase in capital equipment will balance a large reduction in the work force. At the other end of the curve the firm has a large amount of equipment relative to its labor force. If there are not enough workers to use all of the equipment effectively then a small increase in labor may compensate for a large decrease in the amount of capital equipment. The budget line represents the total amount the firm has to spend. As with the indifference curve we understand that, in principle, the concept can be expanded to as many factors or dimensions as we wish.

One might ask what is the most efficient combination of factors that can be used to produce a given product. The answer is that we cannot say until we know the prices of the factors. Just as utility is maximized at the tangency point on an indifference curve, output is maximized at the tangency point on an isoquant diagram. At this point the marginal increase in output from another dollar spent on factor A is the same as that of another dollar spent on factor B. Thus, no improvement in the allocation of factors can be made.

The position of the tangency point depends upon the prices of the factors. Assume, for example, that in India the cost of capital equipment is the same as it is in the United States because it is available on the same world markets, but that labor costs roughly one-twentieth as much per hour as it does in the United States. The optimum combination of labor and capital for U.S. prices would be hopelessly capital intensive for India. And the ideal combination under Indian prices would be hopelessly labor intensive for U.S. prices.

The idea that one cannot make intelligent resource allocation decisions without a good system of prices seems almost self-evident to someone in our economic system. But it has not been universally self-evident. One of the many postbreakup problems in the former Soviet Union has been the lack of a system of prices that reflects costs accurately, for many prices were set administratively in a manner that was not closely related to cost. Such prices make transactions possible, but unlike market-determined prices they do not convey the kind of information that facilitates rational decision making.

PARETO OPTIMALITY

Perhaps the most central idea in welfare economics is that of Pareto optimality. We offer a verbal explanation first and then a diagrammatic presentation that makes use of indifference curve apparatus previously developed. The basic formulation of Pareto optimality is extremely parsimonious but it leads to a considerable richness of results. It can be expressed as follows: *A situation can be considered optimal when it is no longer possible to improve the condition of one party without making at least one other party worse off.* The logic of this is that as long as it is possible to improve the lot of one party without injuring another, the situation cannot be optimal as there is necessarily still room for improvement. When it is no longer possible to improve the lot of one without injuring someone else then one cannot necessarily say that the situation is not optimal.

The original condition for achieving Pareto optimality—that only changes that cause harm to no party can be made—is a very restrictive one. It is hard to think of any significant economic act, public or private, that will not bring some loss to someone. Both Nicholas Kaldor and John Hicks proposed a modification. They argued that a change that imposes a loss on some may still be Pareto optimal if the gainers would be willing to compensate the losers; in other words, if there is gain in net welfare.[3] This is so under the Kaldor–Hicks criterion even if no compensation is actually paid. Note, also, that nothing is said about who are the gainers and the losers. In the case that compensation is paid, the identity of the parties does not matter. But in the case that compensation is not paid, it may very well matter. If a proposed policy change delivered a gain to a wealthy person and a slightly smaller loss to a poor person it would qualify as moving the system toward Pareto optimality under the Kaldor–Hicks criterion even though most of us might not consider it "optimal" under other criteria.

The Edgeworth Box

The concept of Pareto optimality can be illustrated geometrically with the Edgeworth box, developed by the English economist F. Y. Edgeworth. Figure 5.5 shows a situation with two consumers and two goods. Note that any point in the box divides up all of the goods between the two consumers. The box also contains two sets of indifference curves. Consumer X's curves radiate out from the lower left corner and consumer Y's from the upper right corner. Each consumer would like to be on the highest possible curve, that is, a curve as far from his or her own corner as possible.

Can we now say that some points in the box are Pareto optimal and that some are not? Consider point A in Figure 5.6. It does not meet the Pareto criteria because we can see that by moving to point B both parties can be placed on higher curves. Is point B optimal? Again, the answer is "no," as both parties will be on higher curves if we move to point C. At point C the situation is different. The two indifference curves on which the point is located just touch each other at one point. Now, the only way to place one individual on a higher curve is to place the other individual on a lower curve. Point 3 thus is Pareto optimal in that one cannot improve the welfare of one individual without making another worse off.

In Figure 5.7 we see a number of indifference curves and a number of back-to-back tangency points comparable to point C on Figure 5.6. If one imagines that there are an infinite number of indifference curves that can be drawn for each of the two consumers then all of the back-to-back tangency points form the contract curve shown in Figure 5.7. By the logic discussed above, any point on the contract curve is Pareto optimal and any point off it is not. Another way to express the optimality of the points that comprise the contract curve is to say that on the curve "the gains of trade" have been exhausted. If the goods in the system are divided up so that the point that expresses their division is off the curve then there are trades possible that will increase the welfare of both parties. But once the parties represented by the Edgeworth box reach a point on the contract curve,

Figure 5.5
The Edgeworth Box

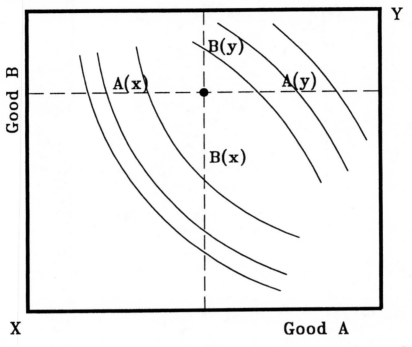

Consumers X and Y are located at opposite corners of the box as shown. The axes of the box are marked off in units of goods A and B. Indifference curves for each consumer radiate out of that consumer's corner. Each consumer would like to be on the highest possible curve (furthest out from his or her corner). Any point in the box divides up all of the goods in the system. For the point shown here, line segment A(x) shows the share of good A that goes to consumer X, line segment B(y) shows the share of good B that goes to consumer Y, and so on.

voluntary trade will cease, as it will not be possible to make any trade that does not diminish the welfare of one party.

Policy Implications

Indifference curves, isoquants, and the more complicated apparatus of the Edgeworth box are essentially devices for illustrating the concept of Pareto optimality. Some policy implications of Pareto optimality follow.

A Pareto optimal allocation of resources cannot occur unless all of the gains of trade can be realized by equilibration at the margin, as was discussed for the consumer using the indifference curve and for the producer using the isoquant. The proper marginal adjustment for the consumer can

Figure 5.6
A Pareto Optimal Point

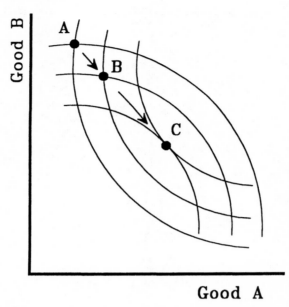

The indifference curves shown here represent an enlarged portion of Figure 5.5. Point A is
not Pareto optimal because it is possible to place both parties on higher indifference curves
by moving to point B. Similarly, point B is not optimal because a move to point C will
again place both parties on higher indifference curves. However, at point C, the condition
of back-to-back tangency makes it impossible to place one party on a higher indifference
curve without placing the other party on a lower curve. Thus, the Pareto condition is
satisfied and point C is Pareto optimal.

only be made by someone who knows the consumer's system of preferences, and the only person who knows that pattern sufficiently well is the
consumer himself. If another individual were to make consumption choices
for the consumer, the chance of this other party knowing the consumer's
preferences well enough to place the consumer at the tangency point would
be remote. If choices are made for the consumer by another party or if
rules, regulations, customs, bureaucratic impediments, or the like limit the
consumer's freedom of choice, then all of the gains of trade will not be
realized and the consumer's situation will not be Pareto optimal.

Thus, the concept of Pareto optimality supports the concept of Consumer
Sovereignty noted in Chapter 1. Comparable comments can be made about
allowing the firm as much discretion as possible. Who can know better the
most efficient mix of resources for the firm to use than the firm itself? To
say that one favors an expanded vision of consumer sovereignty and what
might be termed "producer sovereignty" necessarily defines one's position

Figure 5.7
The Contract Curve

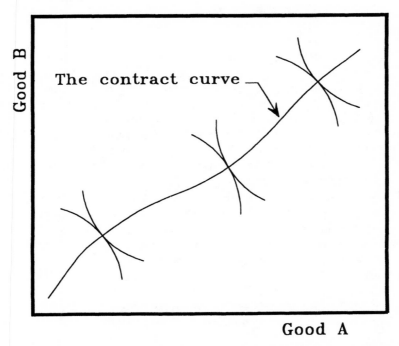

One can conceive of any number of indifference curves in the box and, therefore, any number of back-to-back tangency points. All of those points together constitute the contract curve. Any point on the curve is Pareto optimal and any point off the curve is not.

on regulation to some degree. For, necessarily, if one is a maximalist on consumer sovereignty one must be a minimalist on regulation. One is likely to favor deregulation where possible and to favor regulation only when a clear and strong case can be made for it.

If one has a strong preference for reliance upon the market one will evaluate tax policy partly in terms of the degree to which it distorts or constrains private economic decision making. One will tend to favor a tax structure that treats many classes of individuals and activities in more or less the same manner. This is very different from an interventionist view of tax policy as a major tool for reshaping economic activity. This point is discussed in more detail in chapters 6 and 7.

The modern democratic capitalist state is a major redistributor of income. The concept of Pareto optimality has implications for how this ought to be done. If one is committed to consumer sovereignty, is it not consistent to apply that idea to the consumer whose consumption is made possible by transfers just as well as any other consumer? This suggests that assistance to low-income persons is most efficiently delivered as cash rather than as free or subsidized goods and services (assistance in-kind). Some years ago, when Milton Friedman proposed replacing "the present ragbag" of social programs with a negative income tax, he argued among other things that "it gives help in the form most useful to the individual, namely, cash."[4]

Consider the renter of an apartment in a public housing project in terms of Figure 5.3. The budget line represents both the renter's own income and the amount of subsidy behind the apartment. The renter cannot allocate the entire budget in the way that maximizes his or her utility. Perhaps the apartment costs the authority $5,000 a year to provide but it is rented to the person at $2,500 a year. If the resident, instead of being given $2,500 in housing subsidy, were given $2,500 in cash it is probable that some of that cash would be spent on housing. But it is also probable that some would be spent on other things.

The renter's expenditure on housing with the cash assistance would thus be greater than without it, but less than $2,500 greater. This simply follows from the idea that housing, like most other goods and services, is subject to declining marginal utility. The renter is consuming more housing and less of everything else than he or she would choose to do at that budget. The renter is thus located on the budget line at a point other than the tangency point. He or she is better off with the housing subsidy than without it. But the renter would be still better off with the cash equivalent of the subsidy. Another way to put this is to say that the subsidy costs the donor more than it is worth to the recipient. That would not be the case were the recipient free to spend the subsidy in any manner that he or she chose.

The Limits of Pareto Optimality

Although Pareto optimality is a powerful concept, it has its limitations and it leaves some important questions unaddressed. Its most commonly noted limitation is that it sheds no light on the matter of the distribution of income and wealth. We say that to be Pareto optimal a situation may have no unrealized gains of trade remaining. But we do not address the question of how the parties represented in the Edgeworth box acquired the assets that they bring to the trading process. In the previous discussion we showed that any point on the contract curve is Pareto optimal. But if, as shown in Figure 5.8, Mr. X is very poor and Mr. Y is very wealthy, Mr. X in his poverty may derive little comfort from knowing that there are no further gains of trade to be realized and that his poverty is, therefore, Pareto optimal. He might be much better off in a situation that was not Pareto optimal but in which wealth or income was distributed in a less asymmetrical manner.

The concept of Pareto optimality, by itself, gives us no insight into what

Figure 5.8
Optimal and Non-optimal Points

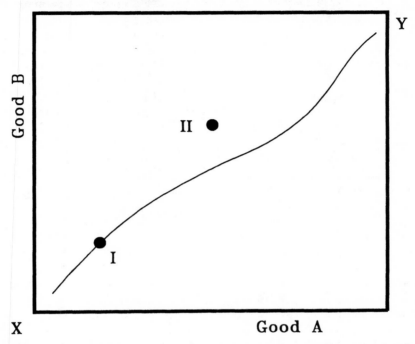

Point I is Pareto optimal in that it is on the contract curve, but note that consumer Y has
many times the income of consumer X. Point II is off the contract curve and thus not Pareto
optimal. Nonetheless, we might prefer point II to point I on the grounds that the greater
degree of equality more than makes up for the lesser degree of efficiency.

would be the optimum distribution of income or what are the effects of
different income distributions upon individuals or society as a whole. Early
neoclassical economists such as Edgeworth finessed the income distribution
question by taking the position that it is impossible to make interpersonal
comparisons of utility. The geometry discussed above requires only that
people be able to order their preferences. But, of course, society does not
have the luxury of finessing the income distribution question that way.
Decisions about income redistribution through taxation, transfers, and subsidies necessarily involve implicit interpersonal utility comparisons. If we
did not believe that an additional dollar of yacht yields less utility to a
wealthy person than an additional dollar of housing or medical care yields
to a poor person, how could we justify taxing the wealthy in order to make
transfers to the poor?

By Pareto's definition, any point on the contract curve is optimal and we
cannot say that one is superior to another. If we could say that we knew

what was the right income distribution then we could say just which point on the contract was the preferred point—the optimum among optimums.[5] But, of course, this is not easily done. We could take a Benthamite view and say that we preferred whatever distribution produced a net maximum of human happiness, assuming that this could be known.[6] But others might object that fairness should be the standard and that income should be distributed on the basis of effort, useful accomplishment, and merit (assuming, of course, that these can be measured). Clearly, the happiness and the fairness standards might yield different results. The philosopher John Rawls argues that all actions must be considered first in terms of their effects upon the least fortunate members of society.[7] Thus, Rawls would be opposed to an action that delivered large benefits to the privileged while imposing much smaller losses on the nonprivileged. But that violates the net happiness standard and may or may not violate the fairness standard. The point is simply that we all do not agree about what are the standards for deciding what is an optimal distribution of income.[8]

Then, too, it is a mistake to believe that one can think about what would be the optimal income distribution without considering what effects that income distribution would have upon society and what society would have to do to reach that distribution. One should not simply consider the Gross National Product (GNP) as a given and then think about how it would be best divided up. The pattern of taxation, transfer, and subsidy will affect economic efficiency, work effort, entrepreneurial effort, and the rate of investment. The economic pie is unlike other pies in that how it is sliced will affect how it grows or shrinks over time. An extremely egalitarian distribution of income might stifle work effort, innovation, and risk taking. An extremely unequal distribution of income may provide the emotional force behind social revolution, and so on. Conservatives have for some years accused modern liberals and advocates of the Western European social democratic model of ignoring the link between redistribution policy and economic performance and, at least in the past, there has been some justification behind this complaint.

If one is to philosophize about what would be the best distribution of income—the optimum optimum discussed previously—it is wise not only to think about the desired end state but also about what would be the "transactions costs" of getting there. Will it require much coercion? How much work effort will people divert from useful activity into resisting the change? Will it require making illegal types of behavior that are now legal? Will it require changing people's values; say, making extreme ambitiousness into more of a fault and less of a virtue than it is now taken to be? In short, to think that there is an ideal distribution of income—if only we could discover it—that exists apart from what sort of society we are and where we are now is an extreme simplification of reality. The issue of how income is to be distributed thus quickly takes us beyond microeconomic theory into the province of the historian, the political scientist, the sociologist, and the philosopher.

The radical economist who believes that wealth and income are distributed in a vastly more unequal manner than they should be is not likely to take the concept of Pareto optimality very seriously. He or she can easily argue that the matter of an "equitable" distribution of wealth is far more important than the matter of marginal efficiency in either production or consumption. The more conservative economist who regards Pareto optimality as a powerful conceptual tool might reply that burdening it with the charge that it does not elucidate the matter of income distribution faults it for not addressing something that it was never intended to address—a bit like complaining that a screwdriver is a useless implement because you cannot hammer a nail in with it.

The question of externalities. For Pareto optimality to prevail there must be an absence of externalities. Assume that you and I trade until we have exhausted all the gains from our trade. Our situation appears to be Pareto optimal. But perhaps in the process of optimizing our own situations we have imposed major losses on another individual who was not a party to our trading process and whose interests, therefore, went unrepresented. Perhaps we did not even know that this person existed. In that case we cannot say that the results of our trading are Pareto optimal. Pareto optimally demands that the parties to the trading process face a structure of true costs and true benefits. This means, if taken literally, that there can be no externalities. All effects upon third parties must be incorporated into the system of prices that the participants in the market face. If complete consumer sovereignty means that large externalities may be imposed upon third parties, then it may be that some restraint on consumer sovereignty actually moves the situation toward Pareto optimality. Thus, although the concept of Pareto optimality and its expression in the Edgeworth box make a prima facie case for consumer sovereignty, there are circumstances that overrule this case. Comparable statements can be made with regard to what might be called "producer sovereignty." Externalities are discussed further in the following chapter.

The behavioral model revisited. The behavioral model behind the idea of consumer sovereignty and Pareto optimality is economic man, one of whose defining characteristics is rationality. The reality, of course, is that some consumers are rational (without endeavoring to define that term) and some are not. As soon as we admit this undeniable point, some of the policy prescriptions that flow from the concept of Pareto optimality seem open to question. For example, if the individual is not rational it may be best to give aid in a way that minimizes the individual's freedom of choice. In that case, cash is the least preferable form of assistance.

The central actor in the model is the individual, economic man. However, the bulk of the U.S. population does not live as isolated individuals, but as members of multiperson households. Thus, a major share of all consumption is not individual but joint consumption.[9] Microeconomists treat the household as if it were an individual, sometimes acknowledging this explicitly and more often simply doing it implicitly. For this substitution to be valid the head of the household, meaning the individual to whom income is paid or transfers are given, must have incorporated the utility functions of the other household members into his or her own utility function.[10] This makes it valid to treat the multiperson household as if it were an individual. In the happy, well-functioning household that assumption may be a good enough approximation of the truth. But the substantial prevalence of divorce, separation, spousal abuse, child abuse and neglect, and the like clearly indicates that there are some millions of households for which it is not a good approximation of the truth. For such households aid that is beyond the discretion of the head of the household may be better. If we give aid in the form of free school lunches the child who gets to school that day gets a good lunch. If we give the aid as cash to a parent for whom the child's welfare is less than a paramount concern we are not so certain how the money will be spent.

Another assumption made previously in this book and also in standard texts on microeconomics is that the utility derived from consumption is received entirely by the consumer. But that is not always the case. As a trivial example, the adult who gives a child a toy may derive just as much pleasure from watching the child play with the toy as the child does in playing with it. The economist Lester Thurow, in a widely cited article on aid to the poor, suggests that the way the recipient spends the aid may be important to the donor.[11] In the jargon of welfare economics, the recipient's actions may appear in the utility function of the donor. In that case cash aid may maximize the recipient's utility but not the utility of society as a whole. Reducing the recipient's consumer sovereignty by giving aid in a constrained form may thus be a move toward Pareto optimality. Note that these arguments do not attack the logic of the Paretian analysis. They simply point out that one must consider in each case how much its assumptions correspond to reality.

NOTES

1. If marginal utilities remained constant, the indifference curve would be a straight line like the budget line and there could be no unique point of tangency. It would thus not be possible to say that some distributions of goods were preferable to others. If marginal utilities increased rather than decreased, the indifference curve would be concave to the origin rather than convex. The highest curve that could be reached with any given budget would be one that the budget line intersected at the axis. Utility would be maximized if the consumer only consumed one good.

2. The view that it is valid to treat all other goods as a single commodity is

the Composite Good Theorem. This was first postulated by John R. Hicks in *Value and Capital: An Inquiry into Some Fundamental Principles of Economics* (London: Oxford Press, Clarendon Press, 1939).

3. Nicholas Kaldor, "Welfare Propositions in Economics and Interpersonal Comparisons of Utility," *Economic Journal* 49 (September 1939) pp. 549–52, and John R. Hicks, "The Foundations of Welfare Economics," *Economic Journal* 49 (December 1939), pp. 696–712.

4. Milton Friedman, *Capitalism and Freedom* (Chicago: University of Chicago Press, 1962), p. 192. Although the United States never enacted a guaranteed income tax as proposed by Friedman, the Earned Income Tax Credit (EITC) of the federal income tax approximates it for low income workers in that, as Friedman suggested, the tax liability of the poor worker is negative. Thus, the flow of payments is not from the filer of the return to the Internal Revenue Service but from the IRS to the filer. It differs from the Friedman proposal in that it applies only to employed persons.

5. This doubly optimum point (it is both Pareto optimal in the ordinary sense and also represents the optimum distribution of income) is sometimes referred to by what the writer regards as a somewhat unfortunate coinnage, the "bliss point." For a brief exposition on this, see Nancy Smith Barrett, *The Theory of Microeconomic Policy* (Lexington, MA: D.C. Heath & Co., 1974), p. 294.

6. After the nineteenth-century British philosopher, Jeremy Bentham.

7. John Rawls, *A Theory of Justice* (Cambridge, MA: Harvard University Press, 1971).

8. In *What's Fair? American Beliefs about Distributive Justice* (Cambridge, MA: Harvard University Press, 1981), Jennifer L. Hochschild examines Americans' beliefs about how justly or unjustly income is distributed. She reviews survey data going back many years and also presents some original data. Her general conclusion is that the majority of the population views the current distribution of income as reasonably fair. She argues that one reason that the United States has never had a strong socialist movement, compared with many European nations, is this perception by a large part of the populace.

9. In 1992 there was a total of 24.0 million one-person households out of a total household population of 250.7 million. Thus, over 90 percent of the household population lived in multiperson households. U.S. Department of Commerce, Bureau of the Census, *Statistical Abstract of the United States,* 113th ed. (Washington, DC: U.S. Government Printing Office, 1993), table 65.

10. This device goes back at least as far as the nineteenth-century British economist Phillip H. Wicksteed. See Chapter 1.

11. Lester Thurow, "Cash Versus In-Kind Transfers," *American Economic Review* (May 1974), pp. 190–95.

CHAPTER 6

The Role of Government, Part 1

This chapter presents a conventional view of the economic role of government. The presentation in this chapter may strike the reader as a bit naive, and the reader may ask, "Is that really how things happen?" The subsequent chapter will provide an adequate dose of skepticism.

In the conventional view the economic role of government is to make the economy function more efficiently and more equitably. Within the market, individuals are guided only by self-interest operating within a framework of laws and regulations laid down by government. The situation is described in Thomas Carlyle's phrase, "anarchy with a constable." But government, standing apart from the market and guided by a concern for the public interest, does those things that the market cannot do at all, serves to correct and adjust the market in those areas where the market works badly, and succors those who, for whatever reasons, cannot survive in the market on their own. This view, albeit stated in an oversimplified way here, is the view that is consistent with American liberalism. It supports the idea of a large public sector and an activist government. It is consistent with the political philosophy of Jimmy Carter or Bill Clinton, somewhat less so with that of George Bush, and still less so with that of Ronald Reagan. In a Western European context it is consistent with the "Scandinavian model," the capitalist economy with a very large public sector, a great deal of public control over the operation of private enterprises, and a great deal of income redistribution.

THE ECONOMIC ROLES OF GOVERNMENT

It is common to classify the economic actions of government as falling into the following three categories, sometimes referred to as a Musgravian classification after the economist Richard Musgrave.[1]

- Stabilization
- Redistribution
- Allocation

In the Musgravian scheme the first two functions should be entirely the province of the national government. The last function, allocation, should be the province of all three levels of government, with the level of government that performs the function corresponding to the area over which the benefits of the function are distributed. The logic behind this division of roles will become apparent.

Stabilization

Stabilizing activities are those intended to stabilize the running of the national economy. This will thus include antirecessionary policy at low points in the business cycle and anti-inflationary policy at high points in the business cycle. Or, in commonly used terms, it will be expansionary at some times and contractionary at others. Stabilization goals can be pursued through fiscal policy (taxes and expenditures) and monetary policy (actions that affect the money supply and the interest rate). It is generally understood that stabilization is the province of the federal government, if only because it would be virtually impossible for 50 state governments to coordinate their actions to pursue such goals.

One link between the macroeconomic issue of stabilization and the microeconomics that is the subject of this book is that they meet on the issue of efficiency. Clearly, if there is involuntary unemployment the economy is not operating at full efficiency, as some resources are not only not in their highest use, but are not in any economic use at all. And efficiency is one of the primary concerns of the microeconomist. Most microeconomic analyses assume full employment but the microeconomist understands that this is a necessary assumption and not a statement of fact.[2]

Theories are sometimes made obsolete by events, and something like that may be happening to the stabilization concept. The old Keynesian wisdom was that governments were to run budget surpluses at the top of the business cycle to reduce aggregate demand and lower inflationary pressures, and to run deficits at the bottom of the business cycle to increase aggregate demand. In a period when the federal deficit is several hundred billion dollars a year even at the top of the business cycle, that option is gone. Then, too, the growing volume of international trade and the growing flows of capital across national borders reduce the capacity of any national government to control the level of domestic economic activity.[3] If the conventional view were being developed in the present economic climate there might thus be somewhat less emphasis on the stabilization role.

Redistribution

Redistribution refers to the redistribution of income, presumably in a downward direction. This is accomplished in part by the pattern of taxes and income transfers. It is also accomplished by the provision of goods and services, for example, public housing or medical care, at below cost.

The Musgravian argument for making redistribution the responsibility solely of the federal government is simply that a standardized pattern of redistribution would avoid causing migration for the purpose of seeking aid. Such migration, unrelated to other economic or personal reasons, would necessarily be inefficient.

A more powerful argument, in this writer's view, turns on the matter of interstate and intermunicipal economic competition.[4] One central fact of state and local government in the United States is the intense competition between places for economic activity. This is driven by the desire to keep local taxes low and local labor markets tight. A policy of generous transfers to lower-income people would necessitate raising taxes, thus making the state or locality less attractive to industry and less attractive as a place of residence for the wealthy, a clearly counterproductive strategy.[5] Thus, if there is to be a high level of redistribution it can only be done by the one governmental unit that does not need to fear interplace competition, namely, the federal government.

Allocation

Allocation refers to actions of government that change the pattern of output of the economy. Clearly, government expenditures on goods and services are allocative. This is true whether the goods and services are directly produced by government or are produced privately. The pattern of taxation and subsidization has allocative effects. Regulations, too, have allocative effects in that they may compel expenditures on some things and forbid or discourage expenditures on other things.

Although separate in concept, the three functions listed above are intertwined in reality. The decision to build public housing is clearly allocative in that it is allocating part of the nation's resources to housing as opposed to something else. It is also redistributive in that it will be rented to poor people at below cost, thus redistributing income downward. By the timing of the expenditures for it vis-à-vis the business cycle, it may also have stabilizing (or destabilizing) effects. In some textbooks transfer payments such as social security and unemployment insurance are referred to as "automatic stabilizers" precisely because they do not move with the business cycle. A program that appears to be a pure transfer program such as Social Security will have indirect allocational effects in that its beneficiaries will spend their incomes in somewhat different patterns than other persons. Thus, changes in the amount distributed through the Social Security program will change the pattern of goods and services produced by the nation's economy.

Reality and the Musgravian prescription. The actual pattern of government activity, while it does not correspond precisely to the Musgravian prescription, does correspond to it roughly. In the realm of stabilization, monetary policy is entirely a federal matter administered through the Federal Reserve System. And it is only the federal government that considers the effect of its fiscal behavior on the business cycle. While it is true that the aggregate effect of state and local fiscal behavior may be procyclical at some times and contracyclical at other times, no state or local government worries about the effects of its actions upon the national economy. Rather, budgetary and financial officers at the state and local levels worry about the effects that national economic trends will have on their revenues, borrowing costs, and expenses.

Not all redistribution is done by the federal government, but the largest programs are federal. Slightly over half of the federal budget in 1992 was devoted to "human resources" which are largely transfer programs. The largest transfer program, Social Security, and the second largest, Medicare, are entirely federal. Medicaid is a joint federal/state program with somewhat more than half of the costs paid by the federal government. The same is true of public assistance. Food stamps are funded entirely by the federal government,[6] and so on. Note, also, that the federal tax system is substantially more progressive than those of the states and localities. The primary reason, as discussed further in Chapter 8, appears to be the matter of interplace economic competition discussed earlier. Allocation is a function of all three levels of government. It occupies the remainder of this chapter.

GOVERNMENT AS A REMEDY FOR MARKET FAILURE

The third of the Musgravian roles of government is allocation. If the market were able to allocate all of the resources of the economy in a way that we thought was satisfactory there would be no allocative role for government. But the market by itself does not do this and that takes us to the subject of market failure.[7] The four types of market failures discussed in this section are (1) public goods, (2) externalities, (3) monopoly, and (4) ignorance.

Public Goods

Public goods are generally defined by or identified by two key properties discussed below, *nonexcludability* and *nonrivalness*. Some economists take the view that the former property alone is sufficient to define a public good. Others take the view that to be a public good the good in question must exhibit both properties.[8]

1. Nonexcludability. To create a market it must be possible to exclude the nonpayer from consuming the good. Otherwise the rational, self-interested individual (economic man) will choose to be a "free rider" and not pay. Thus, nonexcludability, the inability to exclude the nonpayer from consuming the good or service, is one defining characteristic of a public good. If the nonpayer cannot be excluded from consumption then a market cannot be created and the good must either be provided publicly (or by philanthropy) or it will not be provided at all.

2. Nonrivalry. This means that one person's consumption of the good does not interfere with the consumption of that good by another person. The argument for requiring nonrivalry as a criterion for a pure public good is based on efficiency. If the good is truly nonrival in nature then efficiency would require that everyone for whom it had even the slightest utility be permitted to make use of it. Observing the light from the lighthouse may be a matter of life or death for the mariner but only a trivial source of pleasure for the person on the beach. But there is no reason to prevent the person on the beach from "using" this service, as his or her use of it in no way detracts from someone else's use. Another way to put it is that nonrivalry means that the marginal cost of allowing another person to use the service is 0.[9] As noted previously, setting $P = MC$ maximizes efficiency. Thus, for a nonrival good the efficient price is 0. But the market cannot provide goods at a price of 0. That implies public provision. But note that unlike nonexcludability, nonrivalry does not necessitate public provision. It is entirely possible to provide through the market a good that is completely nonrival so long as it is possible to exclude the nonpayer. For this reason nonrivalry is a weaker requirement than nonexcludability.

Some goods are pure public goods and some are pure private goods. Many others display some properties of both. Figure 6.1 shows a number of goods. Those located in the corners are pure cases. Food, like most consumer goods, is a pure case of a private good. The nonpayer can be excluded from consumption and consumption is completely rival. Thus, it is shown in the upper left corner. The lighthouse is a pure public good. It is characterized by nonexcludability and nonrivalry. There is no way to charge for the light from the lighthouse and the fact that I can see its light in no way interferes with your ability to see it. It is thus shown in the lower right corner. National defense is often cited as a pure public good. So, too, is flood control. There is no practical way to protect one house from flood

Figure 6.1
Public and Private Goods

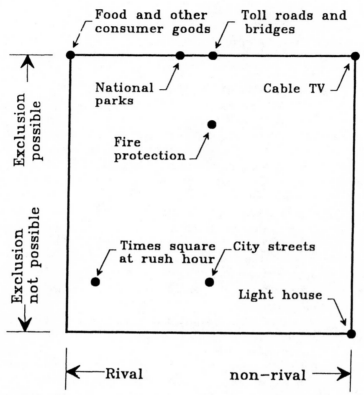

The corners represent pure cases with regard to both exclusion and rivalry. Goods on boundaries but not in corners are pure cases for one criterion and mixed cases for one criterion. Goods inside the box are mixed cases for both criteria.

waters while leaving the adjacent house unprotected because its owner chooses not to pay for flood control. Nor is there any question of rivalry. Mosquito abatement has been cited as another example. Either the entire area is or is not sprayed. It would make no sense to spray one property and not spray the adjacent property. All of these services would thus be located at the lower right corner.

Cable TV is characterized by excludability and nonrivalry. You can be charged a fee for the connection but the fact that you receive the signal does not interfere with anyone else's reception. It is thus located in the upper right corner. The lower left corner, rivalry combined with nonexcludability, is shown without an example. This is because where there is a high degree of rivalry there is usually some way to exclude the nonpayer.

Times Square at rush hour comes fairly close to the lower left corner but is not quite at it. Rivalry is not complete in that while there is serious congestion, one party's use of the area does not absolutely prevent another party from using it. And excludability, while possible in principle, would not be practical. Hence, we show Times Square at rush hour as close to but not quite at the corner.

Toll roads are located along the top border but not in a corner. Exclusion is easily achieved but there is some degree of rivalry in that my use of the road, particularly in peak hours, may impede your use of it. National parks fall in the same category. It is possible to exclude the nonpayer but there is a degree of rivalry, particularly in the peak season. City streets are shown inside the box and not on a border. In general, it is not practical to charge for their use but, in principle, it would be possible to do so.[10] Thus, there is an element of excludability. And there is rivalry at some times of the day. Fire protection is also inside the box. There is an element of exclusion in that it is possible to charge for it in some circumstances. There may also be an element of rivalry in that the same fire company cannot be at two fires at the same time.[11]

Changes in technology will change the boundary between public and private goods. For example, some years ago it could be said that a television broadcast was a public good in that one could not prevent the nonpayer from listening. Thus, the industry evolved as a system in which television broadcasts were free to the viewer and were paid for by advertisers. But now that cable transmission and scrambling devices are available, exclusion is possible and broadcasts can be treated as private goods with the viewer charged either for the connection or by the hour.

Of all types of market failure, the public good for which exclusion is not possible represents the most complete type of failure, for what could be more complete than the total inability to create a market through which the good can be supplied? When government does provide true public goods there is always the problem of deciding what and how much to supply in the absence of price signals from the market. One solution is to estimate how much people would pay if it *were* possible to charge (exclude the nonpayer). This "willingness to pay" approach is at the heart of benefit-cost analysis discussed in Chapter 9.

It is important not to become confused between the economist's meaning of public goods and those goods that are in fact supplied by public funds. Some goods like national defense and mosquito abatement that are supplied by public funds are true public goods in the economist's meaning of the term. On the other hand, public education is not a public good in the economist's meaning of the term in that exclusion is readily possible. It is a private good that we supply with public funds as a matter of political choice. The same is true of public housing or the care offered at a free clinic.

Externalities

In previous chapters we established that setting price equal to marginal cost represented an efficient allocation of resources. But this is true only if the marginal cost figures to which the firm is responding truly represent the real cost of the next unit and the price the buyer pays truly represents the real benefits associated with the next unit. If there are effects that are external to the parties conducting the transaction, say, the firm and the buyer, then the market will not produce optimal results. This is true even if the market fits the model of perfect competition described in the previous chapter.

Assume, for example, that a process of production releases pollutants that affect the life and health of parties who are not party to the transaction. Then, from the viewpoint of society as a whole, the cost figures to which the firm is responding are too low and the firm will produce more units than it should. The last units produced will cost more than they are worth to the consumer. But they will be produced because the firm is only paying part of the costs. The remainder of the costs are, in effect, being paid by parties who are external to the transaction and therefore have no influence on it. Comparable comments can be made from the buyer's side of the transaction. Perhaps the use of the product imposes costs on third parties. For example, driving an automobile affects air quality. In this case the consumer overconsumes because he or she does not respond to those costs imposed on third parties.

External effects or externalities can also be positive. The firm that does scientific research to develop a new product does so for reasons of profit, but in time the knowledge gained will diffuse out from the firm and benefit others in ways that do not show up on the firm's balance sheet. Comparable comments could be made about the expenditures firms make on training their workers. The student may consume higher education purely for reasons of private gain, whether those be anticipated future income, enhanced social status, or the pure pleasure of learning. But if it is true that society in general benefits from having a better-educated population then there are positive externalities associated with this private consumption. In fact, if we did not believe that there were such externalities it would be hard to make the case for the expenditure of public funds on state universities.

One goal, then, of government policy is to cause firms and individuals to "internalize the externalities" so that their behavior is more nearly responsive to the true costs and benefits of production and consumption. The obvious instruments for doing this are taxes for activities that produce negative externalities and subsidies for those that produce positive externalities. Figure 6.2 shows the use of a tax to compensate for negative externalities and a subsidy to compensate for positive externalities. Note that

Figure 6.2
Compensating for Externalities with Taxes and Subsidies

Panel A   Panel B

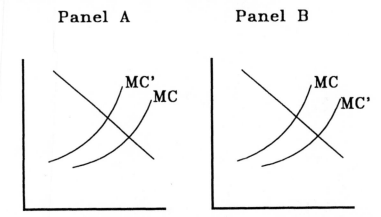

In panel A a tax raises marginal costs from MC to MC' to internalize negative externalities. The equilibrium price rises and the equilibrium quantity falls. In panel B a subsidy lowers the marginal costs to adjust for positive externalities. The equilibrium price falls and the equilibrium quantity rises.

in both cases the adjustment is shown as being made on the supply side. However, the adjustment could also be made on the demand side by taxing the buyer of the product with negative externalities and offering a subsidy to the buyer of the product with positive externalities. As a political matter, whether the tax or subsidy is on the supply side or the demand side may be of considerable importance. But as is shown in Chapter 8, both taxes and subsidies may be shifted to a considerable extent. Thus, there may be a substantial difference between the nominal or de jure and the actual or de facto distribution of burdens or benefits.

Monopoly

In Chapter 4 we discussed monopoly briefly and noted that its presumed inefficiency occurs because the monopolist, if guided solely by the goal of profit maximization, will set marginal cost equal to marginal revenue (see Figure 4.4) and will thus produce too little and charge too much. As noted in Chapter 4, government has attempted to deal with the problem of monopoly by breaking up firms that had a monopoly or near monopoly position. But this is not always practical because monopoly or near monopoly often comes about because there are large economies of scale involved.

The other governmental approach is that of regulation. In the ideal situations, government would compel the monopolist to produce at P = MC.

Figure 6.3
The Case of a Decreasing Cost Industry

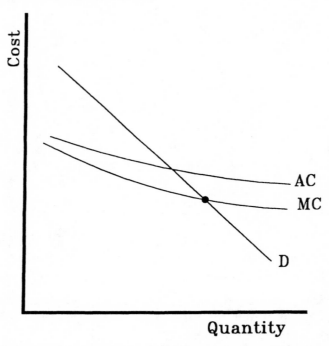

Marginal efficiency would require setting price equal to marginal cost. However, at this point the industry would operate at a loss because price would be less than average cost. Regulation of a monopoly subject to decreasing costs can thus be a difficult problem.

In practice, this is easier said than done. Consider an industry that is subject to continuously increasing returns to scale over the relevant scale of operation, as illustrated in Figure 6.3. Here the marginal cost at any level of production is the lowest cost yet encountered, and therefore is necessarily below the average cost. Thus, marginal cost pricing will force the industry to operate at a loss. The efficient solution would be for government to require the industry to produce at P = MC and then to cover the industry's losses with a subsidy. Such a subsidy would make sense in microeconomic terms, but it would be impossible to defend in political debate unless the debate's audience were restricted to economists and their students.

More commonly, monopolies are regulated on the basis of rate of return. The regulatory agency, usually a state agency, sets a price that permits the monopoly a "fair" rate of return on investment. This may or may not place price and marginal cost reasonably close to each other.

In some cases it is possible to both permit the monopoly to make an acceptable rate of return and achieve marginal efficiency, even though the

Figure 6.4
Two-Part Pricing

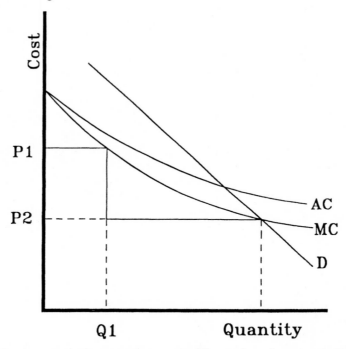

The regulated monopoly charges P1 out to Q1 and then P2 from that point on. This arrangement permits the monopoly to make an adequate return and also achieves marginal efficiency by setting P = MC.

monopoly faces declining costs. This is done through two-part pricing, as
shown in Figure 6.4. An electric utility, for example, might charge domestic
users, say, 7 cents per kilowatt hour (kwh) for the first 500 kwh and then
4 cents per kwh after that. If the average domestic user consumes 1,500
kwh per month, the average user will be paying 5 cents per kwh. If the
average cost of supply, including a normal return to capital, is 5 cents per
kwh then this arrangement will achieve both an adequate rate of return
and efficiency at the margin. Note that this efficient solution requires a
situation in which the user's total consumption is known, so that the user
can be charged different amounts on different parts of his or her consumption.[12]

Perhaps the largest problem with monopoly, and one that cannot readily
be diagrammed, is that a strong monopoly position may cause an enterprise
to become complacent and make less effort to be efficient or innovative.
This is, in fact, one of the problems with regulating a monopoly on the
basis of rate of return—it tends to reduce the impetus to innovate. But

it must be said that some monopolies are quite progressive, as noted before in connection with Bell Labs. Quite evidently, the question of monopoly and efficiency is much more complex than is suggested by any diagram.

Ignorance

As discussed earlier, the perfect market requires perfect information. And, in fact, this requirement is one reason for asserting that the perfect market is an abstraction that can never be fully realized. Improving the quality of information can move the market toward perfection by giving buyers and sellers the means to assess more accurately the true costs and benefits of the choices that they make in the marketplace. Requiring financial disclosure requirements for new stock offers, efficiency labels on refrigerators, mileage data on new car stickers, nutrition information on canned food, and health warnings on cigarette packages and liquor bottles are all ways in which government seeks to improve the market by improving the quality of information.

NOTES

1. Richard A. Musgrave and Peggy B. Musgrave, *Public Finance in Theory and Practice* (New York: McGraw-Hill Book Co., 1984), and earlier editions, chapter 1.

2. The largest conceptual break between neoclassical macroeconomics and Keynesian economics was over this issue. Neoclassical economists assumed that the natural state of the economy was full employment and that unemployment represented only a transitory disequilibrium. In fact, the notion that there could not be overproduction and hence unemployment was enshrined in economic doctorine under the name "Say's Law," after the early nineteenth-century French economist Jean Baptiste Say. In 1936, with the publication of *The General Theory of Employment, Interest and Money* (New York: Harcourt, Brace and World, 1964), John Keynes made the case that an economy could come to equilibrium at below full employment and remain there for a sustained period of time. The interested reader can pursue the subject in any standard introductory economics text.

3. It is generally accepted that the slow recovery of the United States from the recession of 1990 and 1991 was due to recession or slow economic growth in the United States's major trading partners including Japan, Canada, and the European Community. Specifically, poor economic performance by U.S. trading partners held back U.S. economic growth by restraining the growth of demand for U.S. exports.

4. For a picture of the intensity of interplace economic competition in the United States, see J. Castro, "Come on Down, Fast," *Time,* May 27, 1991, pp. 38–42; or R. Guskind, "The Giveaway Game Continues," *Planning* (February 1990), pp. 4–8. For a more detailed discussion of the state of interplace economic competition in the United States and additional references, see John M. Levy, "The U.S. Experience with Local Economic Development," *Environment and Planning* C 10 (1992), pp. 51–60.

5. For a discussion of a municipality (New York City) that did attempt to do a great deal of redistribution and found itself driven to the edge of municipal bankruptcy, see Ken Auletta, *The Streets Were Paved with Gold* (New York: Random House, 1979).

6. For details, see *The Statistical Abstract of the United States,* various years, chapters on State and Local Government Finances and Employment, and Social Insurance and Human Services.

7. The typology presented here is a standard one that can be found in many texts on microeconomics, public policy, and public finance such as Musgrave and Musgrave, *Public Finance in Theory and Practice.*

8. Steven E. Landsburg notes that one can also define a public good by saying that "a good is a public good if one person's consumption increases the amount available to everybody." On reflection the reader will realize that this is tantamount to saying that the good has the properties of nonexcludability and nonrivalry. See Steven E. Landsberg, *Price Theory and Applications.* 2d ed. (New York: The Dryden Press, 1992), p. 472.

9. This is an old idea. In fact, a very clear formulation of it was made by J. Dupuit well before the marginalist revolution ushered in the neoclassical period in economics. J. Dupuit, "On the Measurement of the Utility of Public Works," originally published in 1844, translated in *International Economic Papers,* no. 2. (1952), pp. 83–110. It can also be found in Denys Munby, ed., *Transport* (Baltimore: Penguin Books, 1968), pp. 19–57.

10. In Singapore owners of motor vehicles are charged for the use of streets in the center during some hours of the day. The original system used a fee for a special license. At last report Singapore was planning to switch to an electronic system. The idea of charging motorists for street use was first suggested by A. C. Pigou as a way of dealing with the externalities of automobile use. In the 1960s the economist William Vickrey suggested an electronic system that would be tripped whenever the vehicle crossed a cordon line into or out of the central area. For details on the Singapore experience, see Patrick S. McCarthy and Richard Tay, "Pricing Road Congestion: Recent Evidence from Singapore," *Policy Studies Journal* (Summer 1993), p. 296; and Brian G. Field, "Road Pricing in Practice," *Transportation Journal* (Fall 1992), p. 5.

11. Originally, fire protection in cities was provided on a paid basis. Today, in some exurban and rural areas, fire companies do provide protection on a fee basis. The subscriber to the service gets a plaque that is attached to the house. If the house without a plaque burns, the fire company will do what it can to prevent loss of life but it will not put out the fire. A system like this, however, cannot be used in a densely built up area in which fire can spread from one building to another.

12. For a brief presentation on two-part pricing see Ronald C. Fisher, *State and Local Public Finance* (Glenview, IL: Scott, Foresman, 1988), pp. 332–34.

CHAPTER 7

The Role of Government, Part 2

In the last several decades, a view of the role of government very different from that expressed in the previous chapter has become quite prevalent. Like many heresies, it has come to rival in influence the parent religion from which it sprang. The new view most often goes by the name "Public Choice." It is also referred to as Constitutional Economics, Contractarian Economics, and the Economics of Politics. Like any vigorous heresy it is not monolithic, but includes many different strains.

Public Choice harks back to an old tradition, that of Political Economy, in which politics and economics were one discipline. But for at least the last century, economics has been becoming increasingly mathematical and, to the non-economist, increasingly arcane. Whether it has really become more scientific may be argued, but there is no doubt that it has taken on much of the formalism and intellectual rigor of the natural sciences. In the process, political questions have often been swept off the table. The Public Choice movement places those questions back on the table in a prominent position.

The most central idea in Public Choice is that the proper behavioral model for analyzing political behavior is the same as the proper model for analyzing economic behavior, namely, *economic man*. This may not immediately strike the reader as a major departure but, in fact, it is, and it leads to a view of the economic role of government entirely different from that presented in the previous chapter.

The most prominent name in Public Choice is the economist James Buchanan, who received the 1986 Nobel Prize in Economics for his work in Public Choice. Buchanan, whose teaching and writing career began in public finance shortly after World War II, soon observed that the prescriptions of economists and the behavior of government were quite different and that economists many times ignored the realities of public decision making. Their discussions tended to end when the economic analysis led to a political question. To use his phrase, his fellow economists often wrote as if they lived in a "benevolent despotism." They wrote as if government were a single intelligence intent upon achieving a socially optimum allocation of goods, services, and incomes. When they had examined a situation and recommended the optimizing action, they then felt that their work was done—like the advisor who thinks hard, gives wise advice to the good king, and then goes home for a well-deserved rest. The question of how the political decision about taxes, expenditures, tariffs, regulation, and the like was actually made was dismissed as a political question and therefore not central to the economists' concerns. The reader may recognize that the previous chapter is written from the "benevolent despot" perspective, although that is not explicitly stated. Government is referred to as if it were a single entity or intelligence, and the purity and single-mindedness of its motives is not questioned.

Buchanan and other Public Choice theorists take the view that economic advice divorced from realistic thinking about how governments actually make decisions is often useless. In some cases, economic advice grounded in misconceptions about how governments actually make decisions is distinctly harmful because the end results are radically different from what the politically naive economist expected. In 1978, in a paper delivered in Great Britain, Buchanan stated:

Your economists, and notably Lord Keynes, along with their American counterparts, continued to proffer policy advice as if they were talking to a benevolent despot who stood at their beck and call. This despite Wicksell's clear but simple warning in 1896 that economic policy is made by politicians who are participants in a legislative process, and that economists could not ignore these elementary facts. But British and American economists throughout most of this century continued to seem blind to what now appears so simple to us, that benevolent despots do not exist and that governmental policy emerges from a highly complex and institutional structure peopled by ordinary men and women, very little different from the rest of us.[1]

In the Public Choice view, economics divorced from politics is often a sterile exercise because it cannot give useful policy advice. Thus, a keen understanding of the process by which government makes economic decisions is essential if the economist is to be useful. The central assumption in Public Choice is that the actions of government are best understood if we assume that people in their roles as voters, bureaucrats, and politicians behave very much as they do as workers, consumers, and entrepreneurs—namely, they tend to be rational and to be guided by self-interest. Another way to say this, as noted previously, is to say that economic man is the right behavioral model for political science. It is not necessary to say that people in their political roles are always rational or that they always act in self-interest, but only that these are the best available working assumptions.

Once one accepts economic man as the correct behavioral model for political science, one arrives at a very different picture of the economic role of government from that presented in the previous chapter. One ceases to see government as standing apart from the economy adjusting, correcting, and fine-tuning the economy. Rather, one sees it as being thoroughly enmeshed in the economy. One sees the government not as a single intelligence with a unified purpose, but as a process in which there are many actors and many different and often contradictory motivations.

Government is no longer to be seen as the impartial referee who sets the bylaws by which the economic "game" in the market is played, but a powerful participant in the game, much more powerful than the individuals or firms or other "players," and liable to bend the bylaws to its advantage, always claiming that it did so in the interest of the other players.[2]

The citizen, in his or her role as voter, is not so different in his or her role as consumer. Just as the consumer seeks to make the purchase that delivers the biggest net benefit, so the voter is likely to vote for that candidate who it appears will deliver the biggest net benefit to that voter.

The elected official is, first and foremost, a vote maximizer. He or she has little choice. Regardless of what the politician feels is right or what the politician would do if left to his or her own devices, he or she must offer enough to enough voters to be elected and reelected. The politician who routinely placed his or her concept of the general public interest above that of the voters in his or her home district would soon be defeated by a more realistic opponent. Thus, the electoral equivalent of natural selection guarantees that most elected officials will be the servants of local and specific rather than general interests.

The bureaucrat, also a species of economic man, will, like the rest of us, be guided in large measure by considerations of job security, possibilities for advancement, status, and the like. Just as the employee of a corporation is likely to be guided more by immediate considerations of job security and advancement than by abstract notions of maximizing corporate profit, so too is the bureaucrat more likely to be guided by immediate personal goals than by abstract notions of maximizing net public benefit.

The actions of government are, then, the product of these different interests. Clausewitz said that war is the continuation of politics by other means. The Public Choice theorist might say that politics is the continuation of economic activity by other means. To the notion of market failure discussed in the previous chapter the Public Choice theorists counterpose the concept of government failure. A complete summary of the Public Choice viewpoint is beyond the scope of this chapter, but it is possible to point out a few salient ideas and then a few policy prescriptions.

Public Choice theorists have made much of the concept of "rational ignorance" first ennunciated by Anthony Downs.[3] If a particular piece of legislation has a relatively small effect upon your life and fortunes it is not rational for you to spend much time learning about it. On the other hand, if a few people stand to benefit greatly from it then it is in their interest to be very well informed on it and to lobby for its enactment. Strongly motivated minorities will then use the political process to enact legislation that yields them benefits even though their benefits are smaller than the net loss to the entire body politic. An example cited by the Public Choice theorists James Gwartney and Richard E. Wagner is the U.S. tariff on sugar.[4] They noted that in 1988 the price of domestically produced sugar in the United States was over 20 cents a pound compared to 7 cents a pound on the world market. Because of the tariff two hundred and fifty million Americans each paid $6 more a year for sugar, but 11,000 U.S. sugar growers had an average gross income of $130,000 per farm. Of course, only a part of that $130,000 is profit. A bit of quick arithmetic will show that the growers' net gain or profit was only a fraction of the net loss to the U.S. public as a whole. Then why do we have the import controls? Because an informed and motivated minority has pushed the legislation through Congress past a rationally ignorant majority. The bill that delivers benefits to a small constituency at the cost of larger disbenefits to the populace as a whole fits the Public Choice picture of the economic workings of government very well. It does not fit the benevolent despot model at all. The good king, counseled by his wise court economist, would never permit the powers of his government to be used to produce a net reduction in public welfare.

Public Choice theorists have made much of the concept of "rent-seeking behavior." The concept of economic rent is an old one. Economic rent refers to a gain or advantage that cannot be competed away. In the above example the domestic producer's position in the sugar market cannot be competed away because the law blocks the sale of foreign grown sugar in the United States. The phrase "rent-seeking behavior" and the idea that government is a major venue for rent-seeking behavior appears to have been introduced into the literature by Gordon Tullock, a major Public Choice theorist and a frequent coauthor with James Buchanan.

Rent-seeking behavior is economically wasteful in that it reduces net social welfare. For one thing, the cost to the losing party is often greater than the benefit to the winning party, as in the sugar example. But beyond that the act of rent seeking itself constitutes a waste of resources. The lobbyist who spends his days pressuring congressmen on behalf of his rent-seeking clients is not available to do more useful work and his or her operation uses labor and capital that might otherwise be put to more productive use. Rent-seeking behavior thus reduces the net welfare of society both by creating inefficient arrangements and by diverting energy into the act of rent seeking.

The concept of rent seeking deserves a bit of explication here, for it is a powerful and useful idea, regardless of whether or not one accepts other parts of the Public Choice viewpoint. Agricultural price supports could be considered economic rent in that the farmer is protected from having the prices that he or she receives driven down by competition from other farmers. Rent controls might also be considered a form of economic rent (being careful to distinguish the term *economic rent* from the ordinary meaning of *rent*). The tenant in the controlled unit receives something of value that the tenant in an uncontrolled unit does not, namely, the monetary difference between what the market rent would be and what the controlled rent is. But the advantage that the tenant in the rent-controlled unit possesses cannot be competed away by a potential tenant who offers the landlord a higher rent, for the law prohibits the landlord from accepting such an offer.

There are other examples as well. "Mr. and Mrs. X" enjoy a sense of bucolic privacy in their home in exurbia. They could preserve that condition through the marketplace by buying up adjacent properties so that no one could build near their house. However, instead of pursuing that expensive option they prevail upon the town to zone their area so that no house can be built on a lot smaller than five acres. The bucolic character of their area has now been preserved by law at no cost to them. And their house, because its situation is now guaranteed for the future, is worth more than it would be in the absence of such protection. It may well be that the X's have imposed losses upon those who would like to develop the land near them that are much greater than the gains they have secured for themselves. But that net loss of welfare is not their problem. They now have something of value that cannot be competed away in the marketplace because the law is interposed between their asset and the marketplace. They, too, are enjoying an economic rent.

The concept of economic rent can be applied in the case of labor market discrimination. The party who is favored by the discriminatory behavior is protected by law or custom in his or her job against the competition of individuals from the class of persons that is discriminated against.

A contract between labor and management that sets the wage rate at more than what the equilibrium wage would otherwise be provides the unionized worker with economic rent to the extent of the difference between the negotiated wage and the market wage. The same can be said for minimum wage laws. If the equilibrium wage for fast food workers in a certain locale would be $4.00 per hour then the $4.25 minimum that the law requires (as of 1994) provides those workers with $0.25 per hour of economic rent.

If the law requires that an attorney perform certain routine legal procedures that could, in fact, be equally well performed by a paralegal or other nonlawyer then attorneys are collecting some economic rent. They are being protected from competition that would drive down the fees they receive for these tasks.

Tenure (or its civil service equivalent, the permanent appointment) might be considered an instance of economic rent. The tenured professor is protected from the labor market competition of someone who might do the same work for less money, or better work for the same money, by the fact that he or she is tenured.[5] More generally, seniority rules in employment could be considered a form of economic rent.

These disparate examples are chosen to suggest that the concept of rent seeking has wide applicability. They are not meant to suggest that there are no instances in which economic rent is justified or that there are no instances in which the existence of economic rent is equitable or that there are no instances in which a situation that produces economic rent confers some benefit upon society. As a professor I would offer the argument (obviously self-serving) that tenure does help to protect academic freedom, something that many people value highly. One could argue that seniority rules that give older workers some security in their later years in the workforce have a humane value that does not show up on a balance sheet or a microeconomic diagram.

In the conventional view, government is the remedy for market failure. Public Choice theorists do not deny the existence of market failure. Nor will they deny that government does on occasion succeed in remedying market failure. But the Public Choice theorist will note that tariffs, import quotas, price supports, price controls, tax preferences, excessive regulation, subsidization, and other acts of government frequently cause market failure. The phrase "government failure" has been used to refer to governmentally caused market failure. By and large Public Choice theorists believe that government is more often a cause of than a remedy for market failure.

Public Choice theorists take a different view of income transfers from that presented in the previous chapter. There, we present a picture in which society as a whole formulates a notion of what would constitute the right income distribution and then uses taxation, transfers, and subsidies to move in that direction. Much academic literature assumes that the distribution of income is less egalitarian than is optimal and therefore that anything that moves it toward greater equality is, cet. par., to be favored. In fact, in much academic literature the term *equitable* is confounded with the term *equal* in the sense that any action that moves toward greater equality of income is asserted, often without argument, to be *equitable* or to promote greater *equity*.

The Public Choice perspective is somewhat different. A number of Public Choice theorists have taken exception to the automatic assumption that income inequality is too great and that anything that tends toward equalization is necessarily to be favored.[6] But, more important, they seek to provide a more accurate picture of how transfers actually come into being. The Public Choice theorist does not see government as a being with a single viewpoint formulating a single, internally consistent viewpoint on the matter of income distribution and redistribution and then pursuing goals that flow from that viewpoint. Rather, he or she sees that the powers of government may be used by one group within society to extract money from other groups—the term "plunder" has sometimes been used—and then views the struggle for transfers and preferential treatment as something quite akin to rent-seeking behavior. Individuals and groups use the political process to pursue transfers and special treatment much as they use it to pursue other economic advantage.

PUBLIC CHOICE AND THE EXPANSION OF THE STATE

One of the most striking political phenomena of the twentieth century in the Western world has been the enormous expansion of the state. At the turn of the century government spending as a percentage of GNP in the Western world was, very approximately, in the 10 percent range. In recent years that figure has ranged from the low 30s in the United States to upwards of 50 percent in Scandinavia. A conventional explanation for this historic expansion is that the state has stepped in to pick up the pieces left in the wake of a dynamic and productive, but also often unfair and chaotic, capitalist economy. In other words, the expansion of the state has served to deal with market failures and an unacceptably unequal distribution of income, as well as to assure citizens, through social insurance, some financial stability across their lifespans. A somewhat related explanation is that as people become wealthier and their basic needs are met, they show an increased demand for a variety of public goods; that is, that the demand for that which government provides is income elastic. Thus, the very substantial rise in real incomes in the twentieth century explains much of the expansion of the state.[7]

The Public Choice explanation, as one might suspect, is rather different. The increase in transfer payments is simply the result of "transfer-seeking" behavior akin to the rent-seeking behavior noted earlier. For example, the most powerful lobbying organization in the United States may well be the American Association of Retired Persons (AARP) which, regardless of any more noble sentiments that its literature may express, is basically a huge transfer-seeking apparatus. With its millions of members, a substantial treasury that can be spent on political contributions, and the capacity to mobilize votes, postcards, letters, telegrams, and phone calls on a vast scale it is formidable indeed. We might note that the United States has been more willing to pay for open-heart surgery for senior citizens than for prenatal care for poor teenage girls. Perhaps we should pay for both. But one suspects that the good king, seeking only to extract the maximum net social benefit from each dollar spent, would fund the prenatal care first. More generally, the fact that public funds are spent much more generously on people's last days than on their first days has much more to do with political power than with the results of rationalistic benefit-cost calculations.[8] The effectiveness of transfer-seeking groups, large or small, is amplified by the process of logrolling. Thus, a transfer-seeking lobby that represents only a small number of potential beneficiaries may gain considerable legislative clout through a series of judiciously chosen alliances.

The Public Choice theorist would assert that the direct expenditure and subsidy portions of the government budget, and thus the scope of government, expands in much the same manner as the transfer side. Just as there is a market for goods and services there is a market for legislation. If people who operate motorboats believe that they can get channels dredged and navigation markers installed more cheaply by spending their funds on lobbying Congress or state legislators than by paying for these things directly, they will spend their funds on lobbying. It is the rational, self-interested way for them to behave. If they don't have strength to carry the day by themselves they can make appropriate logrolling arrangements. The legislator who introduces the bill on their behalf will agree to support someone else's bill in return for support on his bill. Perhaps another legislator is introducing a bill on behalf of people who fly light planes and want government to spend more on general aviation airports. Then the motorboat legislator will vote for the airport bill and the airport legislator will vote for the motorboat bill, and so on.

The Public Choice theorist will argue that, considered in toto, this is not the zero sum game that it might appear to be but rather it is a negative sum game. In this example, society will spend more on both motorboat channels and light plane runways than it would if the boaters and fliers had to foot the entire bill themselves. In more formal terms, society as a whole will spend past the point at which marginal expenditure is equal to marginal utility because part of the expenditure is a third party payment. This loss to net welfare is above and beyond the lobbying costs themselves. The Public Choice theorists argue that this sort of behavior is inherent in a majoritarian democracy. The temptation to use the political process to achieve economic goals is simply overwhelming. To expect people not to do it is to expect them to cease behaving like economic man; that is either to cease to be self-interested or to cease to be rational.

BACK TO THE FUTURE

The Public Choice theorists have identified the problem but do they offer a solution? The answer is "yes." Their solution is to move away from majoritarian democracy and toward constitutional democracy. In fact, the field is sometimes referred to as "Constitutional Economics." Public Choice theorists are not per se opposed to deciding public policy matters by majority vote. But they wish that voting to take place within a constitutional framework that places strong limits upon the powers of government. Among Public Choice theorists there is great admiration for the U.S. Constitution and for the men who created it. James Madison stands high in the Public Choice pantheon partly because he recognized the dangers of "faction," meaning the danger that men would organize into groups and parties to exploit their fellows.

Public Choice theorists tend to be admirers of the philosophers to whom the founding fathers looked back, notably Thomas Hobbes and John Locke. They admire the Hobbesian and Lockean notions of the social contract—that the state comes into being by voluntary agreement of those to be governed. That makes the state the creature of its citizens and not citizens the creatures of the state. Thus, they believe that the powers and role of the state, even if a majority believes otherwise, should be limited by the terms of that contract. In fact, many Public Choice theorists write of a *Contractarian State* whose government would be limited to maintaining civil order and providing a limited range of services for which a private market cannot be created, for example, national defense. They then contrast this contractarian state with what they regard as the present hypertrophied state under majoritarian democracy.

A number of Public Choice theorists cite with approval the eighteenth-century Scottish political philosopher Alexander Tytler for what they view as his presience regarding the excesses of majoritarian democracy.

A democracy cannot exist as a permanent form of government. It can only exist until a majority of voters discover that they can vote themselves largesse out of the public treasury. From that moment on, the majority always votes for the candidate who promises them the most benefits from the public treasury, with the result that democracy always collapses over loose fiscal policy.[9]

James Buchanan, in commenting on the great increase in the state's share of total expenditures, noted that though the increase in all states in the Western world in the twentieth century was very large, it has been substantially larger in Great Britain than in the United States. He suggests that this may be because, though it has moved far in the direction of majoritarian democracy, the U.S. government is constrained by a written constitution and the separation of powers written into that constitution. In Great Britain the power of Parliament is far less constrained.

Various policy prescriptions and directions come out of the Public Choice view. All, one way or another, would limit what Public Choice theorists see as the excessive interference in and control of private economic activity by government. Public Choice theorists have devoted much energy to examining the mechanics of voting. One change many of them favor is that of requiring supramajorities (more than a simple majority) for appropriations bills. They argue that this simple change would make logrolling more difficult but would not block really essential appropriations on which there was widespread agreement. In general, Public Choice theorists favor limitations on legislative discretion regarding appropriations. James Buchanan stated:

The Gramm-Rudman-Hollings legislation, although not so desirable from a constitutionalist perspective as an ammendment [requiring a balanced budget] to the United States' written constitution would be, nonetheless reflects a recognition by the Congress that its spending rules, its procedures, were out of hand and that binding constraints are required.[10]

Deregulation, in general, will meet with approval by Public Choice theorists because they view much regulation as serving not the general public interest but rather the interests of small rent-seeking groups. The Tax Reform Act of 1986 reflected some Public Choice influence in that it swept away many tax preferences (tax expenditures). And, certainly, there is no place that more reflects the accumulated effects of transfer- and rent-seeking activity than the IRS code. Public Choice theorists, as one would expect, are free traders. The protective tariff as well as quotas and other nontariff barriers to the free flow of trade are classic Public Choice examples of economic rent and the triumph of factions over the overall public interest.

In the judiciary the Public Choice perspective means a preference for strict constructionism so as not to erode the restraints that the constitution places upon the legislative and executive branches. Justices such as William Rehnquist or Antonin Scalia, who tend to be at the strict constructionist/ original intent end of the judicial spectrum would generally meet with the approval of Public Choice theorists. The rejected Supreme Court nominee, Robert Bork, would also, in general, meet with their approval.[11] On the other hand, an activist liberal such as Supreme Court Justice Harry Blackmun should, in general, meet with their disapproval. His position of judicial activism and his view that the Constitution should be flexibly if not "creatively" interpreted is exactly the judicial philosophy that in the Public Choice view leads to or at least permits the expansion of the state.

What is one to make of the Public Choice viewpoint? The reader may simply accept it. Or perhaps the reader will say that it is not really all that new. He or she might note we have been hearing much in recent years about rent seeking and transfer seeking, though perhaps not by those precise names. To this the Public Choice theorist might say, "Of course you have, and one reason that you have is because we have been dragging those very concepts into the center of the public discourse for the last two or three decades." The reader may reject the Public Choice perspective and say that it is too cynical, that it makes too little allowance for collective common sense and altruism.[12] Many have argued, as noted in Chapter 1, that economic man, whom everyone concerned admits is only a caricature, is not an adequate model for political science. This is certainly a perfectly respectable viewpoint and one that many in political science and other fields hold. But even if one rejects Public Choice as one's overall framework, one might admit that the detailed examination to which it has subjected the interaction between economics and politics is of value and that studying the Public Choice literature leaves one more sophisticated about how things really work.

NOTES

1. James M. Buchanan, *Constitutional Economics* (Oxford: Basil Blackwell, 1991), p. 30. For explication of the reference to Keynes, see Chapter 5 in the same volume, "The Consequences of Mr. Keynes." Briefly, and very simplified, Buchanan argues that Keynes envisioned economic policy as being made by a small, elite, disinterested group with the public interest at heart, rather than as it is actually made. Keynes's prescription for stabilization by running deficits at the bottom of the business cycle and surpluses at the top proved to be disastrous because politicians like the political fruits of deficits but do not like the political pain of higher taxes. Thus, his theoretical analysis gave sanction for an epidemic of deficit financing in Europe and America with its attendant inflation and expansion of national debts. The "Wicksell" referred to in the quote is the Swedish economist Knut Wicksell who wrote in the late nineteenth and early twentieth centuries.

2. Arthur Seldon, in the Introduction, p. x, to James Buchanan, *Constitutional Economics* (Oxford: Basil Blackwell, 1991).

3. See Anthony Downs, *An Economic Theory of Democracy* (New York: Harper, 1957).

4. James Gwartney and Richard E. Wagner, "The Public Choice Revolution," *The Intercollegiate Review* (Spring 1988), pp. 17–26.

5. The professor who feels aggrieved by this notion might reply that he or she is not collecting economic rent, but simply completing the terms of an implied contract by asserting that he or she would never have worked so hard for so little money as an untenured assistant professor, had the possibility of tenure not existed.

6. See Richard Wagner, *To Promote the General Welfare: Market Processes vs. Political Processes* (San Francisco: Pacific Research Institute for Public Policy, 1989), chapter 2.

7. The idea that the public sector would expand in relative terms as society became wealthier and more industrialized was propounded by Adolph Wagner in the late nineteenth century and is sometimes termed "Wagner's Law." For a brief discussion, see Musgrave and Musgrave, *Public Finance in Theory and Practice*, pp. 142–43.

8. For a detailed development of the argument that we underspend on the

young relative to the old, see Sylvia Ann Hewlitt, *When the Bough Breaks: The Cost of Neglecting Our Children* (New York: Basic Books, 1991).

9. Wagner, *To Promote the General Welfare*, p. 135. Wagner credits the quote to William A. Niskanen.

10. Buchanan, *Constitutional Economics*, p. 12.

11. Robert's Bork's book, *The Tempting of America* (New York: Macmillan, Inc., 1990), written after he was rejected by the Senate, provides an extended discussion of strict construction and related judicial issues.

12. See Stephen Kelman, " 'Public Choice' or Public Spirit," in Samuel H. Baker and Catherine S. Elliot, eds., *Readings in Public Sector Economics* (Lexington, MA: D.C. Heath & Co., 1990), pp. 74–86.

CHAPTER 8

Taxes, Grants, and Tax Expenditures

Given the microeconomic emphasis of this book, the discussion of taxation focuses largely on questions of efficiency and the distribution of the burden of taxation. The overarching question of how big the tax-supported sector of the economy should be is beyond the purview of this book, although Chapter 6 on the conventional view of the role of government and Chapter 7 on the Public Choice perspective do have implications for that question. This chapter is divided into three major sections, the first on taxes, the second on grants, and the third on tax expenditures.

TAXES

Two criteria by which we might judge a tax system are *fairness* and *efficiency*. Fairness is not easy to define. One commonly suggested criterion is the user-benefit principle—namely, that the taxes one pays should be in rough proportion to the benefits one receives from public expenditures. This is an old idea that goes back to Adam Smith. Some of our tax system is based on this principle. For example, excise taxes on gasoline are generally earmarked for road funding. To the extent that the amount of gasoline you buy is a proxy for how much you use the public roads, the tax is a user-benefit tax. The municipal government that opts for a user charge for trash collection rather than paying for it out of general revenues is choosing the user-benefit principle, even though the charge is not technically a tax.

The other commonly cited basis for taxation is the ability-to-pay principle—that tax burden should be closely coupled to the income or wealth of the taxpayer. Those with a strongly reformist impulse may go past the ability-to-pay criterion and take the view that one purpose of the tax system, combined with the expenditure side of the budget, is to reshape the distribution of income into a more egalitarian pattern. The income tax is clearly based on ability to pay.

The user-benefit principle and the ability-to-pay principle are at odds with each other. Taxes based on user benefit are likely to be regressive because the use of many public services does not rise proportionately with income.[1] The ability-to-pay principle implies progressivity as embodied in the progressive income tax. Because these two basic principles of taxation are in conflict, universal agreement upon what constitutes a just tax system is not to be had.

The gasoline excise tax and the income tax are at opposite ends of the user-benefit/ability-to-pay spectrum. Much of the total tax apparatus of the nation including sales taxes, many excise taxes, property taxes, and the corporate income tax, lies in a somewhat murky zone between these two extremes. In fact, as will be shown, determining who is the de facto as opposed to the de jure payer of many taxes is often very difficult. Our complex and, in places, ambiguous tax structure in part reflects the fact that the tax structure in a democratic society is necessarily the result of a long history of political compromise.

Taxation within the Federal System

The pattern of taxation varies considerably among the three levels of government. The federal government relies heavily upon personal income taxes, payroll taxes to support the Social Security and Medicare systems, user charges, and corporate income taxes. State governments rely heavily upon sales taxes and user charges. They also make use of personal and corporate income taxes, but at far lower rates than does the federal government. Local governments rely very heavily upon property taxes and user charges. They make much less use of sales taxes than do the states and, in most cases, no use of personal and corporate income taxes.

The entire system contains a large amount of downward transfer. There is a large flow of federal monies to the states and a smaller flow of federal monies that bypasses the states and goes directly to substate governments. In addition, there is a very large flow of funds from state to local governments.

There is considerable logic behind these arrangements. The most salient fact is that states and local governments are in economic competition with each other. No state or local government wants to lose commercial or residential tax base to other areas. Thus, such governments are very much restrained in their taxing behavior by what other jurisdictions do. Localities are especially reluctant to lose wealthier residents to other jurisdictions, for the wealthy are likely to pay more in taxes than they consume in services. Thus, subnational units of government often avoid strongly progressive taxes for fear of driving out the wealthy.

Even a state with a very liberal political complexion will hesitate to tax in a sharply progressive manner for reasons of economic competition. For example, in the 1970s New York State employed a steeply progressive income tax with a top rate of 15 percent, as well as a 4 percent sales tax. The adjacent state of Connecticut employed no income tax and a 6 percent sales tax—clearly a much more regressive system. In due time New York State began to notice that many corporate headquarters were relocating from the New York State part of the New York City Metropolitan area to the Connecticut portion. The phenomenon was easy to understand. The people who made corporate location decisions were people in the top New York State tax bracket who had strong motivation to move the source of their income beyond the reach of the New York State taxing authorities. New York State's top income tax bracket is now 7.875 percent. New York State had no choice. It simply could not afford to continue to lose pieces of its tax base to Connecticut. As of 1991 the top marginal bracket on 48 of 50 state income taxes was under 10 percent. Only Montana at 11 percent and North Dakota at 12 percent topped this figure. By contrast, the highest rate on the federal income tax is 39.6 percent (36 percent plus a 10 percent surcharge on taxable incomes over $250,000).

In general, the smaller the scale of the jurisdiction the more intense the pressure of interplace competition is and the more the jurisdiction will fear to tax that which might prove to be mobile. The relative immobility of property is one reason why the property tax is the tax most heavily relied upon by substate governments. The very limited reliance of substate governments on personal and corporate income taxes and on sales taxes also stems from the fact of interplace competition. When places are small it is easy for such taxes to chase residents, businesses, and retail sales across the municipal line.

The downward pattern of intergovernmental transfers also makes sense for the same reasons. It is the federal government which is freest to tax at high rates without fear of driving away its tax base. It is also easier for the federal government to engage in deficit financing than it is for state and local governments. The immediate reason is that most state governments operate under a constitutional balanced budget requirement. Most local governments also operate under such a requirement, whether it is directly provided for in the state constitution or in state legislation. But the fundamental economic reason is that much local and state debt is held by parties outside of the jurisdiction, whereas most federal debt is owed internally.[2] An external debt is a claim on the real wealth of a community in a way that an internally owed debt is not.

Taxes and Economic Efficiency

At first thought it might appear that the only burden of taxation is the loss to individuals and organizations of the taxes that they pay and the administrative costs of collecting these revenues. But this is not the case. The existence of taxation causes individuals and organizations to modify their behavior so as to reduce their tax burdens. This legal activity, "tax avoidance," imposes an efficiency loss upon the economy because it distorts the allocation of resources. For example, prior to the Tax Reform Act of 1986, commercial real estate received specially favorable tax treatment through the mechanism of accelerated depreciation. This tended to divert capital from other types of investment into commercial real estate. This distorting effect of the tax system was one factor behind the presence of many "see through" (because they are empty) buildings in a number of real estate markets. The wasted resources in this instance constitute an "excess burden" of taxation. Because of preferential tax treatment a dollar at the margin produced less real return invested in real estate than it would if invested elsewhere.

Another loss, not easily illustrated by a diagram, is the resource costs involved in the act of tax avoidance. The accountant who earns a living helping wealthy clients to arrange their business affairs so as to minimize their tax liability is not producing wealth in the normal meaning of the term. Rather, he or she is devoting energy to altering the distribution of after-tax income. The analogy with rent-seeking behavior as discussed in Chapter 7 is very strong.

Perhaps the one tax that, in principle, is nondistorting and thus entails no excess burden is the lump sum or head tax. Here the same amount of tax would be levied on each person regardless of his or her earning and spending behavior. Because nothing the individual did would affect the amount of the tax, individuals would not alter their behavior because of the tax. But despite its theoretical appeal, no government can place major reliance on a head tax. It would be a highly regressive tax that violated most people's concept of fairness.[3] Then, too, a head tax set sufficiently low that the vast majority of the population could pay it would not be much of a revenue raiser. If we start adjusting it by taxpayers' incomes then it is no longer a head tax, but an income tax.

Tax Incidence

With any tax there is little or no ambiguity about who is the de jure payer. But because people and firms modify their behavior in the face of taxation some of the burden may be shifted to other parties. The de facto distribution of the tax burden may thus be considerably different from its de jure distribution.

If one wants to think through the consequences of a particular decision about tax policy one needs to have some ideas about tax incidence, how the de facto as opposed to the de jure burden of the tax falls. In evaluating a tax on gasoline or alcohol or tobacco one should have some notion of whether the major share of the burden will fall on the buyer or the seller. The Health Security Act put forward by the Clinton administration in 1993 proposed, through the "employer mandate," to place a major share of the total cost of health insurance upon firms and, particularly, larger corporations. The first, or certainly one of the first questions to be addressed about this mandate is the question of where that burden would have ultimately come to rest. Would the mandated expenditures have come mostly from profits, or from increased prices, or from reduced wages? Would its ultimate burden have been more or less progressively distributed than if equivalent funds were raised through the personal income tax? Or through a Value Added Tax (VAT)? And so on. Below we discuss the incidence of excise taxes, the corporate income tax, the property tax, and the personal income tax. The simplest tax incidence case to think about is the excise tax.

The Incidence of an Excise Tax

An excise tax is similar to a sales tax except that it applies to a narrower range of goods or services and generally carries a higher rate than a sales tax. One can think of the tax as being paid either by the buyer or the seller. Let us say that a good sells for $1.00 and that there is a 20 percent excise tax on it. One can think of the consumer making two payments, one of $1.00 to the seller and 20 cents to the taxing authority. Alternatively, one can think of the seller as receiving $1.20 and then remitting 20 cents to the taxing authority. The writer finds it easier to think about it the second way. Thus, the following diagrams show the tax as shifting the supply curve. Some writers approach it the other way and show the tax as shifting the demand curve. The end results are the same either way.

Figure 8.1 shows the general approach for analyzing the distribution of the burden of an excise tax. The tax, XO per unit of the good is a cost that the seller must pay. It thus shifts the supply curve S upward to a new position, S', parallel to its old position. The price rises by amount PX and thus the portion of the tax borne by the buyers is PX times the quantity sold. This burden is represented by rectangle I. The seller(s) receives OP less per unit. Thus, rectangle II is the burden borne by the seller. One might think that the tax is a zero sum game, with the buyers' and seller(s') burden exactly equal to the taxing authority's gains. But this is not true, because there is also a loss of consumer and producer surplus shown by triangles A and B. This loss is the "excess" or "deadweight" burden of the tax. Efficiency is achieved by equilibration at the margin. That equilibration prevailed before the excise tax was introduced, but could not subsequently be achieved with the tax wedged in between buyer and seller.

Figure 8.1
The Distribution of the Burden of an Excise Tax

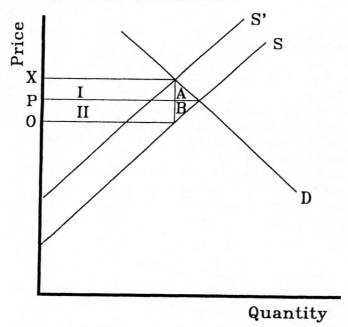

The per unit excise tax is OX. The per unit tax burden is XP for buyers and PO for sellers. The total tax burden is given by rectangle I for the buyers and rectangle II for the sellers. Triangle A shows the loss of consumer surplus and triangle B the loss of producer surplus.

Figure 8.2 shows the situation in which supply is absolutely inelastic and demand is not. Who bears the final burden? The number of units offered will not change. That is the meaning of the absolutely inelastic supply curve. The demand curve will not change either, since changes in the seller's costs do not affect the intrinsic desirableness of the product to the buyer. Thus, the point at which the demand and supply curves intersect does not move and therefore the price does not change. All of the cost of the tax is thus borne by the seller, because the only way that any of the tax burden can be shifted to the buyer is if the price increases. Figure 8.3 shows a reverse situation. Here we assume that demand is absolutely inelastic, but that supply has some elasticity. If the tax is, say, $1 per unit then the tax adds one dollar to the supply curve at any point along its length. We can thus represent the supply curve after the imposition of the tax as being a line parallel to the original curve but shifted upward by the amount of the tax.

In this case the quantity purchased does not change at all. That is the meaning of saying that demand is completely inelastic. The price rises by

Figure 8.2
The Distribution of the Tax Burden When Supply Is Absolutely Inelastic

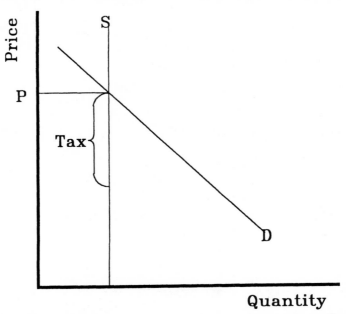

The quantity supplied, by definition, does not change and the tax does not affect demand. Thus, price remains unchanged and the entire burden of the tax is borne by the seller.

the full amount of the tax and thus the entire burden of the tax is paid by the consumer even though it is the seller who is nominally responsible for paying the tax. Another way to state this is that the seller shifts the entire burden of the tax to the buyer.

Figure 8.4 shows an intermediate case in which demand is more elastic than supply. Here, the elevation in market price is relatively small in relation to the tax. Thus, the consumer bears the smaller share and the seller the larger share of the burden. The reader might try redrawing the diagram so that demand is less elastic than supply. Note that as demand becomes more inelastic the situation approaches that of Figure 8.3, and the share of the burden borne by the buyer increases. The general principle from the above examples is that whichever party can least modify its behavior in the face of the tax bears the larger share of the burden. An equivalent way to put it is that the party whose demand or supply is less elastic bears the greater burden.

The same type of graphic analysis that can be applied to excise taxes can also be applied to subsidies by treating the subsidy as a negative tax. In Figure 8.4 assume that the initial supply curve is S2. If the producer is provided with a subsidy per unit equal to the distance AC the new supply

Figure 8.3
The Distribution of the Tax Burden When Demand Is Absolutely Inelastic

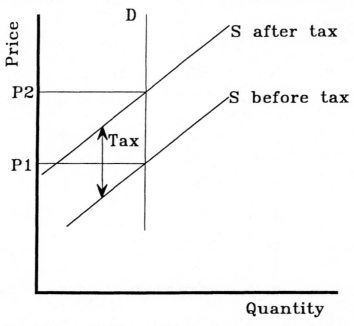

This situation is the opposite of that shown in Figure 8.2. Here, the entire burden is borne by the buyer.

curve is S1 and the price changes from P1 to P. This reduction is only a small fraction of the subsidy. Thus, the buyer captures only that small share of the subsidy and the remainder is captured by the producer. By a similar logic, figures 8.1 and 8.2 can also be changed into diagrams of subsidization rather than taxation.

If subsidies are offered on the demand side the only case in which none of the subsidy will be captured by the supplier is the rare to nonexistent case in which demand is absolutely inelastic. Conversely, if they are offered on the supply side, the only case in which none of the subsidy is captured by the buyer is the equally rare case in which supply is absolutely inelastic. The shifting effects described above illustrate Arthur Okun's metaphor that giving subsidies is like carrying water in leaky bucket. It is only in the rare case that the entire subsidy is captured by the party for whom it is designated.

The very simple cases above illustrate only the immediate or first order shifting of taxes and subsidies. In fact, the effects ramify with decreasing amplitude in what is, in principle, an endless process. For example, the increase in excise taxes on motor fuels passed by the Congress in the summer of 1993 will shift the supply curve of truck transportation to the left.

Figure 8.4
Distribution of the Tax Burden When Demand Is More Elastic Than Supply

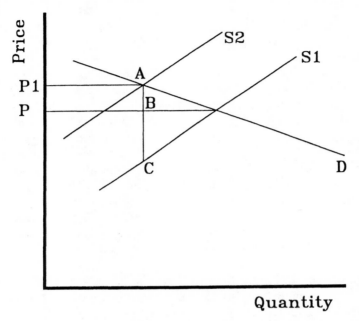

The excise tax has the effect of moving the equilibrium price from P to P1. Line segment AB represents the share of the burden borne by the buyer and segment BC that borne by the seller. In general, the party with the more elastic curve bears the smaller part of the burden.

By the logic suggested above, some of that tax will be shifted forward to customers of the trucking industry. That should increase the demand for rail transportation of goods. If that increase in demand produces some increases in rail freight prices then some of the burden of the tax on motor fuels used by trucks will have been shifted to firms that ship by rail. This, of course, alters the supply curves of those firms and some of their increased costs will be shifted to their suppliers, customers, workers, and so on. In theory, then, to understand fully the distribution of the burden of a tax one should analyze how its effects ripple through the entire economy by means of a "general equilibrium" study of the entire economy. In practice, analyses of tax incidence are more limited. In the heat of political debate the very fact that taxes and subsidies are shifted at all may be obscured.

The Incidence of the Corporate Income Tax

Before discussing the incidence of the corporate income tax a word about the structure of the tax is necessary. If the corporation earns income it generally retains some of that income within itself. This income may be used for investment in a new plant or equipment or for other corporate purposes. The remainder of the corporation's income is distributed to its stockholders, the owners of the corporation. The retained earnings (also referred to as undistributed earnings) are taxed once, at that corporation's tax rate. The distributed earnings are taxed twice: first as corporate income and then as personal income of the stockholders. This double taxation is an unusual feature. In fact, shortly after the tax was introduced in 1909 its constitutionality was challenged on the grounds of double taxation. The Supreme Court, in *Flint v. Stone Tracy Co.,* in 1911 sustained the tax on the grounds that the tax was not double taxation but a charge for the privilege of doing business in the corporate form. These privileges include limited liability in that creditors may not seek recourse from the private assets of the corporation's shareholders or officers, that the corporation may raise capital through the issuance of stock, and a number of others. The incidence of the corporate income tax is simple and straightforward if one makes some simplifying assumptions about how corporations react to the tax. However, when one admits that there is a wide range of corporate responses to the tax, the matter becomes somewhat murky. Let us consider a simple case first.

Assume the corporation is behaving like the model competitive firm in that it maximizes its profits. It hires workers up to the point that the marginal revenue product of the worker is equal to the wage rate and it purchases other factors of production exactly up to the point that marginal cost equals marginal revenues. The firm does its hiring and buying in competitive markets so that it is a price taker. There is thus no way it can force down wages or the prices of the other factors of production. In this case the corporation cannot shift any of the tax to other parties. It cannot alter the demand for its product and it cannot alter the cost structure that it faces. It therefore continues to produce the same amount of product and sell it at the same price. The entire burden of the tax remains with the corporation. That means that the entire burden of the tax falls upon the stockholders. If the stockholders are, on average, persons of above average incomes, as is likely to be the case, the tax is a progressive one. The stockholders are owners of capital, namely, shares in the corporation. Therefore, one can say that the tax is a tax on capital. One can say, further, that in the short term it is a tax on capital in the corporate form. In the longer term, if it is true that markets tend to equalize the after tax return on all forms of capital, it is a tax on all forms of capital.

Note, however, that even in this apparently unambiguous and pure case there may be some indirect shifting of burden. To the extent that the corporate income tax is a tax on capital it will tend to reduce the rate of capital formation. If reducing the rate of capital formation reduces the rate at which GNP grows, then to some extent the corporate income tax may also be a tax on labor because it reduces labor incomes along with the incomes of those who own capital.

Whether corporations actually do behave like textbook profit maximizers, as we assumed above, is an empirical question. A corporation might, instead of aiming for maximum profit, aim for maximum market share subject to some minimum profit requirement. In that case the corporation might respond to an increase in the corporate tax by raising its prices and accepting the loss in market share so as to maintain what it considers an acceptable after tax rate of return. In this case at least some, and conceivably all, of the tax is shifted forward to the consumer. If all of it is shifted forward then it is not a tax on capital at all.

Theory holds that firms price by adjusting so that marginal cost equals marginal revenue. But some corporations use *markup* pricing. The firm computes the average cost of production and adds a percentage for profit. If the corporate income tax is counted as a cost it appears in the price and it is shifted forward.

Joseph Pechman provides an enlightening selection of quotes on the subject from both economists and businessmen, all issued with considerable certainty.[4] Their answers range from some economists who insist that it is only a tax on capital to one corporate executive who insists that all of it is shifted and that the corporation merely acts as an unacknowledged tax collector for the government.

All taxes are ultimately paid by individuals. Thus, to judge the effects of the corporate income tax one must answer the question of "who?" As suggested above that question is a complicated one and economists are not of one mind on the subject. Most economists do not think highly of the corporate income tax, in part because the burden of the tax is uncertain and, in part, because to the extent that it is a tax on capital it may serve to reduce the rate of economic growth. But the tax is here to stay for the foreseeable future. It has been said that "an old tax is a good tax," meaning that it is easier to collect money from an old tax than face the political heat of imposing a new one. Beyond that there is at work here a variant of the "rational ignorance" effect discussed in Chapter 7. The real effects of the tax are complicated and not easy to explain in a sound bite. The politician who proposed eliminating it would quickly be bludgeoned out of office with rhetoric beginning with phrases like "My opponent proposes to eliminate the tax on rich corporations and shift it onto the backs of . . .". Few politicians are that quixotic.

The Property Tax

As noted, the property tax brings in very large amounts of revenue to local governments and districts, most notably school districts. In fact, it is by far the largest tax used at the substate level. It has been subjected to a barrage of academic criticism over the years but it shows no sign of disappearing.[5] In fact, property tax collections in the United States have been growing quite rapidly, from $68 billion in 1980 to $167.9 billion in 1991.[6]

The tax is a very old one, predating the constitution. It is administratively simple. The assessor determines the value of land and structures ("improvements") and the receiver of taxes sends a bill to the owner of record. If the bill is not paid the taxing jurisdiction can, after due process, take possession of the property and sell it to recover back taxes and costs. Unlike personal or corporate income, land and structures cannot be concealed. Thus, a competently administered property tax achieves a very high compliance rate. The yield from a property tax is quite predictable compared with taxes on incomes or sales. The land and structures that constitute the base of a property tax are not mobile in the sense that the base of an income or sales tax is mobile.[7] For all of these reasons, plus the "an old tax is a good tax" aphorism noted earlier, local governments like the property tax.

Old and new views of the incidence of the property tax. The incidence of the property tax is, like the incidence of the corporate income tax, a matter of some dispute. It is not possible to lay out the whole controversy here, but the following few paragraphs sketch out the bare bones of the argument.

In the old view, the property tax was thought to be, on balance, mildly regressive. A large part of the tax was levied on housing. It was argued that since the poor spent as large or perhaps even a larger percentage of their incomes on housing than did the wealthy, the tax, just on that basis, was either proportional or regressive. Then, on top of that, the manner in which the federal tax code treated property taxes made the tax more regressive. The homeowner who itemizes his or her taxes can subtract property taxes from taxable income. At present, when the marginal rate on the federal income tax is 39.6 percent (36 percent plus the 10 percent surcharge for taxable incomes over $250,000), the high-income homeowner can shift $39.60 out of every $100 of property tax burden to the federal government. (Prior to 1981 the top marginal federal tax rate was 70 percent so that the shifting by upper-income homeowners was even greater.) The fact that the wealthy homeowner can shift a larger percentage than the poorer homeowner, of course, adds to the regressivity.

Renters pay property taxes implicitly in their rent, but they cannot deduct these implicit payments from their taxable income. As a group they have much lower average incomes than owners. Thus, the renter/owner difference in tax treatment further adds to the regressivity. Of that portion levied on commercial land and structures some of the burden remained with the property owner and was a burden on capital. Some was shifted forward to the consumers of the goods and services produced in those facilities. How much was shifted forward would depend upon the relative elasticities of supply and demand, as explained in the preceding discussion on the incidence of the excise tax.

The old view seems very convincing and, in fact, was generally accepted for many years. In the 1970s a new view of the property tax emerged.[8] The new view holds the property tax to be essentially a tax on capital. We know that the ownership of capital is skewed toward those with higher incomes. In fact, there is no doubt that the ownership of wealth is substantially more unequally distributed than is income.[9] Thus, if the property tax is a tax on capital it is a progressive tax. But is it a tax on capital? The part of the property tax that falls upon factories, office buildings, stores, and the like would certainly seem to be. Rental housing is no less an income-producing asset than is an office building. If the rates of return on different types of assets tend toward equilibrium with each other then the total effect of the tax is to push down the after tax rate of return on all capital assets. What about owner-occupied housing? If one views an owner-occupied house as a consumption good like shoes, the old view would appear to be the appropriate one. But houses, unlike shoes, are bought for more than utilitarian purposes. They are also, to at least some extent, capital assets. The structure that provides physical shelter is also a tax shelter, a hedge against inflation, and a leveraged investment. The same single-family house that is owner occupied this year may be a rental property next year. In fact, over 10 million single-family units are in rental use at any given time. That constitutes about one-sixth of the single-family housing stock and about one-third of all rental units in the United States.[10]

The new view might apply to a single, uniform property tax rate across the nation. What about the effects of differences in property tax rates among places. These are generally considered to have effects like an excise tax. Imagine two nearby towns that have the same property tax rate. One town then raises its rates. In the town that raised its rates the values of commercial properties fall because the additional tax burden reduces after tax profits and thus makes commercial properties in that town relatively less attractive. Therefore, some of the burden of the tax increase falls upon property owners. Now assume that a few businesses in the high tax town migrate to the low tax town. That shifts the supply curve of those types of businesses in the high tax town to the left. That, cet. par., will push up prices somewhat. That shifts some of the burden of the tax to the consumer. These results are exactly what would occur if the town were to impose an excise tax; the burden would be divided between producers and consumers. Complementary effects will be felt in the nearby town to which firms have migrated. The increased demand for commercial properties will produce higher property prices and thus benefit property owners. The supply curves of the goods and services produced by the incoming firms will shift to the right, pushing prices downward. This will produce gains for consumers but losses for the preexisting suppliers of these goods and services.

Does one accept the new view or the old view? The majority of scholarly opinion appears to favor the new view when looking at the overall incidence of the tax on the nation. But in looking at tax differences and changes in differences between places the excise tax approach just described may be superior. The fact that scholarly opinion on the incidence of the tax could shift so radically and that, even if one fully accepts the new view, the property tax has both capital tax and excise tax aspects points up how difficult it can be to judge the real incidence of a tax.

The Income Tax

The largest tax in the U.S. fiscal system, the federal income tax, is probably one of the least ambiguous with regard to the matter of shifting. The general conclusion of those who have studied the tax is that it is shifted very little because it appears that the supply of labor is little affected by tax rates.[11] If the supply of labor is inelastic then wage rates are unaffected by the income tax. If that is so, then the tax is not shifted from the income earner to another party. The situation is analogous to that in which an excise tax is imposed upon a good whose supply is absolutely inelastic but whose demand does have some elasticity. The equilibrium price cannot change and therefore nothing can be shifted forward. The entire burden remains with the seller—in this case, the seller of his or her own labor. Similar comments can be made with regard to state income taxes. The only caveat here is that differences between tax rates in nearby states may cause some excise effects comparable to those discussed above in connection with the property tax.

The income tax cannot be shifted much, does not appear to affect the level of work effort much, and, within reasonable limits, can be tuned to the level of progressively that society through its representatives in the Congress chooses. Thus, most economists think that it is a good tax.[12] It is obviously less beloved by the public. One reason that the Clinton administration pushed for the employer mandate for health care was that it believed that the public would find it more acceptable than raising the equivalent sums through the federal income tax. Yet it seems very likely that the income tax approach would actually be more progressive than employer mandates that would shift some of the cost forward to the prices of goods and services and some backward to the wage earner. But that would not have been an easy argument to sell politically. Again, the issue of "rational ignorance" arises.

User Charges

As of 1991 all levels of government in the United States took in over $290 billion in user charges. These are fees for services. The services are provided by government but they are not true public goods in the economist's meaning of the term because exclusion is possible and hence, a market can be created. The largest user charge at the federal level is for postal services. At the state level the largest category is for education, primarily at state universities. At the local level the single largest charge is for utilities with hospitals second and water and sewerage third.[13] The user charge is analogous to user-benefit taxation, as exemplified by the gasoline excise tax discussed previously. Services such as sewerage or trash pickup that are paid for by user charges in one community may be paid for by taxes in another. In some cases, say, instruction at state universities, part of the expense is covered by a user charge (tuition), and part by tax revenues.

One rationale for user charges is marginal efficiency. The consumer, in principle, uses the service to the point that marginal benefit equals price. If price is set equal to marginal cost this yields an efficient allocation of resources. As noted in Chapter 6, even in the case of a decreasing cost monopoly, it may be possible to both cover costs and achieve marginal efficiency through a two-tier pricing system.

The user-benefit charge may appeal to many citizens because it seems fair. It may also be attractive simply because it is not a tax. Those who do not use the service will not oppose the charge as they might oppose a tax. To the town board of supervisors the imposition of a user charge may thus be much more attractive politically than an increase in the property tax rate. In a municipality with a large percentage of affluent residents one might expect some resistance to switching from tax-supported to user-charge-supported services on the grounds of tax deductibility. If the service is paid for out of property taxes residents recover part of that through increased property tax deductions on their federal and state income taxes, whereas user charges for the same service are not tax deductible. But in spite of its logic, this argument is not, to the best of the writer's knowledge, raised very often.

One argument against increased reliance on user charges is that it is a move away from the ability-to-pay principle and it reduces the overall progressivity of the combined system of taxes and charges. The person with strongly egalitarian preferences might argue that the "equity losses" outweigh the presumed efficiency gains.

GRANTS

In the U.S. system there is a large downward flow of intergovernmental grants. In 1991, federal grants to state governments totaled $143.5 billion. An additional $19.2 billion of federal aid bypassed state governments and went directly to local governments. The largest single flow was $182.7 billion from state governments to local governments.[14] The term "local governments" includes various quasi-governmental organizations such as school districts, water districts, sewer districts, and the like. Of these, school districts were by far the largest recipients of intergovernmental aid. Much of the growth in federal transfers occurred during the late 1960s and 1970s. Measured as a percent of GNP or as a percent of total state and local expenditures, federal transfers fell somewhat during the 1980s, but still remained at a much higher level than before the 1960s.

It is not easy to say precisely why this large downward flow has come into being, since the 535 members of Congress are not of one mind and all appropriations bills represent a great deal of compromise. However, some possibilities follow. One background condition was noted before. The federal government is less restrained in its taxing behavior by fear of economic competition than are states and local governments. In the 1960s and 1970s the liberal faith in the capacity of government to solve problems led to federal funding for a wide variety of social and environmental programs. Rapid productivity growth in the 1950s and 1960s meant that per capita private consumption could rise at the same time that per capita public expenditures rose. When productivity growth slowed in the 1970s and 1980s the private/public trade-off became more painful.

In the 1960s a Keynesian view of the determination of national income also lent some intellectual support to the idea of large downward transfers. At one time a number of economists believed that if the federal budget reached balance at less than full employment, subsequent surpluses would, by restraining the growth of aggregate demand, prevent the economy from reaching full employment. This effect was termed "fiscal drag." The effects of fiscal drag could be blocked by transfers from the federal government to the states which would then spend the funds. This would increase aggregate demand and push the economy toward full employment. General Revenue Sharing was enacted partly on the basis of the fiscal drag argument. In the present situation of large federal budget deficits the notion of fiscal drag seems unconvincing if not actually perverse. But it was taken quite seriously at one time. Walter Heller, once chairman of President Kennedy's Council of Economic Advisors, was one of its inventors.[15]

A substantial part of total downward transfers is for "human resource" items such as Medicaid. It might be said that we as a society decided that such expenditures were necessary and that, for reasons noted previously, it was more practical for the federal government than for subnational governments to raise the funds. Those with a Public Choice orientation might emphasize the fruits of transfer-seeking political behavior and say that Alexander Tytler predicted it all two centuries ago (see Chapter 7).

Regardless of the exact motivations of the Congress, public finance texts generally justify downward transfers on one or more of the following grounds. But note that there may be a considerable difference between a *justification for* and a *cause* of.

1. *Externalities.* If the public good or service in question has large externalities that transcend the boundaries of the recipient government then the recipient government, left to its own devices, will tend to underfund that activity. The larger government can rectify that situation by assuming part of the cost of providing those goods or services. In effect this internalizes some of the externalities, a concept discussed previously. The principle that the government paying for a service should, in the ideal, correspond in its domain to the area over which the service has its effects is sometimes referred to as the correspondence principle.

2. *Different preferences in public goods between the donor and the recipient government.* If the national government has preferences for public goods that local governments do not have it can encourage local governments to provide these goods through the use of grants.

3. *Differences in local fiscal capacity.* The combined workings of taxes and grants can have the effect of transfering funds from more prosperous to less prosperous subnational units of government. A variation on this theme was suggested years ago by Dick Netzer. He notes that state and local taxes may tend to regressivity because state and local governments are hesitant to tax in a progressive manner for fear of driving out wealthier residents and successful businesses. The federal government has much less fear of the effects of progressive taxation on these grounds. Thus, a substantial reliance on grants by subnational government may move the tax load of all levels of government combined toward greater progressivity.

Types of Grants

To think effectively about grants it is necessary to have some ideas about how grants affect the recipient government. Grants necessarily will change the pattern of expenditures of recipient governments and they will also change the total amount that recipient governments spend. For purposes of discussion let us divide grants into three major categories.

1. *Unconditional grants.* These are transfers that have, essentially, no strings or conditions attached and are not affected by how the recipient government spends its monies. State per capita aid to municipal governments would be an example. Until it was discontinued, General Revenue Sharing from the federal government to the states was an example.

2. *Open-ended matching grants.* Here there is a percentage match with no limit on how much the donor will match. Thus, recipient behavior determines how much the donor will provide. Medicaid funding from the federal government to the states would be an example. Public assistance is another example. Generally, the decision to provide assistance is made by the local government and the funds involved come from all three levels of government. The local decision commits the higher levels of government without any cap on how much they will provide.

Figure 8.5
The Unconditional Grant

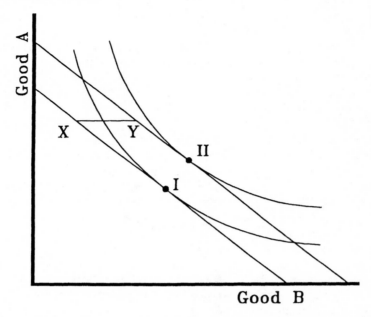

A grant equivalent to line segment xy shifts the budget line to the right parallel to its original position. The recipient government's expenditures move from tangency point I to tangency point II.

3. *Closed-ended matching grants.* Here the donor government provides a certain amount of money for each dollar that the recipient government spends, up to some limit predetermined by the donor government.

The unconditional grant, at least in theory, has only an income effect on the recipient government because it does not change the system of prices that government faces. Both the open-ended and closed-ended matching grants also have a price or substitution effect because they lower the prices to the recipient government of those goods and services that can be funded with that grant. It is thus reasonable to believe that they will affect recipient behavior somewhat differently than will the unconditional grant.

The indifference curve approach presented in Chapter 5 is often used to discuss the differences in recipient behavior between these three types of grants. The geometry is the same. Just think of the recipient government as the utility-maximizing "individual." But retain a little skepticism, because the recipient government really is not an individual and there may be some doubt at times about just whose utility is being maximized.

Figure 8.5 shows the effect of the unconditional grant. The municipal budget line is simply shifted rightward parallel to its original position. The

Figure 8.6
The Open-Ended Matching Grant

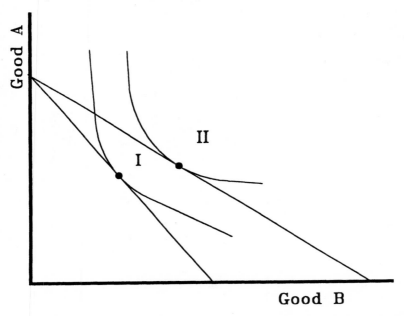

By changing the price of the subsidized item while leaving other prices unchanged, the grant rotates the recipient government's budget line, moving its equilibrium position from point I to point II.

municipality is now free to spend more on both good A and good B. We might posit that the municipality only provides two types of public goods or we might posit that one axis represents a particular good such as education or police protection, and that the other axis represents all other goods. In Chapter 5 we argued that the rational, utility-maximizing individual would prefer to receive a given amount of aid in an unconditional form rather than as reduced prices for a donor-defined range of goods. Exactly the same arguments can be made for municipalities. But, again, reserve a little doubt, as municipalities are not really individuals with a single mind and a single set of preferences.

Figure 8.6 shows the case for the open-end matching grant. Here the slope of the budget line is changed. Assuming a 50–50 match for good B the budget line extends twice as far out on the B axis but still intersects the A axis at the same point. Here we have an income effect, just as in the above case, but also a price effect because the per unit price of good B has been reduced by the matching grant. Total expenditures on good B will rise. This could hardly be otherwise. The market price of the good is unchanged but each unit of the good now costs the municipality half as much

Figure 8.7
The Closed-Ended Matching Grant

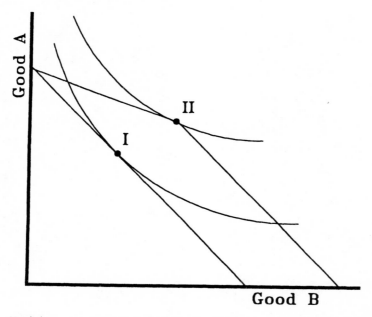

Until the grant reaches its limit the budget line is rotated outward. After the limit it has the same slope as it did prior to the grant. As shown here the grant has both an income and a substitution effect. But if tangency point II occurs below the kink the grant has only an income effect as is the case of the unconditional grant shown in Figure 8.5.

of its own funds. Whether the municipality's own funds expanded on good B will increase or decrease will depend upon the income and price elasticity of the municipality's demand for that good. If the grant is only a very small part of the municipality's income we can ignore the income effect. Then, we can say that if the price elasticity of demand is greater than 1 the expenditure of the municipality's own funds on good B will rise. If the price elasticity is less than 1 then the expenditure of the municipality's own funds will fall. (See the discussion of elasticity in Chapter 3.)

Figure 8.7 shows the case of the closed-ended matching grant. Notice the kink in the new budget line. Up to the limit of the grant the new budget line has a different slope than the old budget line, exactly as in the case of the open-ended matching grant. But, when the limit of the closed-ended grant is reached and no more money will be forthcoming from the donor, the slope of the new budget line becomes parallel to that of the old budget line, since each additional unit of good B is now bought only with the municipality's own funds.

Let us now consider how municipalities will respond to these three types of grants. In the case of the unconditional grant the municipality may choose to allow its expenditures to rise by the full amount of the grant or it may choose to allow its expenditures to rise by only a portion of the grant and thus use the rest of the grant for tax reduction. It could conceivably use all of the grant for tax reduction.

In principle, if the municipality really were a utility-maximizing creature governed by a single intelligence, an unconditional grant would be the same to it as an equivalent reduction in taxes owed by its residents or, to say it another way, an increase in its residents' after tax incomes. The problem for its government would be to strike the right balance between additional expenditures and tax reductions such that at the margin a dollar of grant money spent on public services would yield as much utility as a dollar spent on private consumption. Assume, for example, that this equality at the margin prevailed before the grant and 10 percent of all personal income in the municipality went to taxes that were spent locally. In that case it would be reasonable that of every dollar of grant money received about $.90 would go to tax reduction and about $.10 to increased public expenditures.

In point of fact it has been known for many years that an unconditional grant produces a much larger increase in municipal expenditures than would an equivalent increase in residents' after tax incomes. The fact that the unconditional grant seems to stick with the municipal government rather than be shared with its citizens was termed the "flypaper" effect by Arthur Okun, a usage subsequently popularized by Edward Gramlich. This reality is consistent with the Public Choice view of bureaucratic behavior. It is not what the body politic, behaving in a well-informed and rational manner, would do, nor is it consistent with what the well-informed benevolent despot would do. The "flypaper" effect can be taken as a caution that the theoretical results of formal economic reasoning about what would be logical, collective, utility-maximizing behavior must be tempered by knowledge of the political realities surrounding taxing and spending behavior.

Consider, now, the open-ended categorical grant. This type of grant should, per dollar, encourage a greater increase in municipal expenditure than should an unconditional grant. The argument for this view is that in addition to the income effect that any type of grant has, there is also the substitution effect noted previously. The closed-ended grant might be expected to have somewhat less effect on municipal spending than an open-ended grant of the same matching ratio because of the limit on the maximum size of the grant.

Empirical studies have shown that often the type of grant does not make a great deal of difference in the increase in total spending. In the case of the closed-ended grant we note that a portion of the after-grant budget line runs parallel to the before-grant budget line. If the tangency point is on this parallel segment then the effect, in theory, is the same as that of the unconditional grant. The grant looks different to the donor because it is earmarked, but to the municipality it is just additional revenue.

Our analysis shows that State-local governments spend much more on most functions than is required by statutory requirements to obtain maximum Federal funds. Because most categorical grants are closed ended at relatively low expenditure limits, State-local governments are not stimulated to spend more on targeted services than they are already spending. This results from the effective elimination of the matching substitution or price effect of the Federal spending cap. We find support for the notion that conditional grants which are closed ended at sufficiently low levels of expenditure are equivalent to unconditional, general purpose grants in their impact.[16]

The literature also suggests that in many cases open-ended matching grants are not much more stimulative of total spending than are other types of grants. One possible explanation is that from a municipal point of view, just as from an individual point of view, the best dollar is the dollar that comes with no strings attached. Local officials may become skilled at rendering incoming funds more fungible than donors anticipate. In the contest between donor officials seeking to bind the local officials and local officials seeking maximum fungibility, the locals may win more often than not because they are closer to the scene and know the terrain better. It may also be that in some cases the total amount a municipality may need to spend on a particular function is largely fixed by law, mandate, or technical requirement. In that case its demand for the item may have very low elasticity. If so, its total spending on that item is not very much affected by the substitution effect of the grant. In that situation, all that is left is the income effect. Then, the open-ended matching grant also looks to the municipality very much like an unconditional grant.

The idea that the effects of a diversity of grant types and categories may often be fairly similar does seem to support one policy prescription. It argues for a reduction in the number of grant programs and a bundling together of what were separate small grants. Presumably, then, administrative costs will be reduced without much change in expenditure outcomes. This change was pursued by the Nixon administration under the term "new federalism" and was continued under all subsequent administrations.

THE TAX EXPENDITURE CONCEPT

In an economy in which approximately one-third of the GNP passes through government it is hard to exaggerate the effect upon the economy of the pattern of taxation and expenditure. In 1967, Stanley Surrey, an Undersecretary of the Treasury with a rather theoretical and academic cast of mind, proposed the concept of tax expenditures. The idea was that failure to tax a given stream of income in the manner in which it would normally be taxed constituted, in effect, a government expenditure on or subsidy of that item. But, because tax policy and expenditure policy were decided upon separately, this equality went unrecognized. In a speech in 1967 he said:

through deliberate departures from accepted concepts of net income and through various special exemptions, deductions and credits our tax system does operate to affect the private economy in ways that are usually accomplished by expenditures— in effect to produce an expenditure described in tax language.[17]

The key phrase is, "an expenditure described in tax language." To fail to tax a stream of income that would ordinarily be subject to tax is, in effect, to forgive a debt. And, as suggested earlier, in an algebraic sense to forgive a debt is no different than making a gift. Thus, in a literal or algebraic sense a tax expenditure is just a grant that, in his phrase, is "described in tax language." Surrey argued that in a practical political sense, however, there is a big difference between grants and expenditures on one hand, and tax expenditures on the other.

When Congressional talk and public opinion turn to reduction and control of federal expenditures, these tax expenditures are never mentioned. Yet it is clear that if these tax amounts were treated as line items on the expenditure side of the Budget, they would automatically come under the close scrutiny of the Congress and the Budget Bureau. . . . Instead . . . any examination given to them must fall in the classification of "tax reform" and not "expenditure control." There is a vast difference between the two classifications.[18]

The idea was widely accepted in a very short period of time, and in 1971 the federal Office of Management and Budget (OMB) began to publish an annual estimate of federal tax expenditures.

The basic method by which OMB determines what is a tax expenditure is quite straightforward. Any stream of income that, because of provisions of the federal tax code, escapes federal taxation is considered to generate a tax expenditure. The size of the tax expenditure is OMB's estimate of the amount of revenue that is lost because of this special treatment. Consider a few items in the 1994 column of the tax expenditure summary reproduced as table 8.1. The biggest item in the table is $70.5 billion for "net exclusion of pension contributions and earnings." If employer contributions to pension plans and earnings on funds invested in pension plans were counted as personal income and subject to tax, OMB estimates that in 1993 they would have yielded $70.5 billion in income taxes. The $48.1 billion loss on mortgage interest on owner-occupied homes is arrived at in a similar manner. Had homeowners not been able to deduct this interest

Table 8.1
Tax Expenditures, by Function: 1994 (Figures in millions)

DESCRIPTION	1994
National defense:	
Exclusion of benefits/allowances to Armed Forces personnel	2,400
International affairs[1]	6,795
Exclusion of income earned abroad by United States citizens	1,545
Exclusion of income of foreign sales corporations	1,900
Inventory property sales source rules exception	3,440
General science, space, and technology[1]	2,720
Expensing of research and development expenditures[2]	2,150
Energy	2,865
Excess of percentage over cost depletion: Oil and gas	1,610
Alternative fuel production credit	1,355
Natural resources and environment	2,645
Exclusion of interest on State and local IDB[3] for pollution control and sewage and waste disposal facilities	1,520
Commerce and housing credit[1]	176,780
Exclusion of interest on-	
Life insurance savings	11,215
Owner-occupied mortgage subsidy bonds	1,950
State and local debt for rental housing	1,415
Capital gains (other than agriculture, timber, iron ore and coal)[2]	3,355
Deferral of capital gains on home sales	14,620
Exclusion of capital gains on home sales for persons age 55 and over	6,360
Deductibility of-	
Mortgage interest on owner-occupied homes	48,145
Property tax on owner-occupied homes	14,015
Accelerated depreciation on rental housing[2]	1,280
Accelerated depreciation of buildings other than rental housing[2]	5,430
Step-up basis of capital gains at death	36,050
Investment credit, other than ESOP[4]	3,095
Accelerated depreciation of machinery and equipment[5]	22,065
Reduced rates on the first $100,000 of corporate incomes[2]	5,495
Exception from passive loss rules for $25,000 rental loss	6,245
Community and regional development[1]	2,580
Credit for low income housing investments	1,530
Education, training, employment, and social services[1]	24,040
Deductibility of-	
Charitable contributions (education)	1,960
Charitable contributions other than education	13,090

Table 8.1 (continued)

Credit for child and dependent care expenses	3,585
Exclusion of interest on State and local debt for private nonprofit educational facilities	1,035
Health[1]	83,990
Exclusion of employer contrib. for medical insurance premiums and medical care	63,225
Exclusion of employer share of Hospital insurance tax	13,325
Deductibility of medical expenses	3,735
Exclusion of interest on State and local debt for private nonprofit health facilities	1,770
Deductibility of charitable contributions (health)	1,775
Social Security[1]	24,580
Exclusion of Social Security benefits:	
Disability insurance benefits	1,810
OASI benefits for retired workers	19,025
Benefits for dependents and survivors	3,745
Income security[1]	98,225
Exclusion of workmen's compensation benefits	4,270
Net exclusion of pension contributions and earnings:	
Employer plans	70,475
Individual Retirement Accounts	6,410
Keoghs	3,840
Exclusion of other employee benefits:	
Premiums on group term life insurance	3,715
Special ESOP rules (other than investment credit)	3,095
Additional deduction for the elderly[5]	1,945
Earned income credit	4,435
Veterans benefits and services[1]	2,060
Exclusion of veterans disability compensation	1,815
Deferral of interest on savings bonds	1,475
General purpose fiscal assistance[1]	47,280
Exclusion of interest on public purpose State and local debt	15,040
Deductibility of nonbusiness State and local taxes other than owner-occupied homes	27,195
Tax credit for corporations receiving income from doing business in United States possessions	5,045

[1]Total (after interactions). [2]Normal Tax method. [3]Industrial development bonds. [4]Employee stock ownership plans. Includes investment credit for rehabilitation of structures, energy property, and reforestation expenditures. [5]Pre-1983 budget method. [6]Data on calendar year basis.

Source: U.S. Office of Management and Budget, Budget of the United States Government, annual.

from their taxable federal income, IRS would have, by OMB's estimate, taken in another $48.1 billion in tax revenues. The $15.0 billion tax expenditure on "public purpose state and local debt" means that because interest on municipal bonds is exempt from federal income taxation, the IRS collected $15.0 billion less than it would have had this stream of income been subject to tax; and so on.

The calculations are made under the assumption that behavior would not be changed were the tax exemption to be removed. But, of course, much economic behavior is heavily conditioned by tax considerations. Thus, the numbers in the table should be taken as rough indicators and not literally. For example, if the homeowner mortgage interest deduction were to be eliminated, some homeowners might choose to pay off their mortgages rather than carry them because the after tax cost of carrying mortgage debt would have gone up. Then, too, if the deduction was removed the prices of owner-occupied housing would probably drop, since the tax shelter advantages of homeownership would have been diminished. As housing prices dropped the average size of new mortgages would decline. Thus, the amount of mortgage interest paid would be less in the absence of the exemption than in its presence. We should also note that the numbers in the table cannot be added to produce a meaningful result. This is because removing one tax expenditure would alter economic behavior and that would affect the size of the other income streams whose exemption from taxation constitutes the other tax expenditures. The elimination of the tax expenditure for the exclusion of employer contributions to medical insurance premiums and medical care would reduce the demand for medical care and thus reduce doctors' incomes. That would then reduce the amount of money doctors had to spend on home mortgages which would then reduce the size of the homeowner mortgage interest tax expenditure, and so on.

Despite the above caveats, the tax expenditure concept is a powerful one for thinking about public policy. It serves to remind us, as Surrey noted, that it is a mistake to consider the tax side and expenditure side of the budget in isolation from each other. Tax expenditures show up as powerful elements in the consideration of public policy issues. The medical insurance tax expenditures shown in Table 8.1 have been a major forces in increasing the demand for medical services. That increase in demand has helped to increase medical expenditures as a percentage of GNP. That effect, in turn, constituted some part of the political force behind the Clinton administration's 1993 health care proposals embodied in the Health Security Act. Not all of its results have been bad, of course. It has lowered the after tax cost of health insurance and thus enabled some people to obtain health care that they would not have obtained in its absence. The increased expenditures on medicines and medical equipment that it made possible may have increased the rate of development of new pharmaceuticals and medical equipment. This tax expenditure reshaped the bargaining between labor unions and corporations because a dollar of tax exempt health insurance benefits was worth more to many workers than a dollar of taxable wages. Whether, on balance, this particular tax expenditure was a good idea is not to be resolved in this chapter. The point is that one cannot fully understand our present health care situation without knowing about it.

In the same way, one cannot fully understand U.S. housing markets without knowing about the $48.1 billion homeowner mortgage interest tax exemption and the $14.0 billion homeowner tax expenditure on homeowner property taxes. That combined $64.1 billion tax expenditure dwarfs any federal housing program done through the expenditure side of the budget. In fact, it tends to favor suburbanization, which would seem to place it in opposition to federal programs designed to help urban areas attract housing investment. That brings us back to the point that in an ideal budgetary process, the expenditure side and the tax side of the budget would be considered as a whole—not separately.

The tax expenditure concept is widely accepted, as the annual publication of a tax expenditure budget by OMB indicates. It is not, however, universally accepted. Some conservatives object to the concept on the grounds that it seems to suggest that government has some sort of natural claim on all assets and income and that failure to assert this claim is a gift. A more sophisticated objection, in the writer's view, is that looking at each tax expenditure on its own and then summing all of the tax expenditures is misleading. The argument is made that a better way to decide whether an industry or activity receives a favorable tax treatment is to look at its total tax burden as a percent of income. It might well be that an industry did benefit from one or more tax expenditures but that it, because of other tax treatment, still paid an above average rate of tax.

Is a tax expenditure the same as a grant? In an algebraic sense the answer would appear to be yes. If I tell you that you do not have to repay the debt that you owe me is that not the same as my giving you an equivalent sum? In that sense they would appear to be the same. In a political and psychological sense they may be very different. Grants appear in the federal budget and must be voted on periodically. Tax expenditures come from provisions in the IRS tax code and have much less visibility. They endure until the code is amended. Then, too, if one has received a grant it is hard to deny to oneself that one is receiving money. It is much easier to get used to special tax treatment and begin to take it as one's right.

NOTES

1. Taxes are regressive if they take a smaller percentage share (though they might take a larger absolute sum) of high incomes than low incomes. They are

proportional if they take the same percentage of low and high incomes and progressive if they take a larger percentage of high incomes.

2. As of 1990, federal debt was about $3,266 billion. Foreigners held only $313 billion in federal bonds and other securities, or roughly 10 percent of the total. See tables 449 and 1317 in the *Statistical Abstract of the United States,* 112th ed., (1992).

3. Her attempt to make heavy use of the head tax at the local level was a major factor in forcing Margaret Thatcher out of the Prime Minister's position in Great Britain in 1991. The specific source of the objection, even within her own party, was the fairness or regressivity issue. See Glenn Frankel, "Thatcher's Replacement Completes Policy Reversal by Dumping Poll Tax," *Washington Post,* March 25, 1991, p. A18.

4. Joseph Pechman, *Federal Tax Policy* (Washington, DC: The Brookings Institution, 1987), p. 135.

5. The academic criticisms of the tax are well presented in Dick Netzer, *The Economics of the Property Tax* (Washington, DC: The Brookings Institution, 1957). This book was considered to be the definitive work on the property tax for many years.

6. *Statistical Abstract of the United States,* 113th ed. (1993), table 468.

7. Over a period of years, property taxes and property tax differentials between places will affect the expenditures on construction and maintenance. In some cases high property tax rates and weak or declining property values may encourage abandonment or, in the extreme, arson. Then, too, on very rare occasions a structure may be demolished so that the owner of the property no longer has to pay property taxes on it. In these indirect and long-term senses one might say that improvements are mobile in the face of the property tax.

8. For an early presentation of the new view see Henry Aaron, *Who Pays the Property Tax* (Washington, DC: The Brookings Institution, 1975).

9. Frank Levy and Richard C. Michel, *The Economic Future of American Families: Income and Wealth Trends* (Washington, DC: The Urban Institute, 1991), p. 50. While the top 5 percent of all families earn 16 percent of all cash income, they hold slightly half of all wealth. Conversely, the bottom 20 percent of all families earn 5 percent of all income and their net wealth (assets–debts) is negative.

10. *Statistical Abstract of the United States,* 113th ed. (1993), table 1242.

11. The Musgraves note that the income tax should discourage work by reducing the after-tax income of an hour of work. On the other hand, if the marginal utility of income rises as one has less income the tax should increase work effort. These two effects may cancel each other. See Musgrave and Musgrave, *Public Finance in Theory and Practice,* p. 404. This writer should note that as a very aggregate piece of evidence, the length of the work week in the United States has remained at about 40 hours for almost half a century, despite a very large increase in real after-tax income. This suggests that work effort is certainly not highly sensitive to the after-tax hourly wage. Many microeconomics texts discuss the possibility of a backward bending supply curve for labor. For a time increases in wages would evoke increases in work effort. But past some level of wages the diminishing marginal utility of income would reduce work effort and the curve would begin to bend back toward the vertical axis (wages plotted on the vertical axis and hours worked on the hor-

izontal axis). To the writer's knowledge empirical support for the backward bending supply curve is not very strong.

12. At very high marginal rates the tax may produce a great deal of tax avoidance that makes the de jure marginal rates and the effective rates very different. It is also argued that at very high marginal rates entrepreneurial effort is reduced with a consequent loss for the entire economy. This was part of the reasoning behind the Tax Reform Act of 1986 that cut the top marginal rate on the federal income tax to 28 percent and balanced that with the elimination of some tax shelters to make the act "revenue neutral."

13. *Statistical Abstract of the United States,* 113th ed. (1993), table 468.

14. Ibid., tables 468 and 488.

15. For the genesis of "fiscal drag," see Walter W. Heller et al., *Revenue Sharing and the City* (Baltimore: Johns Hopkins University Press, 1968).

16. Roger H. Bezdek and Jonathan D. Jones, "Federal Categorical Grants-in-Aid and State-Local Government Expenditures," *Public Finance* 43, no. 1 (1988), p. 53.

17. Stanley S. Surrey, *Pathways to Tax Reform: The Concept of Tax Expenditures* (Cambridge, MA: Harvard University Press, 1973), pp. 3–4. *Statistical Abstract of the United States,* 112th ed. (1992), table 449.

18. Ibid.

CHAPTER 9

Benefit-Cost Analysis

For the firm engaged in producing for profit, or considering whether to begin to produce a particular product or service, there is no need to think about whether the benefits to society are greater or less than the costs to society. The market signals—what the firm can sell the product for and what it must pay for the factors of production—are sufficient information. If there are externalities involved, that is not the firm's problem. Society may choose to ignore them or it may choose to intervene in the market through subsidies, charges, special tax treatment, or regulation. Those interventions will affect the firm through the market signals that it receives. But the externalities themselves are not the firm's problem.

For a government supplying or considering whether to supply a public good, the situation is quite different. In the case of the pure public good there can be no price signals from the demand side of the market to tell government how much to supply or how much that which it does supply is worth to society. Unlike the firm, government should be concerned with externalities since, as we have suggested earlier, the existence of externalities is a prime justification for the presence of government in the economy. In the case of a quasi-public good for which government charges, a major problem is to determine what price or system of prices is the most economically efficient when viewed in terms of the entire society. This is a vastly more complicated question than that facing the firm. For the firm the question is much smaller—what price or system of prices best suits the firm's goal, whether that goal is profit maximization or a related goal such as sales volume or market share.

The tool developed to help government evaluate projects is benefit-cost analysis. It would be naive to say that major investment decisions are made solely on the basis of benefit-cost studies, since political considerations weigh heavily in almost all major spending decisions. It is fair to say, however, that benefit-cost studies help to clarify the pros and cons of investment decisions and, generally, help to move the decision-making process toward greater rationality. Well-done, objective benefit-cost studies can help to tip the scales against bad projects and toward good projects. It is also accurate to say that benefit-cost studies are required for many types of federal funding and requested by the Congress and government agencies for many cases where they are not formally required. For someone who will be involved in policy formulation or policy analysis, some knowledge of benefit-cost analysis is highly useful even if one is never going to do such a study. Writing about his experience in the Congressional Budget Office in 1986–1987, Edward Gramlich notes:

But I also was surprised to see just how often benefit-cost analysis is actually used in Washington. The Congressional Budget Office prepares analytical reports on different policy issues—acid rain, minimum wages, public employment, matching grants, cost efficiency in the provision of health care, national defense. I found my old benefit-cost experience being called upon more or less continuously as I reviewed reports in these areas . . . [1]

The goal of a benefit-cost study is to make as complete an accounting as possible of the benefits and costs to society of a proposed project or program. Both the benefits and the costs are presented in terms of their present value so as to permit direct comparison. The benefit-cost analyst is thus able to say what appears to be the net benefit, positive or negative, of that proposed action. Usually, not all of the costs and benefits can be quantified. It is the task of the analyst to quantify that which legitimately can be quantified and to present as clearly and as systematically as possible that which cannot be quantified.

BASIC CONCEPTS OF BENEFIT-COST ANALYSIS

Most of the basic concepts in benefit-cost are drawn from finance and from microeconomics. A few of these are presented below.

The rate of discount. A given payment to be received at some time in the future is worth less than that same payment if received now. Assume that you hold an ironclad guarantee to receive $100 a year from now. Assume also that the present rate of interest is 6 percent. In that case, if you had $94.34 now you could put it away at 6 percent interest and one year from today you would have $100. The calculation for this is: $94.34 × 1.06 = $100.

If we discount $100 by 6 percent for one year we arrive back at $94.34. The calculation for this is: $100 × 1/1.06 = $94.34. Note that 1.06 and

1/1.06 are reciprocal quantities. If you want to carry a present sum into the future you use an *interest* rate. If you want to bring the value of a future sum back into the present you use a *discount* rate.

Interest rates reflect risk, anticipated inflation, and the increase in real wealth that investment in the production of goods and services can generate. The discount rate reflects these same things, but looking backward to the present rather than looking forward from the present.

Discounted present value. The discounted present value of a stream of benefits or payments is found by cumulating the discounted values as shown below. If one were to receive a payment of $100 a year from now, and four successive annual payments, all discounted at 6 percent, the present value would be calculated as shown:

$$\text{Present value} = 100 \times 1.06 + 100 \times 1.06^2 + 100 \times 1.06^3$$
$$+ 100 \times 1.06^4 + 100 \times 1.06^5 = \$421.24$$

The reciprocal relationship also prevails. If $421.24 is put away now at 6 percent interest it will be just sufficient to generate $100 payments in the same years noted above.

Expectations about inflation can have major effects on interest rates, as can readily be seen in the financial pages of the newspaper. Inflation can be dealt with in either of two ways:

1. All calculations can be done in terms of real values. If this is the choice, the discount rate used should be the real rate of interest. This figure is the nominal rate of interest adjusted for inflation. For example, if the nominal rate of interest is 7 percent but the rate of inflation is now 3 percent then the real rate of interest is about 4 percent. And that is the figure that should be used.

2. The calculations can be done in terms of the nominal values that the analyst expects to prevail in the future. For example, assume that one expected benefit from a highway project is savings in travelers' time. Presumably, as the value of the dollar declines with inflation, the monetary value of travelers' time will increase. If the analyst expects 3 percent inflation and a minute of travelers' time is currently valued at 20 cents, then a minute of travelers' time a year hence should be valued at $20 \times 1.03 = 20.6$ cents and a minute of travelers' time two years hence should be valued at $20 \times 1.03^2 = 21.22$ cents.

The first approach is simpler and more commonly used. But either is acceptable. The important thing is not to mix the two approaches.

Consumer surplus. This concept was discussed in Chapter 3. The concept of consumer surplus is used to estimate the benefits of a project. If a price is charged, for example, a toll on a road, one counts as benefits not only the revenues received but also the estimated consumer surplus in the space between the price line and the demand curve. Where there is no charge the entire area under the demand curve is consumer surplus.

Producer surplus. This concept was also discussed in Chapter 3. In totalling up the benefits of any project it is also necessary to include net benefits to producers.

SOME BASIC CONSIDERATIONS

One basic decision in any benefit-cost study is deciding over what area costs and benefits are to be considered. For a large project the nation might be considered the proper area of concern and benefits or costs accruing outside of the nation would be ignored. For a few studies effects beyond the nation's boundaries should be considered. For many studies the boundary may be a city or state or geographic region within a nation. But in any case, some boundaries must be established. The results of the study may vary greatly, depending upon how the boundaries are defined. If a public works project will facilitate economic growth within a municipality the results of the benefit-cost study bounded at the municipal line may come out very favorably. But if some of that growth will come because firms move in from neighboring communities, then a study that drew its boundaries at, say, a regional level might show a much less favorable result.

Within the boundaries of the study it must be decided whether to take a general equilibrium approach or to hold the rest of the world constant. For example, one cost of a construction project is labor. Should the benefit-cost analyst simply consider the cost of hiring labor for the project or should the analyst also consider the effects that hiring for the project will have on wage rates elsewhere in the economy? As a generality, the larger the project is, the more case there is for the general equilibrium approach.[2]

The choice of discount rate is another major decision. But what discount rate should be used? For capital investments one choice is to use the collective judgment of the capital markets. The interest rates on long-term, low-risk investments, say, AAA corporate bonds or 30-year government bonds, tell us at what rate the capital markets discount the future. An alternative discussed in the benefit-cost literature is the *social rate of discount.* This is a figure somewhat lower than that which we get from the capital markets. The argument begins with the proposition that we as a society underinvest and overconsume. If this is so, then we should invest more. The law of diminishing returns suggests that the rate of return on additional investment will be lower than the current rate of return at the margin. This suggests that some investment at rates of return below the present interest rates established in the capital markets is justified. There is considerable literature on the social rate of return.[3]

The choice of discount rate is often a very important issue. Both the present value of the costs and the benefits are affected by the choice of

Table 9.1
The Present Value of a Sum of Payments Discounted at 10 Percent

Initial amount	Discount rate	Term in years	Total	Increment in last year
$1,000	10%	10	$6,144.57	$385.54
$1,000	10%	20	$8,513.56	$148.64
$1,000	10%	30	$9,426.91	$57.31
$1,000	10%	40	$9,779.00	$22.09
$1,000	10%	50	$9,914.81	$8.52
$1,000	10%	100	$9,999.27	$.07
$1,000	10%	200	$10,000.00	$5.27 x 10^{-6}
$1,000	10%	Infinity	$10,000.00	$.00

Source: Calculated from the computer program in the box below.

discount rate. If the costs and the benefits accrue at different times the choice of discount rate can have a very large effect upon the ratio of benefits to costs and thus upon the decision about whether or not to proceed with a project. This will be apparent in the sample benefit-cost analysis presented subsequently.

With any rate of discount greater than 0, the present value of a given future cost or benefit shrinks and ultimately disappears. Table 9.1 shows this effect for a sum of $1,000 discounted at 10 percent per annum. Note that the increase in present value from year 100 to infinity is only $10,000.00 − $9,999.27 = 73 cents.[4]

If one uses a smaller discount rate the future disappears more slowly, but it ultimately does disappear. An annual stream of $1,000 payments discounted at only 1 percent has the values shown in Table 9.2.

The reader who has access to a personal computer that can be programed in BASIC can quickly gain a feeling for the effects of discounting by entering the following brief program and then trying different payment sums, discount rates, and terms (number of years). Just run the program and respond as the computer asks you for the sum, discount rate, beginning year, and end year. After you have entered the end year the machine will do the calculations and print out the present value and, below it, the amount that the present value changed in the last year of the computation.

```
Ok
list
10 INPUT "discount rate as a decimal   ",RATE
20 INPUT "sum   ",SUM
```

(continued)

```
 30 INPUT "beginning year   ",A
 40 INPUT "end year   ",B
 50 FOR J = A TO B
 60 X = SUM * 1/(1+RATE)^J
 70 TOTAL = TOTAL + X
 80 NEXT
 90 PRINT "TOTAL"    TOTAL
100 PRINT "AMOUNT ADDED IN LAST YEAR"    X
Ok
run
discount rate as a decimal  .06
sum   1000
beginning year   1
end year   30
TOTAL 13764.84
AMOUNT ADDED IN LAST YEAR 174.1104
Ok
```

Discounting the future makes sense in financial terms, because, as noted earlier, the discount rate and the interest rate are reciprocal quantities. It also makes sense because of the general uncertainty of life. But it does not necessarily make sense to everyone under all circumstances. For example, to one who thinks that we should exercise a sense of environmental stewardship for those who will follow us a hundred or a thousand generations from now, any discount rate greater than 0 is too big, because any discount rate greater than 0, as shown in the above tables, ultimately reduces the value of any future event to an infinitesimally small quantity. If you took the view that some unique natural features might become increasingly valuable as population increased, you might even make the argument that in some cases we should use negative discount rates.

Still another question that may have to be decided is whether or not to value resources used in a project at their market price or some other price.[5] One commonly cited example is that during the Great Depression much labor and capital was idle. The opportunity cost of employing such resources was thus very low. If the opportunity cost was less than the wage rate or payment necessary to bring that labor or factor into employment then the price the analyst uses, the *shadow price,* should be less than the market price. Incidentally, in conditions of tight labor or factor markets one might make the argument that the shadow price should be higher than the market price.

The case for shadow pricing is weakest when markets are functioning well. In the case of perfect markets and an absence of externalities one cannot make a case for shadow pricing at all. Where there are large exter-

Table 9.2
The Present Value of a Sum of Payments Discounted at 1 Percent

Initial amount	Discount rate	Term in years	Total	Increment in last year
$1,000	.01	100	$63,028.90	$369.71
$1,000	.01	200	$86,331.39	$136.69
$1,000	.01	500	$99,309.32	$6.91
$1,000	.01	1,000	$99,995.26	$.04
$1,000	.01	5,000	$99,999.76	2.47×10^{-19}
$1,000	.01	infinity	$100,000.00	

Source: As above.

nalities, large elements of monopoly, or other factors that prevent an efficient adjustment at the margin, then one can make a case for shadow pricing. But even here, a caveat is necessary. The fact that the market is not setting prices very well does not necessarily imply that an administrative or planning apparatus will set them any better.

In the perfect benefit-cost analysis all costs and benefits would be counted once, and no costs or benefits would be counted more than once. No accounting of benefits and costs can be complete, but double counting can be avoided. Consider, for example, a new metro stop. One clear benefit is the time savings for travelers. But what about the increased rents that apartment owners near the stop will realize? Those should not be counted because they are simply the capitalized value of time savings, and those savings have already been counted. What about increased property values? These, in turn, are just the capitalized value of the increased rents accruing to the savings of travelers' time. These, too, should not be counted. In fact, counting both increased rents and increased property values would be triple counting.

Valuing Human Life

Many projects have consequences for human life or health. For example, the per-mile fatality rate on interstate highways is about one-tenth that for local, nondivided roads. Thus, part of the benefit from a project that replaces a two-lane road with a divided roadway is reduced loss of life. How do we value a human life? No entirely satisfactory method has been developed, yet the problem cannot be ignored. We cannot think clearly about how much to spend on safety if we have no idea at all of how much we value a life. The most commonly used method is to use labor market data to see how much more compensation workers require to accept an additional amount of risk.

Policy analysts typically estimate the value of life from labor markets because the availability of information on risks in labor markets and the associated wage rates that workers receive enable estimation of the market-generated risk trade-off. Analysts interpret the observed market trade-off between dollars and mortality risk as an indication of the compensation a worker would forego for a reduction of risk. Then they statistically extrapolate to generate the dollar value of life.[6]

To use an example from the article quoted above, assume that statistical studies showed that it took $50 more income to induce workers to take an otherwise comparable job that entailed an additional risk of dying of 1 chance in 100,000. Then we would conclude that the value of life as revealed by this data was $50/(1/100,000) = $5 million.

Note that this method attempts to determine the value of life to the person himself or herself by inference from the person's behavior in the market. There is no attempt to find some intrinsic value of life or to estimate how much one's life is worth to other people. The method has some obvious problems. Do workers really have good data on job-related mortality risk so that the inferences from their behavior have meaning? Is there a linearity problem? The worker who is willing to take a 1/100,000 risk for $50 might not be willing to take a 1/2 risk for $2,500,000. Despite these and other objections that can be raised, the consensus among policy analysts and others concerned with the valuation of life is that this is the best available method.[7] Note that this method implicitly assumes that society should assign the same value to people's lives that they themselves appear to do. Perhaps that is the ultimate extension of the concept of consumer sovereignty. In the land of the benevolent—or malevolent—despot, very different assumptions might be made.

A BENEFIT-COST EXAMPLE

To illustrate the concepts of benefit-cost analysis, a very simple highway project example is presented here. Typically, in highway projects the major benefits are time savings, vehicle operation cost savings, and savings in human life and health due to safer roadways. The major costs are typically right-of-way acquisition costs, construction costs, and maintenance costs. We assume the following for this project.

Benefits

1. Time savings. We assume 10 million trips a year with an average time saving of 10 minutes per trip and an average of 1.25 occupants per vehicle. We assume that on average motorists and passengers value their time at $.20 per minute. In actuality, the motorists' value of time might be estimated from survey data or inferred by seeing how travel volumes have been influenced by impositions of or changes in tolls. The value of the time saved in a year is thus:

$$10,000,000 \times 1.25 \times 10 \times .20 = \$25,000,000$$

In this simplified example we have not considered the possibility that building this highway will reduce traffic volumes on other roads. If that resulted in higher travel speeds on those roads, then a more complete accounting would also consider those time savings.

2. Vehicle operation costs. We assume that the new road shortens the average trip by one mile and assign a per-mile vehicle operations cost of 25 cents. Savings in vehicle operations costs are thus:

$$10,000,000 \times .25 = 2,500,000$$

3. Savings in human life. On the basis of mortality experience on the old road and expected mortality on the new road, we assume that one life per year will be saved. On the basis of wage differentials by risk of death in different occupations we arrive at a figure of \$3,000,000 per human life.

Costs

1. Right-of-way acquisition costs. These are assumed to be \$90,000,000, payable one year from now.

2. Construction costs. These are assumed to be \$100,000,000 each year in years two, three, and four.

3. Maintenance costs. These are assumed to be \$500,000 per year beginning in year 5 and continuing at that rate for each succeeding year.

We assume a time horizon of 30 years and thus calculate no costs and benefits after that point. To keep matters simple, all calculations are done in real dollars rather than adjusting for inflation.

Note that we are assuming no charge will be levied for the use of the new road. This means that anyone who will derive even the smallest increment of utility from using this road rather than some other path will use it. Thus, the entire area under the demand curve in Figure 9.1 is consumer surplus. Were a toll to be levied the benefits would now be the remaining consumer surplus shown by triangle A and the revenue shown by rectangle B. The consumer surplus shown by triangle C would be lost. This is the excess burden of the charge analogous to the excess burden of taxation discussed earlier.[8] Table 9.3 shows the present value of project benefits and costs calculated for three different discount rates.

The reader will note that the results of the study vary greatly, depending upon which discount rate is used. The costs are not greatly affected by the discount rate because most of them occur in the near term. The benefits, on the other hand, drop off very sharply as the discount rate is increased because they begin later than the costs and extend far into the future. The project that looks advisable at a 4 percent discount rate looks very ill-

Figure 9.1
Consumer Surplus and Benefit-Cost Analysis

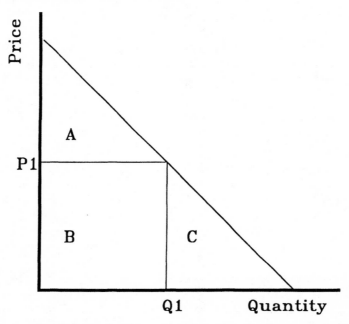

In the absence of a toll the road will be used down to the point that marginal utility equals 0. In this case the entire area under the demand curve is consumer surplus. If a toll is imposed at P1 causing road use to fall to Q1, consumer surplus is triangle A and revenues are rectangle B. Triangle C is the loss of consumer surplus. That loss is the excess burden of the toll.

advised at an 8 percent discount rate. If partisans on opposite sides of an investment decision squabble about what discount rate to use it is thus understandable. If, for example, the proponents of a dam want to use a discount rate of 2 percent while the Sierra Club wants to use 6 percent, this simply indicates that both parties understand the mathematics of discounting.

Which is the right rate to use? The writer would suggest that in this illustration 4 percent is the best of the three choices. Because we are doing all of the calculations in real dollars with no adjustment for inflation we should use a real rather than an inflation-adjusted discount rate. If we decide to use the capital market as our guide to how to discount the future we see the following. As of this writing (Spring 1995), the interest rate on the 30-year federal government bond was about 7.0 percent. Inflation at this time is somewhat under 3 percent. That gives us about a 4 percent real interest rate on a long-term, essentially risk-free investment. The above rea-

Table 9.3
Hypothetical Benefit-Cost Data at Three Different Discount Rates
(Figures x 1,000)

Benefit or cost	Annual amount	Years in which accrued	Present Value at		
			4%	6%	8%
Value of time saved	$25,000	5 thru 30	341,554	257,493	198,641
Veh. operating cost saved	$2,500	5 thru 30	34,155	25,749	19,864
Value of lives saved	$3,000	5 thru 30	40,986	30,899	23,813
Cost of acquisition	$90,000	1	86,538	84,906	83,333
Cost of construction	$100,000	2,3,4	266,836	252,171	236,620
Cost of maintenance	$500	5 thru 30	6,831	5,150	3,973
Total benefits			416,695	314,141	242,318
Total costs			360,205	342,227	242,318
Net benefits			56,490	-28,086	-83,608
Benefit/cost ratio			1.157	.918	.743

soning is based on the assumption that we decide to use the collective wisdom of the capital markets rather than shadow pricing, as noted before.

The reader will note that where benefits exceed costs so that the project shows positive net benefits the benefit-cost ratio exceeds 1. When the costs exceed the benefits so that the net benefits are negative the benefit-cost ratio is less than 1. If the reader plots the discount rate against the benefit-cost ratio data in the table, he or she will note that the project shows a zero net benefit and therefore a benefit-cost ratio of 1 at a discount rate of approximately 5.5 percent. That discount rate at which the project shows a benefit-cost ratio of 1 (just breaks even) is referred to as the Internal Rate of Return (IRR). Sometimes IRRs are calculated with the idea that the higher the IRR the more desirable the project. But at least one authority on benefit-cost analysis, Gramlich, argues that this can be misleading at times and that, in any case, it gives us no more guidance than we get from considering net benefits.[9] The benefit-cost ratio can be used to rank projects in terms of benefit per dollar. For this reason it may at times be useful to compute the benefit-cost ratio as well as net benefit.

The example, of course, leaves out a great deal. For example, the new road may have air quality effects that should be counted. There may be gains and losses to producers as traffic patterns change, and so on. Then, too, there may be effects that are impossible to reduce to dollar terms but that should be taken into account. For example, there may be urban design considerations that should weigh in the decision to build or not to build. The benefit-cost analyst may not be able to monetize these but should at least lay them out systematically so that they can be considered.

NOTES

1. Edward M. Gramlich, *A Guide to Benefit-Cost Analysis,* 2d ed. (Englewood Cliffs, NJ: Prentice-Hall, 1990), p. ix.

2. For a discussion of the general equilibrium approach, see ibid., chapter 5.

3. See E. J. Mishan, *Cost-Benefit Analysis* (New York: Praeger, 1976), chapter 32, as well as other references indexed under "social rate of time preference."

4. The $10,000 value at infinity can be calculated from the formula for the sum of an infinite series. This is $1/(1 - r)$ where r is the ratio between terms. In the case of a 10 percent discount rate the ratio is .9. Thus, the calculation is $1,000/(1 - .9) = $1,000/.1 = $10,000$. For the case of the 1 percent discount rate in the following table the equation would be $1,000/(1 - .99) = $1,000/.01 = $100,000$.

5. The general term for a price established by the economists or other analysts is "shadow price." Mishan defines it as "the price an economist attributes to a good or factor on the argument that it is more appropriate for economic calculation that its existing price, if any." See Mishan, *Cost-Benefit Analysis,* p. 81. In years past, socialist theoreticians saw the shadow price as a way in which a planning bureau could achieve the efficiency of the marketplace without the actuality of the marketplace. In retrospect this seems theoretically plausible but rather naive. See, for example, Oskar Lange, *On the Economic Theory of Socialism* (Minneapolis: University of Minnesota Press, 1938).

6. Michael J. Moore and Kip W. Viscusi, "Doubling the Estimated Value of Life: Results Using New Occupational Fatality Data," *Journal of Policy Analysis and Management* 7, no. 3 (1988), p. 476.

7. Another standard that has been used is the discounted present value of future earnings. But this is fraught with problems. It implies that people's lives have no value other than economic value and that the lives of highly compensated workers are worth more than those of other workers. In general, it yields lower values for human life than the method described in the text. Still another method has been to use jury awards in cases involving highway fatalities.

8. We have assumed that the road is a pure public good in that its use is completely nonrival. If that is not so then tolls would, by reducing traffic volumes,

improve the quality of service for those who did use it. That would, in turn, change the demand curve because the road would now be delivering a somewhat different quality of service.

9. Gramlich, *A Guide to Benefit-Cost Analysis*, p. 100.

PART II

SELECTED APPLICATIONS OF MICROECONOMIC PRINCIPLES

This section of the book contains a number of selected topics designed to illustrate basic concepts presented in Part I.

CHAPTER 10

Rent Controls

Rent controls are of interest for this book primarily because of the light they shed on the more general subjects of price controls and market interventions. Thinking through some of the many secondary effects of rent controls should make one a more subtle thinker about market interventions in general, regardless of whether or not one has a particular interest in housing markets as such.

In the United States rent controls were introduced during World War I and then dropped shortly after the end of war. Rent controls were reintroduced by the federal government during World War II. In 1947, two years after the war's end Congress repealed rent controls. For a time only New York State retained controls, primarily in New York City. During the inflationary 1970s, tenant pressure for controls grew and a number of municipalities adopted controls, often under state "local option" legislation. As of the end of the 1980s about 200 municipalities in the states of New York, New Jersey, Massachusetts, Connecticut, and California had controls. There are also controls in the District of Columbia. The "rent control capitol" of the United States is New York City, which has had controls of one type or another continuously since 1943.

THE MECHANICS OF RENT CONTROLS

The basic mechanics of controls are fairly simple, though there are many variations on the theme. Generally, rent control begins with a freeze on rents in that part of the rental stock that is to be controlled. Often the freeze is from the date of the passage of the control legislation. In some cases there is a rollback provision to nullify the effect of last-minute increases before the freeze date.

Because landlords' costs rise with inflation, most rent control ordinances have some mechanism for periodic increases in the permissible rent. Commonly, this is an annual, across-the-board adjustment. Some ordinances also provide for an individual appeals process in which a landlord may appeal for an increase above the across-the-board increase on the basis of his or her particular situation. Both proponents and opponents of controls would probably agree that setting the legal rent unit by unit or building by building would be superior in principle to across-the-board adjustments. For one thing, all buildings do not have the same structure of operating costs nor do their operating costs represent the same percentage of total costs. For another, the freezing of rents when the legislation is enacted may lock the landlord who happens to be operating at a loss at that moment into a permanent money-losing situation even if subsequent across-the-board adjustments are reasonable. But administratively a building-by-building adjustment process is too complicated to be practical.

In an attempt to prevent controls from inhibiting new construction, most rent control ordinances exempt buildings constructed after a certain date from controls.

To prevent the quality of controlled units from deteriorating through disinvestment, some ordinances contain provisions that permit tenants to withold a portion of their rent if the property violates some provisions of the building or housing code. In effect, an administrative remedy replaces the discipline of the market.

Under some rent control systems tenants acquire a permanent right to occupy their housing unit without a lease. They become "statutory" tenants. In an uncontrolled market, rent is fixed by lease, but in a controlled market this function of the lease is lost. Then, too, if the control system includes vacancy decontrol or any other arrangement that permits a rent increase when the tenant moves out, the statutory status prevents the tenant from being forced out. Where controlled rents and market rents differ appreciably, having status as a statutory tenant can be of considerable monetary value, a point to which our discussion will return.

When a municipality decides that it should move toward decontrol of rental units a common scheme is vacancy decontrol. The intention is to protect tenants from large and sudden increases in rent that might occur if controls were abruptly lifted. Under vacancy decontrol an apartment loses its controlled status when the tenant moves. In some cases the apartment may be permanently decontrolled. In other cases the apartment may be rented once at market rates but then again comes under rent control with subsequent rent increases limited to the annual adjustment noted earlier.

THE POLITICAL REALITIES OF RENT CONTROLS

Most economists take a negative view of rent controls. For reasons that will be discussed, the market distortions are numerous and significant and controls often reduce both the quality and quantity of the rental housing stock. As an income redistribution device rent control is quite inefficient. So why are controls frequently enacted? Denton Marks suggests:

In an environment in which both supporters and opponents of a policy are well organized and have much to gain (especially relative to income) both individually and collectively, it is reasonable that the outcome that pleases more voters dominates. The policy is more attractive if it confers significant benefits on the more numerous group without burdening the government budget so that there is neither an explicit tax increase nor an explicit subsidy.[1]

Marks's comment about the lack of explicit taxes or subsidies is an important one. Controls permit a municipality to deliver an income subsidy to some of its constituency without any immediate public expenditure. The transfer comes from landlords of controlled properties, not from the public treasury. If tenants are numerous compared to landlords that has its obvious political attractions.

To Marks's comments the writer might add several additional points. One is that the economic effects of controls, while not difficult to comprehend, are not self-evident to the average voter or politician. They are just complicated enough not to be compressible into a sound bite or a bumper sticker. Thus, they are hard to use in political debate. Then, too, when these arguments are deployed by property owners they tend to be discounted because they are so clearly self-serving.

Second, rent controls appeal to populist sentiment. The poor tenant is a figure who evokes sympathy. The landlord does not. Thus, in the political combat over controls the proponent of rent controls appears to many to occupy the moral high ground. Controls are often seen more as a matter of fairness or justice than as a matter of economic policy. In Boston, which has had controls since 1972, the city agency that administers controls is the Rent Equity Board. Thus, the concept of fairness is enshrined in the legislation itself.

Finally, controls tend to create few immediate problems. Rents are fixed, usually, at current levels so most landlords do not feel much immediate burden, nor do tenants receive much of an immediate windfall. It is only with the passage of time that market and controlled rents diverge sharply and a variety of dislocations and distortions begin to appear. The relative absence of problems in the short term helps to make controls a salable political proposition.

The overall political context of rent controls also needs a few words. Controls tend to be enacted in jurisdictions of liberal political complexion. In a politically conservative atmosphere notions about the virtues of the marketplace and the importance of property rights militate against them. In fact, a number of states have passed legislation that expressly forbids local governments to impose rent controls. When controls are enacted they often have a strong pro-tenant bias, since if tenant political power did not exceed landlord political power the controls would not have been enacted. One place in which protenant bias often shows up is in the matter of periodic rent adjustment, a point to which we shall return.

THE MARKET EFFECTS OF RENT CONTROLS

The simplest, or what we might call the first order effect of controls was shown in Figure 3.7. By fixing the legal price below the market clearing price, controls create a condition of permanent shortage or, in other terms, a permanently uncleared market is created. Because the figure depicts the short-term situation the supply curve is shown as having very little elasticity. How large a shortage is created depends primarily upon how much below the market clearing price is the controlled price and how elastic is the demand for rental housing.

Figure 10.1 shows a somewhat less obvious effect of controls. Controls tend to promote overconsumption of housing in the controlled sector. This shifts some demand into the uncontrolled sector and elevates prices there. By overconsumption we mean that some people who are able to obtain controlled units will consume more space than they would if they had to pay the market clearing price. For example, an empty-nest couple in a five-room apartment might move to a three-room apartment if they had to pay market rent for their five-room apartment. But if a controlled five-room unit rents for no more than an uncontrolled three-room unit it makes no sense to move. An affluent suburban couple who like to come into Manhattan or Boston or the District of Columbia for a weekend or two each month may maintain a controlled apartment there. If they had to pay the market rent they might give up the apartment and instead rent a hotel room for a few days each month. How much controls elevate rents in the uncontrolled sector will depend in part upon the relative sizes of the two sectors. If the controlled sector is large relative to the uncontrolled sector then, cet. par., the elevating effect should be larger. Then, too, the effect should be larger if there are similar types of units in both sectors—that is, if there is a high degree of substitutability between some controlled and uncontrolled units.

Figure 10.2 shows another frequent though not inevitable effect of controls. In the long term controls tend to reduce the supply of rental housing. That is, they shift the supply curve to the left. One might wonder how this

Figure 10.1
Shifting Demand into the Uncontrolled Sector

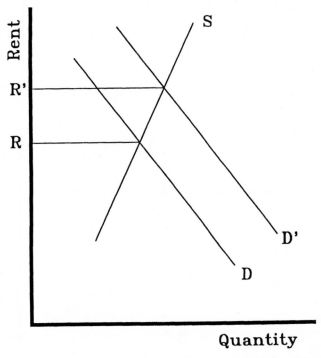

Overconsumption by some in the controlled part of the housing market shifts some demand
to the uncontrolled sector, moving the demand curve from D to D' and elevating rents in
that sector from R to R'.

can be, given that most jurisdictions that impose controls exempt new units,
and that unsatisfied demand from the controlled sector may drive up rents
in the uncontrolled sector. The main answer is that the real estate investor
has no guarantee that units now exempt from controls will not subsequently be brought under controls. Thus, a substantial part of the value of
an investment made under current rules can be destroyed by subsequent
legislative acts. Anthony Downs notes that New York City has twice imposed controls on units that were exempt at the time they were built. He
also notes that "Many major insurance companies will not make mortgage
loans on rental housing projects in rent-controlled cities, no matter what
exemption clauses exist in the ordinances."[2] It must be admitted, however,
that it is not inevitable that controls will depress new construction. Downs
notes, for example, that in Los Angeles, where controls are much less dra-
conian than in New York City, investors seem to have no fears that units

Figure 10.2
The Effect of Controls Upon Supply

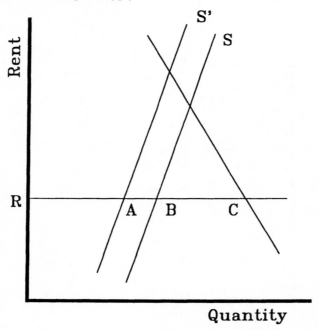

If investors fear future extension of controls the supply curve of housing may be shifted to the left. If rents are fixed at R and controls shift supply from S to S' then the shortage will increase from BC to AC.

now free of control will be subsequently controlled, and thus there appears to be no depressing effect upon new investment.

As will be shown subsequently, controls may also shrink the supply of rental housing by encouraging conversion to nonrental uses, notably condominiums and cooperatives or, in the extreme, by promoting abandonment. Controls are generally enacted where there is a feeling that there is a shortage of housing. By shortage we do not mean the economist's definition of a situation in which the market does not clear because the quantity demanded exceeds the quantity supplied. Rather, we mean a less precise layman's meaning that, somehow, there is not as much housing as there should be in some particular price range(s). In some cases no finding at all regarding rent levels is necessary. For example, in 1974, New York State enacted the Emergency Tenant Protection ACT (ETPA) that permitted municipalities to declare "rental emergencies" and impose controls on previously uncontrolled units if the municipality simply made a finding that its vacancy rate fell below 5 percent. But because of both the overconsumption and the discouragement of new construction noted above, controls are likely to further depress the vacancy rate and further contribute to the perception of shortage. Thus, controls are likely to be self-perpetuating.

OTHER SIDE EFFECTS

The side effects of controls are numerous, and they demonstrate the principle that it is hard to intervene in a market just once, because the act of interference will usually produce side effects that call for further intervention. The permanently uncleared market or perpetual shortage of controlled units will bring into being mechanisms by which people attempt to deal with the shortage.

One phenomenon is "rationing by inconvenience." To the cost of obtaining a controlled unit must be added the inconvenience of much trampling of streets, rushing to the newstand to get the newspaper with the real estate classified ads the minute it comes out, and the like. Shortages, of course, also bring into being black markets. If the apartment in question would rent for $1,000 a month on the open market but is controlled at $600 a month there will be potential renters who would be happy to pay the legal rent plus $200 a month under the table or, perhaps, a one-time bribe of a few thousand dollars to obtain the apartment. Controls may thus create a category of economic crimes.

In principle, price controls can be backstopped by rationing. In order to buy the product one needs not only to have the money but also the ration coupon. If the number of ration coupons matches the number of units available then, in principle, rationing by inconvenience is eliminated since there is no longer any excess demand that can be legally expressed. The motivation for illegal transactions or "black markets" is, however, not eliminated. During World War II, the United States did apply a combination of price control and rationing to a number of goods such as gasoline and meat. But clearly, rationing is not a feasible option in peacetime housing markets.

In New York City, controls of long standing have also created a peculiar category of property rights in that having the legal right to occupy a controlled apartment is a right that may be worth some thousands of dollars year after year. Under law and administrative procedure the right to occupy a rent-controlled apartment has been a transferable right in that when the tenant dies (or moves) the tenant's spouse or other relative may continue in tenancy. The question of which spouse gets to keep the rent-controlled apartment may also be an issue in divorce and separation proceedings. Whether the same rights of succession apply to persons who do not constitute family in a common meaning of that term (related by "blood, marriage, or adoption") has been the object of litigation. In *Braschi v. Stahl Associates* the issue was whether Mr. Braschi could continue to occupy the controlled unit after his longtime companion died. Seven years after the death of his companion the Court of Appeals ruled in Mr. Braschi's favor, citing a history of "emotional and financial commitment and interdependence." In a subsequent ruling the State Court of Appeals ruled that the State Division of Housing and Community Renewal could by administrative act extend the succession rights afforded relatives to some classes of nonrelatives. The agency subsequently extended these rights to "life partners of unmarried people, the disabled, the aged and the poor."[3] One might note that only one of the four categories is an economic category.

The Public Choice theorist might note that the above illustrates the concept of rent-seeking behavior. The semantics are confusing because it is the tenant who engages in the rent-seeking behavior even while paying rent in the normal meaning of the word. The tenant, or the tenant organization, seeks to use the political and legal processes for protection from the market in order to obtain something of value from the property owner, namely, the right to occupy an apartment at below its market rent. The use of noneconomic means to obtain a protected economic position is the essence of rent seeking. At first glance the situation might appear to be a zero sum game activity with the algebraic sum of tenants' gains and landlords' losses equal to zero. But the Public Choice theorist would argue that the situation is really a negative sum game because the labor expended by attorneys, administrators, and the contending parties themselves is labor that produces no wealth. It is merely labor diverted from productive activity into a struggle over the division of existing wealth. Then, too, there are the various distorting effects previously noted.

The effects of controls ramify through housing markets, producing a large variety of side effects. In New York State one major effect of rent controls was to accelerate the conversion of rental apartments into condominiums. Landlords facing lowered profit margins or actual operating losses, and hence declining values of their properties, were frantic to get out from under rental housing. Conversion to condominiums was the obvious way out. In fact, one attorney who specialized in condominium conversions referred to the process as "the most sophisticated form of abandonment." One thing that made condominiums attractive to buyers was the favorable tax treatment, because the individual who owns a condominium unit can deduct his or her share of mortgage interest and property taxes from his or her federal and state taxable income. The property owner doing the conversion is thus selling not only an apartment but also the right to benefit from a tax expenditure. Of course, not all tenants in rent-controlled buildings were happy about the conversion process. The tenant who did not want or could not afford to purchase a condominium apartment was in danger of being forced out into the housing market where controlled apartments are hard to find. This generated political pressure to resist conversions and that soon was manifest in legislation that made the conversion process more difficult. Thus, the original legislation controlling rents brought into being other legislation to deal with the side effects of controls.

Controls tend to shift property tax burdens. The reduced income-earning capacity of controlled properties limits their ability to pay property taxes. Sooner or later this becomes reflected in lower assessments and, therefore, lower tax bills. The shortfall must be made up by higher taxes on other types of property. This takes us back to Marks's comment about no "explicit" tax effects. There may be implicit tax effects, but it takes a bit of economic reasoning to realize that this may be the case. In the writer's experience in observing the adoption of controls, the tax shifting effect is rarely considered.

Perhaps the most significant effect of controls in many jurisdictions is the reduction in the market value of controlled properties. Lawrence Smith and Peter Tomlinson, in studying rent controls in Toronto, Ontario (all but three of Canada's provinces have some form of rent controls), found that between the adoption of controls in 1975 and 1980 the value of rental properties in the city fell by 51 percent after adjusting for inflation.[4] Some decrease in the value of rental property is inevitable simply because controls limit profit potential without in any way limiting the potential for losses. Thus, even the most fairly and carefully administered system of controls would produce some loss of owners' equity. In the Toronto case much of the loss of value occurred because the process of rent adjustment was biased in a pro-tenant direction. Smith and Tomlinson note that during this period apartment operating costs went up by 75 percent but that permitted rent increases totalled only 39 percent. The spread between cost increases and rent increases occurred with great rapidity because the time period in question, 1975–1980, happened to be a period of rapid inflation in Canada. Had prices been more stable during this time the gap between costs and rents would have widened more slowly and the loss of value would have proceeded less dramatically. The end results, however, might well have been the same.

The reduction in the market value of rental properties has various consequences. Two of them, conversion to condominiums and the shifting of tax burden, were noted above. In many cases the reduction of property value encourages disinvestment. The owner decides that the property is essentially doomed in the long run and so tries to squeeze out maximum profit in the short run by putting as little money as possible into repairs and maintenance. If this process goes on long enough the property may become so run down that even if controls are lifted the property cannot be saved. Abandonment, or, if the property owner is unscrupulous, arson to collect fire insurance, may be the building's ultimate fate. In the case of Toronto some rental property values fell so sharply that owners demolished buildings in order to obtain the sites upon which to build condominium apartments. In order to block the loss of rental housing the city enacted legislation that limited the floor area ratio (FAR) of any building built upon the former site of a rental unit. In terms of preserving the rental housing stock this made sense, but note that a land use control was applied not on any usual urban design basis, but simply on the rent control status of a building.

Because of the sharp slowdown in new construction, the provincial government began to subsidize new residential construction. Thus, explicit subsidy costs that had not been foreseen when controls were instituted began to appear.

Rent controls have an element of income redistribution in them and are advocated, in part, upon that basis. The image of the wealthy landlord exploiting the poor tenant has considerable force in public debate. Controls clearly do transfer income from property owner to tenant if we take the free market rent as a baseline. If the average landlord is wealthier than the average tenant, which is undoubtedly the case, some downward redistribution of income results. But as an income redistribution measure it is relatively inefficient, since not all landlords are rich nor are all renters poor. In the summer of 1993, the New York State legislature passed legislation that permitted vacancy decontrol on apartments renting for $2,000 a month or more. The law also permitted decontrol even if the tenant did not move out—providing that the tenant was earning $250,000 or more per year. Subsequently, the New York City council voted to expand the state decontrol provisions so that any apartment would be decontrolled after its rent reached $2,000 per month, even if the current tenant did not vacate.[5] Even this minor modification to prevent controls from delivering windfalls to the very well-to-do was strongly resisted in the city council on the grounds that it might set a precedent for further weakening of controls.

IS THERE EVER A CASE FOR CONTROLS?

The case against controls is strongest where the market works well—where it tends to clear and where there are not undue barriers to the entrance of new suppliers. Where the market is blocked from operating in its normal manner there may be some case for controls, especially over a limited time period. Consider the situation in 1943 when Congress imposed rent controls upon the entire nation. Large numbers of people had to move from one part of the country to another because of war mobilization. Sudden increases in housing demand occurred near military bases and war plants. But the usual market response to increased demand, namely, an increase in supply, was blocked because construction materials and labor were preempted for the war effort. Thus, in the absence of controls rents in some cities would have zoomed upward, transferring large amounts of wealth from tenants to landlords. Here, controls seem justified. They did not address the underlying problem of inadequate supply, but they did address the equity issue. Congress's response—enacting controls during the war and then removing them shortly thereafter—made sense. In more normal circumstances the danger is that controls will create conditions, namely, a restriction of supply and an increasing gap between market and controlled rents, that will make their elimination more and more difficult and painful as time passes.

NOTES

1. Denton Marks, "On Resolving the Dilemma of Rent Control," *Urban Studies* 28, no. 3 (1991), pp. 415–31. Note: This article also contains an extensive bibliography of books and articles on the subject of rent control, both in and outside of the United States.

2. Anthony Downs, *Residential Rent Controls: An Evaluation* (Washington, DC: The Urban Land Institute, 1988), p. 18.

3. Alan S. Oser, "Altering the Rules on Who May Take Over Apartments," *New York Times*, Real Estate Section, January 16, 1994, p. 7. See also Diana Shaman, "Apartment Succession Rule at Issue," *New York Times*, Real Estate Section, November 12, 1993, p. 30.

4. Lawrence B. Smith and Peter Tomlinson, "Rent Controls in Ontario: Roofs or Ceilings," *American Real Estate and Urban Economics Journal* 9, no. 2, (Summer 1981), pp. 93–114.

5. James C. McKinley, Jr., "Council Vote Lifts Control on Luxury Units in Future," *New York Times*, March 22, 1994, p. B3.

CHAPTER 11

Zoning: The Economics of Land Use Regulation

Zoning, like the rent controls discussed in Chapter 10, is a regulatory activity of government with major market effects. Its goal is not redistributive like rent controls, but rather its explicit goal is to facilitate land use planning and to deal with the externalities of land development. Although zoning has major effects on the market for land and through that on the markets for housing and commercial structures, its economic side is often not clearly perceived by planners, local government officials and, perhaps most important, by citizens. Rather, zoning is most commonly seen in regulatory, legal, or design terms. A discussion of its economic side is included in this book primarily because it is instructive in illustrating the economic ramifications of regulation. It also illustrates that regulations, just as well as market transactions, can have significant externalities.

Zoning is probably the most commonly used form of land use control in the United States. It is used in almost all cities, the great majority of towns, and most suburban areas.[1] It is also used in many exurban and semi-rural areas. In brief, zoning is a system that divides a municipality into a number of zones and then specifies in considerable detail what type of development is permitted in each zone.[2] The zoning map shows the location of each zone with sufficient precision that one can readily place any parcel of land in the municipality within its correct zone(s). The zoning ordinance specifies exactly what may be built in each zone. For example, for a particular residential zone the ordinance might specify that only single-family houses may be built in the zone, that the minimum lot size is 40,000 square feet, that the house must be set back at least so many feet from the front, rear, and side lot lines, and so on. For a multifamily residential zone the ordinance might specify how many units may be built per acre, how many parking spaces must be provided per unit, how high buildings may be, the maximum percentage of the lot area that may be covered by structures, and many other design details. Comparable comments can be made for commercial zones. The ordinance will specify what commercial uses are permitted, how much floor space is permitted per acre, and a wide variety of design details like parking requirements, access requirements, maximum building heights, and the like. In brief, the ordinance specifies to what uses any given piece of land may be put, the maximum permitted intensity of use, and a great many site and structure design details.

Zoning ordinances and maps are typically prepared by municipal planners or planning consultants. However, in principle, they may be prepared by anyone. They acquire the force of law when they are adopted by a resolution of the municipal governing body. Like any piece of legislation, a zoning map or ordinance may be amended or repealed. Much zoning legislation contains a formalized appeals process. But even if it does not, the possibility of appeal is always implicit, since any interested party can attempt to get the legislative body that enacted the zoning legislation to change it.

Zoning is a process by which government restricts the uses to which privately owned land may be put. If in the absence of zoning anything would be permitted, then one can say that zoning is a system of prohibitions. It, in effect, says to the property owner: "You may not put commercial uses in a residential zone, you may not build more than so many units per acre, you may not build over a certain height, you may not build more than so many square feet of floor space per acre, and so on. Note that if all land was owned by government there would be no need for zoning. Government, as owner, would be able directly to control what was built where. Zoning, in effect, gives government some of the rights of ownership, namely, the power to exercise some control over how land will be used. But note that it cannot compel use. It can only influence use by forbidding some types or intensities of use.

That government has the right to exercise some control over the use of privately owned land is not apparent from a reading of the Constitution. Rather, it is a right that has emerged from a series of court decisions beginning in the late-nineteenth century and continuing to the present day. The Supreme Court case that definitively established the right was *The Village of Euclid v. Ambler Realty Co.*, decided in 1926. The constitutional issue is this. The Fifth Amendment states, in part, "nor shall private property be taken for public use without just compensation." It has always been clear that government could, through the power of eminent domain, take private property, but it was also clear that government had to pay fair market value for what it took. When government zones property it may, in effect, take part of the value of that property by preventing it from being used in what would otherwise be its most profitable use. Yet no compensation is paid. The burden of the Euclid and many subsequent decisions is that a reasonable amount of restriction to serve a valid public purpose is a legitimate exercise of the police power of local government and does not constitute a "taking."[3] Thus, no compensation is required. Of course, exactly how much restriction can be done before a taking has occurred and exactly what constitutes a valid public purpose can be argued, and many an attorney earns a comfortable living litigating such matters. The exact limits of the zoning power emerge from the body of case law and thus continue to change over time.

The popularity of zoning as a type of land use control stems from one salient characteristic. It is essentially costless to municipal governments. The same or greater control could be had through public ownership of land or through the purchase of easements from property owners by government.[4] But these routes could be very costly. The only direct costs that zoning imposes upon a municipality are administrative costs or, in the event that a property owner chooses to litigate, legal costs.

ZONING AS A POLITICAL PROCESS

Zoning maps and ordinances acquire force only when they are adopted by a municipality's legislative body. Zoning is thus a political act. Therefore, before we look at the economic effects of zoning we briefly consider it as a political phenomenon.

In the land of the good king advised by his wise court economist, the zoning power would be used in accord with sound, marginalist principles to achieve, as nearly as possible, Pareto optimal results. Zoning confers benefits by dealing with the externalities of land development, as noted. It also imposes losses in many cases by preventing land from being developed in its most profitable use. The path to Pareto optimality would be to use the zoning power only when the gains outweighed the losses and to stop at the point at which the marginal gains from zoning equaled the marginal losses from zoning. This is essentially the same notion of adjustment at the margin that we discussed in connection with the profit-maximizing firm. The Kaldor–Hicks criteria that the gainers would, in principle, be willing to compensate the losers would be maintained.

In the above view, one thinks of government as a single intelligence with a unitary view of the public interest, the viewpoint from which Chapter 6 was written. In the writer's view it is more useful to use the Public Choice perspective and consider zoning as the outcome of a political process that reflects individual interests rather than a unitary public interest. The economist best known for this perspective is William Fischel.[5]

Following Fischel's general line of argument, consider the matter of residential land in a small town that is part of an expanding metropolitan area. At one time most of the land in the town was owned in large, subdividable blocks and the landowners who held these blocks were the dominant group in town politics. As a group they had much to gain from growth. Now the town has grown and political power is predominantly in the hands of residents whom Fischel, in one article, terms "lodgers." They may own their own homes or they may rent. In either case their salient characteristic is that they do not own developable land and thus do not stand to profit from growth. Rather, they stand to gain from limiting further development. Stopping or slowing development will preserve the low density pattern of development that they like and spare them from noise and congestion.

Using the zoning power to limit growth may also benefit present residents by holding down tax rates. This effect is achieved in two different ways. First, by holding down density the municipality may be able to avoid certain expenses that come with denser development, such as the switch from volunteer to professional fire protection. Second, zoning for low densities has the effect of zoning out less expensive housing types and also, through this housing price effect, less affluent residents. Thus the town will tend to allow in only those housing units and residents who, at current tax rates, yield more in tax revenues than they consume in additional services. Some years ago the economist Dick Netzer made the analogy between this type of municipal behavior and a club that becomes gradually richer by refusing to admit anyone as a new member who is not at least as wealthy as the average present member.

Among the lodgers, those who are homeowners may have still another reason for using the zoning power to restrict growth. The market value of the lodger's house is likely to be higher if additional housing that might compete with it is not built. Campaigning for a zoning law that protects the house that one owns from the competition of new housing is clearly an example of rent-seeking behavior. The effort to zone out less expensive housing may also have the effect of achieving a degree of class or race segregation. No court will sustain a zoning law that has such exclusion as a motivation. But untangling the various motivations, some respectable and some not, that may lie behind a municipality's zoning policy is not easy.

ZONING AS FREE GOOD

The use of zoning is essentially costless to the populace of the town. Since it is free it will, in principle, be used down to the point at which the marginal value obtained from additional use is zero. That suggests that it will be used to restrict growth even when the gains to the lodgers are much smaller than the losses that the restrictions impose on others.

In situations in which there were no transactions costs and no constraints on trade, the owners of property and potential residents would observe that the losses imposed on them were greater than the gains delivered to the lodgers. They would approach the lodgers and offer to make compensating payments. In terms of the Edgeworth box diagram discussed in connection with welfare economics, the position that divides up all of the resources in the system would move to the contract curve (see Figure 5.7), producing a Pareto optimal result.

This optimizing move does not occur because there is no mechanism by which such payments can be made and the gains of trade thus realized. The fact that such mechanisms do not exist is summarized by Fischel in the phrase "incomplete assignment of property rights." The town has one of the rights normally associated with property ownership, namely, the right to exert some control over how the property is used. But it lacks another right usually associated with property ownership, namely, any rights of sale. Thus, trade is blocked. Allowing more development might produce a large gain for the property owner or would-be resident at the cost of only a small loss to the lodgers. A compensating payment to obtain permission would make both parties better off, but there is no mechanism by which such payments can be made.

Before leaving the matter of politics, one other point needs to be made. In most cases municipalities tend to resist residential development much more than they resist commercial development.[6] This is understandable in fairly simple tax and labor market terms. A substantial share of local government expenditures comes from locally raised taxes, predominantly the property tax. And most local governments operate under some pressure from their residents to simultaneously hold down tax rates and provide adequate services. It is residential growth that brings in population that needs the full panoply of municipal services. A zoning policy that discourages population growth but encourages commercial growth thus looks like a way to hold down pressure on the tax rate. Then, too, a zoning policy that slows population growth appears to have desirable labor market consequences for the resident population. Commercial growth without corresponding population growth tightens the labor market in which residents must find employment. A policy of restricting commercial growth more than residential growth would have the reverse effect. Some years ago, commenting on the possibility that a municipality would seek to slow population growth by choking off employment growth and then letting population growth slow as a secondary effect, William Alonso stated: "It amounts to choosing poverty, unemployment and old age. In brief, it amounts to choosing to be Scranton, and this is a choice that few will make."[7]

The consequences of the greater tendency to restrict residential than commercial growth are discussed subsequently.

THE ECONOMIC EFFECTS OF ZONING

Zoning has economic consequences because it changes the effective supply of land. That, in turn, changes the price of land and the cost of housing
and commercial buildings. Those changes will, in turn, affect many aspects
of the municipality including the size of its population and the amount of
economic activity within the municipality. The changed pattern of prices
for homes and commercial buildings will also change the composition of
the population and employment profile of the municipality. Changed land
supply conditions in one municipality will affect the markets for land in
any other community whose housing or commercial land markets are
linked to those of the first community—that is, where there is any degree
of substitutability between land in the two communities.

In the case of land for single family homes, zoning may have the apparently paradoxical effect of simultaneously raising the price of land when
measured by the building lot while lowering it when measured by the acre.
Assume that the most profitable use for a tract of land would be development at a density of four houses to the acre, but that the zoning stipulates
a maximum density of one unit to the acre. The one-acre lot will, no doubt,
be worth more than the quarter-acre lot. But, making the reasonable assumption that additional land for a single-family house will be subject to
diminishing marginal utility, it is reasonable to assume that it will not be
worth four times as much as a quarter-acre lot.

The cost of houses will also be affected. The house built on the one-acre
lot is likely to cost more than the house built on the quarter-acre lot for
several reasons. In addition to costing more, the larger lot will be more
expensive to develop for purely physical reasons. It will typically require
more grading and longer utility lines. In a subdivision of one-acre lots there
will need to be more feet of road per house than in a subdivision of smaller
lots, and so on. Then, too, builders, in general, will be reluctant to put
low-cost houses on high-cost lots.[8]

If the municipality zones a large amount of land for low-density development, the overall reduction in the number of potential building lots will
shift the supply curve for housing to the left and this will elevate the equilibrium price of houses throughout that municipality. Because one type of
housing is substitutable to some extent for another, the effects will ramify
to types not directly affected. Thus, reducing the supply of building lots
for single-family houses might elevate rents for apartments and vice versa.

Reducing the supply of housing in one municipality will affect housing
markets in all communities for which there is any degree of substitutability.
Demand that cannot be met in one municipality will show up as additional
demand in other municipalities. If supply is highly elastic in these other
municipalities the increased demand will show up primarily as an increase
in quantity. If supply there is relatively inelastic, perhaps because these

municipalities also zone restrictively, then the increased demand will manifest itself primarily in higher prices. In either case, it is clear that restrictive zoning in one municipality can deliver gains to property owners in other communities and losses to renters or would-be buyers in other communities.

Zoning, because it introduces artificial constraints into the land market, can deliver large gains and losses to participants in that market. For gains, consider the following. Suppose that a 100-acre tract would be worth $40,000 per acre if it could be developed for condominium apartments, but that the zoning law permits only single-family houses on one-acre lots, in which use the tract is worth only $10,000 per acre. If the owner of the property can get the zoning changed he or she has made a $3,000,000 capital gain ($30,000 per acre × 100 acres). The motivation for politicking and public relations activity, litigation and, in the extreme, bribery is considerable.

A very common strategy among suburban developers is to approach the owner of such a restrictively zoned parcel and buy an option on the property. The developer then uses all of the political, legal, and public relations options available to try to get the zoning changed. If the developer is unsuccessful he or she simply lets the option lapse. If successful in changing the zoning, the developer buys the property for the price stipulated in the option, generally a figure not far above what the land was worth in the original zoning category. In this case the developer has, in effect, made a substantial capital gain before the first shovelful of dirt is moved.

If one examines the pattern of land use in many suburban communities one sees that much commercial development was done on land previously zoned for low-density residential use. The scenario just described explains why it is often more profitable to build upon land that has been rezoned than upon land that originally had appropriate zoning. In the latter case the land sells at its true market value. In the former case the land price is artificially depressed by the unrealistic zoning. This situation can tend to subvert the goals of municipal land use planning because it provides a powerful motive for building in places other than those earmarked for development.

Zoning, as was just described, can deliver "windfalls." But it can also deliver "wipeouts." When land is upzoned, that is, rezoned to a less intensive category or use, the property owner suffers a capital loss. Just consider the previous scenario run in the reverse direction.[9]

The effects of zoning on the value of any one piece of property are relatively easy to determine, since the value of land in various uses is generally known. A more complex question is what is the effect of zoning on the total value of land in the community. Clearly, the value of an individual parcel will be reduced if it is zoned for a lower intensity of use or, more generally, if it is zoned in any way that prevents it from being put to its most profitable use. However, that act of zoning may increase the value of other parcels of land in at least two different ways. First, it may increase their value simply by shrinking the supply of competing land. If the zoning law prohibits the building of townhouses on parcel A, that increases the value of parcel B on which townhouses are permitted. Second, the zoning on a parcel may reduce the negative externalities (noise, traffic, etc.) that would otherwise flow from its development. That, in turn, may increase the value of nearby properties. Thus, when the above effects are considered it is not possible to say, a priori, whether zoning increases or decreases the total land value in a municipality. A detailed empirical study of the municipality and its zoning controls would be needed to make a definitive statement.

METROPOLITAN AREA EFFECTS OF ZONING

If a large number of municipalities in a metropolitan area practice zoning in the manner suggested earlier—substantial restriction on residential construction and little or no restriction on commercial development—what might be the consequences at the metropolitan level? Assume, for simplicity, that the area consists of a central city and a ring of suburban towns. Assume further that many of the towns zone in the manner of the town described above. What consequences follow? First, population densities will be lower in the restrictively zoned suburban towns than would otherwise be the case. The population blocked from settling in the suburban ring will end up either in the central city or in exurbia beyond the ring of suburban towns. Given the major dispersing forces at work in many if not most U.S. metropolitan areas, the writer suspects that for most metropolitan areas most of the displacement will be to the periphery rather than toward the center. But even if this is not so, the effect will still be a spreading of the metropolitan area because of that part of the growth that is displaced peripherally. The more dispersed metropolitan pattern will have consequences for environmental quality, for the costs of providing public services, and for time and money costs of transportation.[10] We might argue about exactly what these consequences are, but it is clear that there will be some and that they are externalities stemming from the process of numerous body politics within the metropolitan area, each pursuing its own self-interest. The analogy with externalities flowing from the pursuit of self-interest by individuals and firms in a market process is quite strong.

Some of the winners and losers are easy to identify. The losses to landowners have been noted previously. Those persons who want to live in the suburban ring but are not able to do so have clearly suffered a welfare loss. Many of those living in the suburban ring will also have suffered a welfare loss because they will be paying more in rent or more to purchase a house than they would have had to if the zoning had not restricted residential development. Those who own housing in the suburban ring will gain because zoning controls will limit the amount of new housing that can be built to compete with the existing housing. Winners and losers can also be identified outside of the housing realm. Businesses that would have profited from additional customers or a larger labor supply will be losers. Some workers may benefit because they are protected from competition in the labor market from the workers who would have moved into housing that would have been built had zoning controls not blocked its construction.

If the entire metropolitan area, or at least a large part of it, functions as a single housing market, zoning controls in some municipalities will elevate housing prices in other municipalities, even if the latter do not themselves zone restrictively. Beyond the suburban ring in exurbia there will also be winners and losers. By and large, those who own property in these other municipalities will gain and those who must buy or rent in the face of higher prices generated by the demand displaced from the suburban ring will be losers.[11] Labor markets and business operations will be affected by the outward displacement of population growth in a manner analogous to what happens inside the metropolitan ring. To the extent that zoning controls in the suburbs retard the movement of population out from the central city there will be housing market and labor market effects within the city, too.

It has been argued that restrictive zoning laws create class and racial segregation and this point has been the object of much litigation. If a part of a municipality is zoned so that only expensive housing can be built on it, it unquestionably produces class segregation because residency there is limited to more prosperous people. Given that Blacks, as a group, have lower incomes than Whites, it will by the same pricing mechanism produce some degree of racial segregation even in the absence of any individual discrimination. This general line of argument has, since the 1960s, been accepted by the courts in a number of decisions, and there now exists a substantial body of case law on it.[12] There is also legislation in some states designed to encourage or compel local governments to make some provisions in their land use controls for low- and moderate-income housing to reduce the segregating effects of restrictive zoning.

The exercise of zoning power by a large number of municipalities, each without regard to effects beyond its own borders, contributes to a scattered pattern of land use. This is because, as noted, many local governments restrict residential development while simultaneously not restricting or, in fact, actively competing for, commercial development. The corporate headquarters sited by itself in a sea of low-density, residential development is the ultimate result of a pattern of restricting residential growth while seeking out commercial development that will contribute nicely to the tax base but will require few additional public services. Many planners feel that it is an inefficient form of development. For example, scattered commercial development is virtually impossible to serve with public transportation. But from the view of the individual municipality, the behavior that produces this pattern is entirely logical.

IF ZONING IS SUBOPTIMAL, WHAT CAN BE DONE?

Above it was argued that zoning is suboptimal for several major reasons. First, as Fischel's phrase "an incomplete assignment of property rights" suggests, there are not adequate mechanisms by which gains of trade can be realized. Second, the act of zoning has relatively few explicit costs to the community. Thus, it can be treated like a free good and overused. Finally, zoning powers are vested in units of government that are much smaller than the geographic area over which the effects of zoning are felt. Thus, much of the effect of a municipality's zoning actions is felt externally to the municipality and does not weigh in its decision making.

Fischel's overall solution to the problem of the suboptimality of zoning is to move toward a zoning system that permits more trade and negotiation, to make zoning a more "fungible" process. In point of fact, zoning practice is moving in the direction that Fischel suggests. For example, in some cities builders are allowed to build higher than the normally permitted limit if they agree to provide a certain number of housing units. The theory is that this will balance the housing market effects stemming from providing additional commercial floor space. In a number of communities, residential builders may be permitted to build at more than the usually specifed number of housing units per acre if they will provide a certain number of units at below market rates for "low and moderate income" households. Here the builder gets the additional density that he or she wants and the community moves toward its "affordable housing" goals. A full discussion of these sorts of arrangements is beyond the scope of this chapter but is covered in detail in the urban planning literature.[13]

In principle, some of the externalities of zoning could be eliminated by moving the power to zone, or at least some of the power to zone, to a higher political level. This idea is analogous to the correspondence principle discussed in connection with public finance. But this solution would have its problems; zoning would certainly become more complicated than the present system and would lead to decision making by persons far from the scene and less well acquainted with the facts than are local people. In that each piece of land has some element of uniqueness in regard to topography, access, soil conditions, relationship to nearby land uses, and the like, this is not a trivial objection.

There is another issue that, though it cannot be quantified, strikes this writer as very important. The power to plan and to control land use is one of the major powers of local government and one in which citizens often take great interest. Because it is a function of local government it is one in which citizens can readily participate. It is one in which a few citizens with strong feelings can often swing the outcome. This has its advantages and disadvantages. But it must be said that moving zoning powers to a higher and therefore less accessible level of government would be a major disempowering of the citizen. That loss of control over one's environment has a psychic cost, quite apart from whether or not the objective quality of decision making were to be increased or decreased. To the extent that power is removed from the community and vested in a more distant entity, the community is weakened. In the writer's view, that is a serious matter.

Charles Tiebout suggested many years ago that each community offers a unique package of services matched by a package of taxes and that the potential resident, like a consumer, can choose the most suitable package.[14] Thus, variety in municipalities increases net welfare by providing what is, in effect, consumer choice. If it is true that some of this intermunicipal difference stems from the different use of planning and zoning powers, then moving those powers to a higher level of government is likely to diminish the variety of communities and hence the amount of choice available to the potential resident. That, presumably, would be a net welfare loss.

As a practical political matter there is no real chance of moving major control over local zoning to higher political levels. There are in many states some state-level controls on land development, particularly in environmentally fragile areas. But in the overwhelming majority of cases these controls constitute another level of control. They do not supersede local controls.

If we were to be guided by the correspondence principle, we might argue that the appropriate level for some supralocal control over zoning decisions would be at the metropolitan area level, because that is the level that often corresponds to the level at which the land market effects of zoning are felt. But we do not have metropolitan governments in the United States. We have, in some metropolitan areas, Councils of Governments (COGs), but their powers are extremely limited.

We are thus left with one main path to improving the process. This is the Fischel solution of making zoning more open to negotiation and bargaining so that some gains of trade can be realized. And, as noted, this is the path in which zoning is moving. In some cases zoning may be made more efficient by pressure from the courts. For example, in a number of cases regarding restrictive zoning the courts have required that regional housing needs be considered or, at least, they have been willing to hear testimony about regional housing needs. To that extent some externalities now may be internalized in municipal zoning decisions.

NOTES

1. The only major city in which it is not used is Houston. For a discussion of the Houston case, see Bernard H. Siegan, *Land Use without Zoning* (Lexington, MA: Lexington Books, 1972).

2. Numerous books contain general accounts of zoning. See, for example, John

M. Levy, *Contemporary Urban Planning*, 3d ed. (Englewood Cliffs, NJ: Prentice-Hall, 1994); Frank So and Judith Getzels, eds., *The Practice of Local Government Planning* (Washington, DC: International City Management Association, 1988); Daniel R. Mandelker, *Land Use Law* (Charlottesville, VA: The Michie Co., 1982); and Peter L. Buck, ed., *Modern Land Use Control* (The Practicing Law Institute, 1978). Recent developments are also covered in the periodicals *Planning* and *Zoning Digest*.

3. The term "police power" may be somewhat misleading. It merely refers to the power of government to regulate private activity to protect the public interest.

4. An easement grants the party purchasing the easement the right to make some use of part or all of the property (such as the right to run utility lines through the property) or it binds the owner of the property not to make certain use of the property. As an example of the latter case, an agricultural preservation easement might bind the farmer from whom it was purchased to not convert the property to nonagricultural use. Such easements have been used by local governments that wanted to preserve some agricultural land in areas where market forces would have caused the conversion of farmland to more remunerative purposes.

5. William Fischel, "The Property Rights Approach to Zoning," *Land Economics* 54., no. 1 (February 1978), p. 64; William Fischel, "Introduction: Maxims for Research on Land Use Controls," *Land Economics* 66, no. 3 (August 1990); and William Fischel, *The Economics of Zoning Laws: A Property Rights Approach to Zoning* (Baltimore: The Johns Hopkins University Press, 1985).

6. In fact there is a very intense competition for economic development among states and municipalities involving, for the nation, many billions per year in public capital investments, subsidy, and tax abatement. It is not uncommon for the same municipality that uses its zoning powers to sharply slow residential growth to spend considerable sums of public money promoting economic growth. For a brief account of the local economic development process and references to the literature see John M. Levy, *Economic Development Programs for Cities, Countries and Towns*, 2d ed. (New York: Praeger, 1990).

7. William Alonso, "Urban Zero Population Growth," *Daedalus* (Fall 1973), reprinted in *Management and Control of Growth*, vol. I. (Washington DC: The Urban Land Institute, 1975), pp. 405–14.

8. There is a substantial literature on the relationship between land use controls and single-family house prices. For an early example, see George Sternlieb and Lynne B. Sagalyn, *Zoning and Housing Costs* (New Brunswick, NJ: Center for Urban Policy Research, 1972). For a more recent example, see Henry O. Pollakowski and Susan M. Wachter, "The Effects of Land Use Constraints on Housing Prices," *Land Economics* 66, no. 3 (August 1990), pp. 315–24.

9. This terminology comes from Donald G. Hagman and Dean J. Misczynski, eds., *Windfalls for Wipeouts: Land Value Capture and Compensation* (Chicago: American Society of Planning Officials, 1978).

10. While this scenario is generally accepted and makes sense to this writer, it is not universally accepted. For a dissenting view, see Benjamin Chinitiz, "Growth Management: Good for the Town, Bad for the Nation?" *Journal of the American Planning Association* 51, no. 1 (Winter 1990), pp. 3–8.

11. The only exception to this statement would be if the supply of buildable land in exurbia were, in effect, infinitely elastic. But this is not a realistic possibility.

Even if the supply of undeveloped land appears very large compared to the size of the developed area, building requires public capital investment in the form of roads, water lines, sewer lines, and the like. Thus, the supply of land that is actually available for development at any given time will be such that increasing demand will push up prices.

12. The best-known series of cases in this connection are the Mt. Laurel, N.J. cases collectively known as Mt. Laurel I, II, and III. For a brief account see Levy, *Contemporary Urban Planning*, pp. 119–20.

13. See ibid, chapter 9, and So and Getzels, *The Practice of Local Government Planning*.

14. Charles Tiebout, "A Pure Theory of Local Expenditures," *Journal of Political Economy* 64 (October 1956), p. 422.

CHAPTER 12

Selling the Right to Pollute

In this chapter we discuss the sale of pollution rights and the use of pollution taxes, two closely related techniques. Both are grounded in a proposition presented in the first half of this book—that one way to move toward a Pareto optimal allocation of resources is to have institutional and market arrangements that permit the gains of trade to be realized. Recall that in the Edgeworth box (Chapter 5) the contract curve, which contains all of the Pareto optimal distributions of resources in the system, is the locus of all those points for which the gains of trade have been exhausted.

The idea that we might create a market in rights to pollute or that we might tell people that they may pollute just so long as they pay the required tax per unit of pollution strikes some people as peculiar or even morally offensive. After all, we don't create markets in the right to commit murders and periodically auction off so many murder rights to the highest bidder. Nor do we tax murders and say that it is alright to commit one so long as one pays the tax on it. But this moral objection to pollution rights and taxes comes from a misunderstanding that takes a bit of explaining.

Unless we go back to an original state of nature that prevailed before humans learned to use fire, some pollution is inevitable. When you get into your fuel efficient car to drive to a Sierra Club meeting you still become a polluter the instant you turn the ignition key. The question is not whether or not to pollute, but what balance to strike between human needs on the one hand and preservation of the natural environment on the other hand.

THE OPTIMAL LEVEL OF POLLUTION

Pollution confronts us with two sets of costs: the damage that the pollution we do not abate causes, and the costs of abatement. In principle, the

Figure 12.1
The Efficient Level of Pollution Control

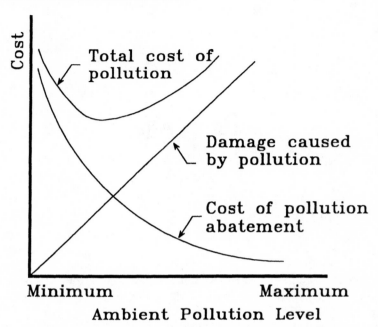

The costs of damage done by pollution are shown as linear and the costs of abatement as exponential, an expression of the law of diminishing returns. These costs are added vertically to get the total cost curve. The efficient level of control corresponds to the low point on the total cost curve.

optimal level of pollution control would be that point at which the total of damage costs and abatement costs was least. This is the low point on the total cost curve in Figure 12.1. The curve was produced by the vertical addition of the cost curves for abatement and for pollution damage. In general, the low point will be achieved when, at the margin, a dollar spent on pollution abatement produces exactly one dollar of environmental benefit. In the figure the cost of pollution damage is shown as linear. This may be so for some pollutants and not for others. The cost of abatement is shown as an exponential function. That seems reasonable in that in many pollution control processes like sewage treatment one does encounter diminishing returns. The first few percent of pollutants is removed at much lower marginal costs than the last few percent. To really know exactly where the optimal point lies we would need to have perfect knowledge of how the physical world works and perfect wisdom in knowing how to value all things, both present and future.

Obviously, we are a long way from that level of knowledge and wisdom.

But the basic logic of the diagram is intuitively reasonable. It seems sensible to believe that there is an optimum environmental quality that does not lie at either end of the horizontal axis. The left end of the spectrum would represent an unacceptably and unhealthfully low standard of living. While it may not seem intuitively obvious in a prosperous First World that spending large sums of money to achieve small increases in environmental quality can increase human mortality and morbidity, this is in fact the case.

Regulations to promote health and safety that are exceptionally costly relative to the expected benefits may actually worsen health and safety, since compliance reduces other spending, including private spending on health and safety. Past studies relating income and mortality give estimates of the income loss that induces one death . . . to be around $9 to 12 million.[1]

The extreme right hand side of Figure 12.1 would represent, at least in the short term, a very high material living standard in a very degraded environment. Clearly, neither would be optimal.

Consider the obvious point that there are efficient and inefficient ways to reduce pollution. If we could reduce pollution more efficiently, that would be represented in Figure 12.1 as a shift to the left of the marginal cost of abatement curve. That would move the intersection between the two cost curves as well as the low point in the total cost curve to the left, that is, to the cleaner end of the horizontal axis. It would also lower the low point on the total cost curve. Thus, the more efficient abatement techniques are, the more abatement can be achieved with a given level of expenditure or the less can be spent to achieve a given level of abatement, or some combination of both effects can prevail.

IS THE STANDARD REGULATORY APPROACH EFFICIENT?

The initial approach to pollution abatement, and still the major one, was direct regulation. A few activities were absolutely prohibited and more were regulated in terms like parts per million or grams per mile. There is no question that environmental quality has been improved by these methods. For example, airborne lead has been reduced to a very small fraction of its previous total by phasing out and then banning leaded gasoline. Automotive emissions of carbon monoxide and unburned hydrocarbons have been sharply reduced by compelling manufacturers to equip cars with exhaust systems that meet per mile standards. And so on.[2]

The question is whether it is possible to achieve pollution abatement more efficiently than with flat regulation. Applying the same regulatory standards to all emitters of a particular type of pollutant is likely to be less than perfectly efficient because at the point that each polluter stops spending on abatement, the amount of abatement that each achieves per dollar

Figure 12.2
The Inefficiency of Flat Rate Regulation

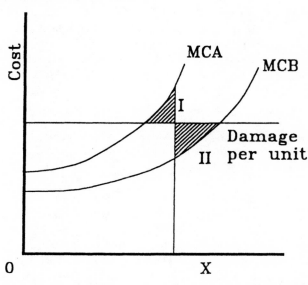

Lines MCA and MCB represent the marginal costs of abatement for firms A and B. Assume a flat rate regulation requires both firms to abate OX units. Area I represents firm A's abatement costs in excess of benefits and area II represents the opportunity cost loss of firm B stopping while the marginal benefits still exceed marginal costs.

is likely to be different. If, at the margin, pollution reduction per dollar is different for the various pollution emitters then the process of abatement does not meet the test of efficiency at the margin.

Figure 12.2 illustrates this point. Both firms have to meet the same regulatory standard of, say, parts per million. The firms have different abatement cost structures. Perhaps this is because of different scales of operation, different type of production process, different locale, or any other reason. As shown in the figure, firm B stops abating while its marginal cost of abatement is less than the marginal benefit from additional abatement. Clearly, it would be efficient from an aggregate point of view if the firm continued to spend on abatement up to the point where marginal costs and benefits were equal. But the firm will not do that because it does not have to. It will only abate up to the point that it meets the regulatory standard. On the other hand, firm A continues to spend on abatement past the point at which the marginal costs of abatement equal the marginal benefits of abatement. That, too, is not efficient. But the firm must do it because it must meet the regulatory standard. If one considers the picture presented in the figure as the complete situation, it is evident that if firm A abated a little less and firm B abated a little more the same total amount of abatement could be achieved at a lower cost. Alternatively, a larger total abatement would be achieved at the same cost. Either way, society would be better off. Both pollution tax and pollution rights schemes are grounded in this fundamental idea of adjustment at the margin. In that sense they are both variations on a theme.

POLLUTION TAXES

With a pollution tax the polluter pays a sum for each unit of pollution emitted. If it is cheaper to abate the pollution than to pay the tax the polluter abates. If it is more expensive to abate than to pay the tax then the polluter pays the tax. Abatement takes place up to the point at which the marginal cost per unit of abatement exceeds the tax rate. How much abatement will be achieved depends upon the abatement cost curve and the tax rate.

One might ask whether the taxing authority really knows the benefit achieved per unit of pollution abated. The answer is that such things are not known with any precision. There is uncertainty about the exact effects and pathways of most pollutants, and there is always room for argument about just what value to place upon the effects to the extent that they are known. Thus, the figure the agency uses is only the roughest of approximations. But the same point can be made about regulatory standards. To set the standard properly the regulatory agency would have to have a figure for benefit per unit abated to lay off against the probable costs that it was imposing on the industry and its customers through the standard. Therefore, the fact of imprecise knowledge about the costs to society for a unit of pollution is not, by itself, a point in favor either of flat regulation or of the tax approach. In fact, the tax approach, because it requires that the regulatory agency focus upon the costs of abatement, is consistent with the federal government's requirement that its agencies do cost-benefit studies for major new regulations, a policy begun under President Reagan.

The box on page 182 shows a hypothetical case for an industry made up of two firms of equal size. We assume that in the absence of any emissions regulations both firms will emit the same amount of pollution. We then assume that our goal is to reduce total emissions for the industry by 90 percent. We also assume that the two firms have different cost structures.

As the calculations in the box show, the same total abatement is achieved with less cost with a properly calculated tax than with a simple regulatory standard. Note that we have not counted the taxes paid by the firms as part of the cost. From an aggregate or society-wide point of view, the taxes represent a transfer of wealth but no creation or destruction of wealth and therefore should not appear in any cost calculations. The taxes collected from firm B represent that much less in taxes that have to be collected

Assume that two firms compose the entire industry. Each firm, if unregulated and untaxed, would emit 10 units of pollution per day. The firms, for any one of a number of reasons, will face different marginal cost schedules if required to reduce the amount of pollution that they emit. Firm A's schedule is one in which marginal costs rise monotonically. Firm A's costs rise with the square of the number of units. These figures are shown below.[3]

Units Abated	Plant A Total Cost	Plant A Marginal Cost	Plant B Total Cost	Plant B Marginal Cost
0	0	0	0	0
1	1	1	.2	.2
2	3	2	1.0	.8
3	6	3	2.8	1.8
4	10	4	6.0	3.2
5	15	5	11.0	5.0
6	21	6	18.2	7.2
7	28	7	28.0	9.8
8	36	8	40.8	12.8
9	45	9	57.0	16.2
10	55	10	77.0	20.0

Assume that the goal of the regulatory authority is to reduce pollution emissions by 90 percent (abate 18 units). If it requires each firm to abate 9 units firm A will have to spend $45 and firm B $57 for a total cost of $102.

Alternatively, the regulators, after examining the cost structures of the two firms, might decide to set the pollution tax at $13 per unit emitted. Facing this tax structure, firm A will then decide to abate 10 units and firm B 8 units. The abatement costs are now $55 for firm A and $40.80 for firm B for a total of $95.80. From a social perspective the tax solution achieves the same pollution abatement effects while saving $6.20 in pollution abatement costs. Note that the $6.20 saved is equal to the difference between the marginal cost of the 9th unit for firm B (which was not abated) and the 10th unit for firm A (which the firm did abate when confronted with the tax).

The story is not quite over, because firm B must pay $26 in taxes for the two units of pollution that it still emits. This matter is discussed further in the text.

elsewhere. Furthermore, they are an attractive sort of tax. Most taxes fall upon good things and create a so-called "excess" or "deadweight" burden of taxation as discussed previously. But here, we are taxing a bad rather than a good and thus there may not be an excess burden of taxation.

From the firms' perspective the situation in the above example is not quite so rosy. The taxes pushed firm A to abate the 10th unit and so it is worse off to the extent of its marginal costs for unit 10. Firm B is also worse off because the taxes on the two units that it still emits are higher by a small amount than the marginal cost of abating the 9th unit, as it would have done under the regulatory system. The firms' executives and stockholders are not likely to be pleased by the pollution tax approach, even if they can be shown that society in the aggregate clearly is better off. In point of fact, business has not generally been favorably disposed to the pollution tax approach even though one would generally expect businesses to favor market-based over regulatory approaches. Pollution taxes have been slow in coming in the United States and business opposition or lack of enthusiasm is one reason. Oddly, business opposition has often gained strength from some environmentalists and others whom one does not normally think of as business allies because of the "right to pollute" sorts of arguments raised earlier. But the overall logic of pollution taxes is strong and it is likely that they will gradually find their way into the U.S. tax structure.

The ozone tax enacted in 1990 may be the first true pollution tax in the United States and is considered to be highly successful. Andrew Hoerner notes that it has "rendered the EPA regulations of the ozone depleting chemicals moot, by encouraging producers to reduce production lower than the caps in every year so far."[4] In 1993 the proposed carbon tax (motivated by the greenhouse effect) did not have enough support to make it through Congress and the increase in the gasoline tax that finally appeared in the 1993 tax bill was much smaller than its proponents had hoped for. Nonetheless, the fact that these two proposals made as much progress as they did may be harbingers of more pollution taxes in the future. Pollution or effluent taxes are currently in widespread use in Western Europe.

ARE SUBSIDIES A GOOD ALTERNATIVE?

Pollution taxes have much to recommend them by way of economic efficiency. Unfortunately, they have the political disadvantages noted above. Cannot similar efficiencies be achieved with subsidies? After all, is not a subsidy just a negative tax? Certainly, subsidies would not encounter opposition from industry and they may look better politically. They have the connotation of helping someone to do a good thing, whereas pollution taxes have the connotation of allowing someone to continue doing a bad thing just so long as the tax is paid.

While this line of argument seems plausible, economists have for many years realized that pollution control subsidies are likely to be a good deal less efficient than pollution taxes.[5] Consider the situation in which government imposes a strict standard on emissions of some pollutant produced in manufacturing a particular product and then provides subsidies to aid manufacturers in purchasing emission control equipment. The subsidy has two opposing effects. By encouraging the purchase of the equipment it will reduce emissions per unit of product produced. But by lowering the manufacturer's cost curve it will cause more of the product to be produced, as compared to how much would be produced in the presence of the regulations but the absence of the subsidy. Whether the total amount of emissions will rise or fall depends upon which effect predominates. Consider a situation in which the per unit reduction in emissions is moderate, the elasticity of demand for the product extremely high, and pollution control costs are a large percentage of total production costs. Here the increase in the number of units produced might be a larger percentage than the decrease in pollution per unit with the result that the total emissions increase.

CREATING A MARKET FOR POLLUTION RIGHTS

Although the technique is dissimilar, the concept of a market for pollution rights has an underlying similarity to that of the pollution tax, namely, proper adjustment at the margin. Legislatively, the pollution right concept may fare better because is not quite so likely to run into opposition from business. It will, however, encounter the same sort of (in this writer's view, misguided) opposition to the "right to pollute" as will the pollution tax.

To begin, we describe a current Environmental Protection Agency (EPA) pollution rights program. We then consider the logic behind the program. Subsequent to the passage of the Clean Air Act in 1990 the EPA set up a market for pollution rights concerning emissions of sulphur dioxide (SO_2), one of the primary causes of acid rain. About two-thirds of all SO_2 discharged into the atmosphere is emitted by coal-fired electric generating plants, so the program was geared to the electric power generating industry.

The pollution rights being traded became operative in 1995 but the trading began earlier. Initially, electric utilities were assigned so many pollution allowances, each of which entitled them to emit one ton of SO_2 per year. The number of units was based upon the utility's fuel consumption during the late 1980s. The number of allowances, about 8.95 million, was set so that by the year 2010, total SO_2 emissions in the United States will be about ten million tons lower than they were in 1980.[6]

For each ton of SO_2 the utility emits it must have one allowance. If the emissions exceed the number of allowances the utility has, it must pay a fine of $2,000 per ton in excess. The allowances are tradable through an auction process run by the Chicago Board of Trade (CBOT) acting as a contractor to the EPA. Allowances not used in one calendar year may be carried over into a subsequent year.

There has been some discussion of opening a futures market in pollution rights analogous to present-day futures markets in commodities. In that way a new utility could reduce uncertainty about its future allowance expenditures by buying contracts that would guarantee its ability to buy a stated number of allowances for a known price on a given date. As with present futures markets in pork bellies, wheat, aluminum, and so forth, the market for pollution rights would become a vehicle for speculation.[7]

If a utility has carried-over allowances or knows that it will not need all of its allowances for the coming year it may choose to sell its allowances. If the utility knows that it will generate more SO_2 than it has allowances it will have to buy allowances from another utility. The function of the CBOT is to establish a smoothly functioning market for these allowances. As of 1994 trades were made in the general range of several hundred dollars per ton. The rate of trading was relatively slow because the fines for a utility exceeding its allowance did not begin until 1995.

Utilities that now have more allowances than they need to cover their own emissions will still be motivated to reduce emissions because it will give them still more allowances to sell. Utilities that are over their allowance will be motivated to reduce emissions so that they need to buy fewer emissions. If the system works as expected, an efficient marginal adjustment will occur. Utilities will spend on pollution abatement up to the point that their abatement costs exceed the price of purchasing allowances. That price will be set in the market maintained by the CBOT.

The system is flexible over the long term in that the EPA can adjust the pressure it puts on the industry to reduce its total emissions by either reducing the number of allowances or adjusting the number of pounds of SO_2 that one allowance covers. In fact, such a change is planned for Phase II of the program, scheduled for the year 2000. The system should be readily enforceable in that SO_2 emissions will be measured by sensors in generating plant smokestacks.

What about new generating plants? New plants will come into the market with no allowances and thus must purchase them from existing holders. For the utility company thinking about building a new plant the expectations about the future price of allowances will be an important consideration. Presumably, as the system operates and more trades occur, the price of allowances will become more predictable. What about the case in which a new plant cannot come into the industry because its fixed and operating costs plus the cost of its emissions allowances will not permit it to break even? The economist would argue that if it cannot cover all of its costs, including the allowances, then it should not come into being.

THE INITIAL ASSIGNMENT OF RIGHTS

The participants in the market at the time the rights program is being set up are being given something of value, namely, the allowances. The utility that gets 100,000 allowances at a time when allowances are expected to trade at $300 each is getting a set of rights with an apparent market value of $30 million.

Does it matter how these initial rights are distributed? Obviously, it matters to the individual participants in the market. But, in a well-functioning market, it should not matter to society as a whole. The initial distribution of rights should not affect the price at which the market ultimately settles. This idea that the initial distribution of rights does not matter is generally referred to as the Coase Theorem, although Ronald Coase himself did not explicitly state it as a formal theorem.[8] Coase's arguments have been very widely cited and discussed and the term "Coase Theorem" found its way into the literature several years after he published. If the Coase Theorem is correct, it is a very liberating idea for designers of economic policy, since it means that they can focus on getting the market-signaling mechanisms set up correctly and not worry so much about initial allocations of rights.

EXTENDING THE SYSTEM

As noted, the system, as originally set up, was limited to electric utilities. This makes sense in that utilities constitute most of the major emitters and their emissions are readily monitored. However, as of 1994 EPA was working on plans to extend the system through an "opt-in" program for non-utilities.[9] The idea of the program as stated in EPA literature is to allow manufacturing firms to reduce their SO_2 emission levels below "baseline" levels and then sell the resulting unused allowances to utilities. Again, the basic idea is simply to have the task of emission reduction done by whichever party can do it most efficiently.

EFFICIENCY ACROSS CATEGORIES

Permitting trades across industries, in the above case utilities and manufacturers, in the case of the same pollutant is a step toward greater efficiency in pollution control, since it takes us further toward the goal of proper adjustment at the margin. A further step, and not an easy one to take, would be to permit trades across different types of pollutants. In principle this would mean that at the margin the dollar spent on abating pollutant A would achieve as much environmental improvement as the dollar spent abating pollutant B or C or D, and so on. If one thinks of various pollutants as constituting risks to human life or human health then one might argue that the really efficient system would, at the margin, achieve the same degree of risk reduction for a dollar spent on risk regardless of the source of the risk. At this time we are very far from such a system. Typically, standards are set for one pollutant or one risk at a time and the best we can do is to achieve economic rationality in the pursuit of that one goal.[10]

NOTES

1. Randall Lutter and John F. Morral III, "Health Health Analysis: A New Way to Evaluate Health and Safety Regulations," *Journal of Risk and Uncertainty* (January 1994), pp. 43–66. The term "health health" refers to balancing the risk from a specific hazard against the more general risks that accrue from the lower level of private spending occasioned by mitigating this hazard. For the relationship between per capita income and longevity on a country-to-country basis, data on per capita GNP and life expectancy can be found in the Comparative International Statistics chapter of the annual *Statistical Abstract of the United States* (various years).

2. For an overview of trends with regard to a number of pollutants, see *Environmental Quality: Annual Report of the Council on Environmental Quality* (Washington, DC: U.S. Government Printing Office. The series has been published annually since 1971.

3. The marginal cost function for plant B is the arbitrarily chosen relationship $MC = n^2 \times .2$ where n is the number of units.

4. Andrew J. Hoerner, "The Infancy and Early Childhood of Pollution Taxes," *Tax Notes*, November 12, 1992, pp. 855–58.

5. For an early analysis of this point, see William J. Baumol and Wallace E. Oates, *The Theory of Environmental Policy* (Englewood Cliffs, NJ: Prentice-Hall, 1975), especially chapter 12.

6. This simplified description is drawn from communication with staff of the Acid Rain Division of EPA and from program documentation including EPA430/F-92/018 and EPA430/F-92/017.

7. The terms "speculation" and "speculator" often have a bad connotation, but speculation often performs a useful function. The speculator who buys when prices are low and sells when they are high drives up low prices and drives down high prices and thus stabilizes the market. By so doing the speculator makes the market a safer and more predictable place for producers and buyers and thus facilitates productive economic activity. Another way to put it is to say that one function of the speculator is to absorb market risk.

8. Ronald H. Coase, "The Problem of Social Cost," *Journal of Law and Economics* (October 1960), pp. 1–44.

9. The Opt-in program is described in EPA publication EPAA430-F-93-013.

10. To get a sense of how much difference there now is in the marginal effect of a dollar spent on different types of risk reduction, the reader might look at table 6 in the Lutter and Morrall article cited above. The reader might also examine some of the recent articles on Superfund in the risk management literature. See, for example, David E. Burmaster and Robert H. Harris, "The Magnitude of Compounding Conservatisms in Superfund Risk Assessment," *Risk Analysis* (April 1993), pp. 135–40.

CHAPTER 13

The Minimum Wage Controversy

In 1938, Congress passed the Fair Labor Standards Act that established a national minimum wage of 40 cents per hour. The minimum has been periodically raised by Congress and the percent of all wage earners to whom it applies has been increased. Since 1991 the minimum has stood at $4.25 per hour. It currently covers over 80 percent of all workers.[1]

Early in 1993 the Clinton administration's Secretary of Labor, Robert Reich, advocated an increase to $4.50 and annual indexation to adjust the minimum wage for inflation. In late 1993 the administration decided to postpone its minimum wage request, for political considerations. The administration's health plan had aroused large amounts of opposition in the business community because of its employer-mandate provisions, and so it seemed like an unpropitious time to also ask for a minimum wage increase.[2]

Liberals and those on the political left generally favor increases in the minimum wage and certainly do not doubt the basic wisdom and fairness of having a minimum wage. The reverse is true of many businessmen and many conservatives. Among economists the wisdom of minimum wage legislation has been a matter of some interest and there is now a large literature about it. While there is substantial though not universal agreement about the economic mechanisms involved, there is less agreement about the magnitude of the effects of minimum wage legislation. Disentangling the effects of minimum wage legislation from the effects of other and often more powerful variables is not an easy task. Various studies show a substantial range of results.[3]

For much of the labor market the minimum wage is almost entirely irrelevant because the equilibrium wage is substantially higher than the minimum wage.[4] We confine our discussion to that part of the labor market

Table 13.1
Characteristics of Workers at or Below the Minimum Wage, 1992

Employed fulltime	37%
Employed part-time	63
Age 16 to 24	52
Age 16-19	30
Employed in services	80
Employed in manufacturing	12
Employed in public sector	8
Male	38
Female	62

Source: Statistical Abstract of the United States, 1993 (113th edition), table 676.

in which equilibrium wages are below the minimum wage. At present that is about 4 percent of total employment.

WHO ARE THE MINIMUM WAGE WORKERS?

In 1992 the Bureau of Labor Statistics estimated that there were a total of 4,762,000 workers employed at or below the minimum wage of $4.25 per hour. A few characteristics of these workers are shown in Table 13.1. All figures are rounded to the nearest whole percent.

The overall picture is one of a large amount of youth employment and a large amount of part-time employment, primarily in services. The figures do not tell us anything about the workers in the income range just above the minimum wage—those who would fall under the coverage of the law were the wage raised to, say, $4.75. But the chances are that their characteristics are not very dissimilar to the characteristics of those now at or below the minimum wage.[5] The part-time and youth employment percentages have important implications for the distributional effects of the minimum wage and also for its efficacy or lack thereof as an antipoverty tool.

ARGUMENTS PRO AND CON

The case for raising the minimum wage, which is really just an extension of the case for having a minimum wage law at all, is often put in the following way. Among the poor there is a subcategory generally referred to as the "working poor." These are, as the term implies, persons who are employed but whose wages are too low to lift them and their dependents, if any, above the poverty line.[6] As of 1993 the poverty line for a household of four was $14,763. At the current $4.25 minimum wage a full-time (2,000 hours a year) worker will earn only $8,500. Thus, it is argued that an increase in the minimum wage is needed to lift many households out of poverty.[7]

A related argument is that the minimum wage is so low that it is not very competitive with public assistance. It is argued that raising the minimum wage will make work more competitive with public assistance for people with relatively weak skills and will thus draw them away from welfare dependence.

Finally, increases in the minimum wage are advocated on the grounds that by raising the wages of low-paid workers relative to higher-paid workers, the overall degree of income inequality in the United States will be reduced.

The argument most commonly advanced against the minimum wage is that it will reduce employment among low-skilled workers. It is also argued that even if an increase in the minimum wage produces some increase in the absolute income going to the poor or some decrease in income inequality in the United States, it is an extremely inefficient way to achieve these goals.

At a more aggregate level it is argued that raising the minimum wage will push up labor costs and thus be inflationary. Some opponents also argue that to the extent that minimum wage legislation reduces employment it reduces the GNP and imposes a loss upon the entire economy. Finally, it is argued that raising the minimum wage may weaken U.S. firms in the competition with low-wage, overseas manufacturers, thus shrinking manufacturing employing and increasing the balance of payments deficit. We turn first to the most serious objection, the matter of job losses.

The Minimum Wage and Employment

What follows is very simplifed in that it treats unskilled labor as a single entity for which there is a single equilibrium wage. In fact, in the absence of a minimum wage law the wages of those who would be affected by it would be spread out over a wide range from near zero to up to the legal minimum. Even in the presence of the law there is a considerable spread of wages below the minimum, both because of evasion of the law and because not all workers are covered by it.

The employment argument is a simple supply-and-demand argument. We assume that the equilibrium wage in the market in question is below the minimum wage. If it is not, then the minimum wage is a moot issue. In the neoclassical theory of wage determination, employers hire as long as the marginal revenue product of additional labor exceeds the wage rate. Given that labor, like all factors of production, must be subject to diminishing returns, the demand curve for labor must slope downward just as do other demand curves. If that is so, then replacing the market-determined wage with a legislated wage above the equilibrium wage will reduce total em-

Figure 13.1
The Minimum Wage and Employment

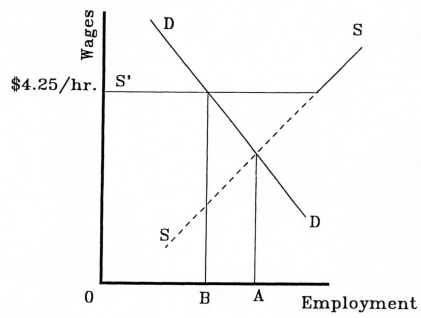

In the absence of a minimum wage the supply of labor is line SS and the amount of labor
employed is OA. When the minimum wage is imposed the dashed portion of the labor
supply curve becomes irrelevant and the labor supply curve becomes S'S. The amount of
labor employed falls to OB.

ployment. Note that this is the same argument that is made with regard to
unions. One thing the union seeks to do by bargaining and the threat or
actuality of striking is to set a wage above that which would be set in the
market.[8]

Figure 13.1 shows the above argument. The supply curve for labor in
the absence of the minimum wage as shown in this figure begins in the
lower left corner. But the minimum wage renders irrelevant that portion of
it shown as a dashed line because the law prevents employers from hiring
anyone at below $4.25 regardless of their willingness to work for less than
$4.25. Instead the supply curve in the presence of the law extends hori-
zontally from the wage axis until some point at which no more labor will
be forthcoming at $4.25. At that point the supply curve in the absence of
the law and the presence of the law are the same.

As shown in the figure the law causes employment to fall from OA to
OB. Clearly, the law has created winners and losers within the low-skill labor category. Some workers who were employed at below the minimum

wage are now employed at the minimum wage. On the other hand, some workers who were previously employed below the minimum wage are now unemployed. Which effect outweighs which is a question of elasticity. If the elasticity of demand for labor is extremely low the gains for the many who remain employed will outweigh the wage losses for the very few who lose their jobs. If the elasticity of demand is higher, then the reverse will be true.

Elasticity estimates vary. Brown, Gilroy and Kohen present a range from different studies.[9] Estimates are often broken down by age, sex, and race of worker. Estimates by type of work rather than by type of worker would probably reflect labor market realities better but the data is easier to develop the other way. A large number of estimates fall in the .1 to .3 range. Thus, one will often see a statement in the literature to the effect that for every 10 percent increase in the minimum wage a reasonable expectation is a 1 to 3 percent drop in the amount of unskilled labor employed. In general, elasticities seem to be higher for teenaged than for adult workers. Very recently, a small number of articles have disputed the idea that minimum wage laws produce any reduction in labor demand. These have been based on studies of relatively small markets. Both for methodological reasons and because they so flatly contradict both standard economic theory and the results of numerous earlier studies they, at this time, represent a minority view of the matter.[10]

To see the relationship between the elasticity of the demand for labor and the effects of a minimum wage law, let us assume that in some particular sector of the low-skill labor market the equilibrium wage would be $3.75 rather than $4.25 and that the elasticity of demand for labor is .1. Assume, for ease of calculation, that 1,000 workers are employed at $3.75 per hour. The hourly wage bill is thus $3,750. The increase from $3.75 to the new minimum of $4.25 is 13.3 percent. At the assumed elasticity of demand of .1, employment will decline by 1.33 percent or 13 out of 1,000 workers. The new wage bill will be 987 × $4.25 = $4,194. Or, one can say that 987 workers will each be ahead by 50 cents per hour for a total of $493.50. Thirteen workers will each have lost $3.75 for a total per hour loss of $48.75. Clearly, at this low elasticity, wage gains for the many outweigh the wage losses for a few. If the reader does the same calculations for an elasticity of .5 he or she will see that 67 jobs will be lost and the wage bill will now be $3,965 per hour. Wage gains for those who keep their jobs still outweigh wage losses for those who lose their jobs but the gap between gains and losses has been narrowed considerably. At an elasticity of 1.0 the situation is a break-even one and at elasticities greater than 1 the total wage bill begins to decline.

Microeconomic literature often treats the act of work as a disutility which workers balance, at the margin, against the utility of income. Thinking of work only as a disutility might be called, to quote a bumper sticker the writer has seen, the "a bad day at the beach is better than a good day at the office" theory of work. If one adheres to this theory, the job losses produced by an increase in the minimum wage appear even less serious because now one must add back into the total picture the gains from the fact that some people now no longer face the disutility of work.

In the writer's view, regarding work simply as a disutility is a mistake. One's work (or nonwork) is a big part of one's identity. It affects one's sense of self-worth; it may affect how one sees one's relationship to society; it affects what other people think of one; and so on. Low-wage jobs for people with little or no prior work experience may be much more important in the long term for getting started and for establishing an employment history than for the actual dollars they bring in. The point is that the disemployment effects of a minimum wage have more consequences than can be measured in a wages-lost-by-some-versus-wages-gained-by-others analysis or in a utility-of-income-versus-disutility-of-work calculation.

Opponents of the minimum wage generally find the argument that a higher minimum wage will draw more workers into the labor force to be fundamentally illogical. It is true that more people would be willing to work at higher wages and that the higher wage would make work relatively more attractive compared to welfare. But if the higher wage shrinks the number of jobs, then increasing the minimum wage will just, in the manner of price support programs in general, produce a surplus. In this case the surplus will be composed of people who would be willing to work at the legislated wage if only the job existed. It is hard to see how one draws people into the labor market by reducing the number of jobs available to them.

The Minimum Wage and Income Redistribution

Minimum wage increases are often advocated on the grounds that they will make the distribution of income in the United States more equal. This seems entirely reasonable, for a higher minimum wage will do a lot more for the incomes of dishwashers than it will for the incomes of stockbrokers. Econometric studies suggest that, indeed, an increase in the minimum wage will have an equalizing effect. But they also suggest that the effect will be much smaller than one might suspect.

The redistributional effect is weak because minimum wage earners are distributed more or less evenly across the entire family or household income spectrum. In the bottom decile of the income distribution there are many households with no wage earner. And in the upper deciles, where many households contain more than one worker, there is often one household member who is working at a minimum wage job. William Johnson and Edgar Browning, in 1983, estimated that of all workers earning the minimum wage or less, 11.5 percent came from households in the bottom decile of the income distribution. But they also estimated that 11.1 percent came from households in the top decile.[11] For the remaining eight deciles the figures occupied a remarkably narrow range, from a low value of 9.0 percent for the 7th decile to a high value of 10.6 percent for the 9th decile.

If an increase in the minimum wage adds, say, $500 a year to the income of a family in the bottom decile, that will produce a much larger percentage increase in household income than it will if it adds $500 to the income of a family in the top decile. Thus, spreading a similar increment of income across all deciles will produce some income equalization. But it is obviously an inefficient way to do it. If we take the bottom two deciles of the household income distribution as a rough proxy for the poor, then about four-fifths of the beneficiaries of the minimum wage increase fall in the nonpoor category.

If the reader is surprised that such a large percentage of minimum and below minimum wage workers are from nonpoor households, he or she might look back at the part-time and youth figures in Table 13.1. These figures are consistent with and help to explain the Johnson and Browning estimates of the distribution of minimum wage earners across household income deciles. That distribution makes it clear that the full-time minimum wage earner who is the sole support of a household is a small minority of all minimum wage earners. If full-time minimum wage earners who are the sole support of their households were in the majority, then most minimum wage earners would necessarily be found in the bottom two household income deciles.

Fine-Tuning the Minimum Wage?

Given the large percentage of part-time and youth workers at or under the minimum wage, could it be tuned to deliver benefits to older workers who are more likely to be heads of households and yet not discourage entry into the labor force? One suggestion has been to set the minimum wage lower for workers under a certain age. For example, we might set the minimum for workers under 21 at $3.00 per hour and the minimum for workers over 21 at $4.75. An arrangement like this was proposed by the French government in the spring of 1994, but students rioted and the government backed off.[12] Suppose U.S. students were less vociferous or the U.S. government less easily intimidated. How would it work?

The idea makes sense in that it addresses two different groups for which we have two different goals. The question is whether its goals would be defeated by an obvious side effect. If the youth wage were set substantially lower than the adult wage would adults start losing jobs to youths? If most minimum wage jobs are relatively low skilled and can be learned quickly, then years of experience do not make an employee much more valuable. In that case, to use the above numbers we would probably see adults who could not be paid less than $4.75 per hour losing their jobs to teenagers whose minimum is $3.00 per hour. We might see jobs that are now full-time jobs being split into two or three part-time jobs specifically to switch them from adult to youth jobs. In that case, the split wage would be counterproductive in terms of raising the incomes of working poor households. As noted, if not belabored, in previous sections of this book all proposed market interventions should be examined for side effects that may nullify the intent of the intervention.

Who Pays the Bill?

If an economist is someone whose mantra is "there's no such thing as a free lunch," it is appropriate to ask who pays the bill. Assume that mainstream analysis of the effects of an increase in the minimum wage is correct—total wages paid to low-wage workers increase and the amount of labor that they supply decreases. Then the supply curves of firms that employ low-wage labor or that are themselves supplied by firms that do must shift to the left. This effect will show up in higher prices and, presumably, lower profits. Perhaps some costs will also be shifted to higher-wage workers in the form either of reduced wages or job losses as the firm's higher costs reduce the number of units that it can sell. More generally, one might say that it is spread throughout the economy. In their econometric analysis Johnson and Browning simply treat it as causing a price increase that is borne by consumers in proportion to how much they spend.[13]

How Much Would an Increase in the Minimum Wage Matter?

If the elasticity figures cited earlier are correct, the disemployment effects of an increase in the minimum wage would not be huge and total wages paid to low-income workers would rise somewhat. On the other hand, the figures on the distribution of minimum and subminimum wage earners across household income deciles make it clear that the number of households lifted out of poverty by an increase in the minimum wage will also be small. Thus, it also appears unlikely that many households will experience enough increase to lift them off the public assistance roles. Most of the wage gains, though they will accrue to low-income workers, will accrue to households that are not low income.

It seems reasonable that to the extent that a higher minimum wage reduced employment it would lower GNP. But if, say, 100,000 relatively low-productivity jobs were lost from a labor force in the 120 million range, the percentage decline in GNP would be miniscule. The inflationary effects of modest wage increases would probably also not be very large. If, let us say, wages for several million workers, a majority of them part-time, rise by 50 cents per hour, that increase would be a very tiny fraction of a GNP currently in the $6 trillion range. The effect of an increase in the minimum wage on manufacturing employment and on the U.S. balance of trade will also be small because only about one job in thirty in manufacturing is a minimum wage job.

In the writer's view the most serious negative effect would be that an increase in the minimum wage would eliminate some entry-level jobs and that would prevent some young people from ever getting a foothold in the labor market. That would be a potentially serious long-term effect for a relatively small number of people. This writer is not aware of any study that has made an attempt to quantify this effect, nor is the writer convinced that we have enough good labor market theory to be able to make a successful attempt at such quantification.

On balance, it appears to the writer that an increase in the minimum wage will have neither the major poverty-reducing nor the major job-destroying effects that proponents and opponents have claimed.

NOTES

1. Since 1950 the rate had been changed 19 times with the rate increasing from $0.75 to the 1991 figure of $4.25. The longest interval between changes was 1981 to 1990. Average wages in the United States have increased faster than the minimum wage. Thus, the minimum wage was 54 percent of the average wage in 1950 but 37 percent of the average wage by 1992. See table 675 in the *Statistical Abstract of the United States*, 113th ed. (1993).

2. See Steven Greenhouse, "Labor Official Retreats on Higher Minimum Wage," *New York Times*, October 30, 1993, p. L9.

3. An extensive review of the literature up through the early 1980s can be found in Charles Brown, Curtis Gilroy, and Andrew Kohen, "The Effect of the Minimum Wage on Employment and Unemployment," *Journal of Economic Literature* (June 1982), pp. 487–528.

4. It can be argued that when the minimum wage is raised it creates a wage compression effect that causes pressure for wage increases in the region above but reasonably close to the new minimum.

5. One thing that suggests this, though it certainly does not prove it, is that the characteristics of those listed as "below $4.25" are not radically different from the characteristics of those listed as "at $4.25."

6. The poverty line is calculated by the Bureau of Labor Statistics each year and varies with household size. It was based upon a multiple of the amount required for an adequate diet for a household of a given size and has subsequently been adjusted each year for inflation. It is thus an absolute rather than a relative measure of poverty. A brief description of the measure is offered in the Income, Expenditures and Wealth chapter of the *Statistical Abstract of the United States*. For a statement of the origins of the measure see Mollie Orshansky, "Counting the Poor: Another Look at the Poverty Profile," *Social Security Bulletin* (January 1965).

7. I have used the term "household" here. The term "family" is also widely used. Household means the one or more people occupying a single dwelling unit.

The term family, as used by the Bureau of the Census, implies a household of more than one person with its members related by blood, marriage, or adoption. All families are households but not all households are families. Family income figures as recorded by the Bureau of the Census tend to be somewhat higher than the larger category of household incomes.

8. It can be argued that in some cases union activity can also have a job expanding role through work rules or no layoff provisions. In this case the effects of unionization and of minimum wage legislation are not entirely analogous.

9. Brown, Gilroy, and Kohen, "The Effect of the Minimum Wage on Employment and Unemployment."

10. David Card, "Do Minimum Wages Reduce Employment: A Case Study of California," and "Using Regional Variation in Wages to Measure the Effects of the Federal Minimum Wage." Both articles appear in *Industrial and Labor Relations Review* (October 1992).

11. For an elegant and widely cited study, see William R. Johnson and Edgar K. Browning, "The Distributional and Efficiency Effects of Increasing the Minimum Wage: A Simulation," *American Economic Review* (March 1983), pp. 204–11.

12. Alan Riding, "Jubilant French Students Celebrate Wage Victory," *New York Times,* April 1, 1994, p. A3(N).

13. Johnson and Browning, "The Distributional and Efficiency Effects of Increasing the Minimum Wage: A Simulation."

CHAPTER 14

The Economics of Interplace Competition

The discussion of various forms of competition presented in the first half of this book is about the competition between firms. The firms' decisions are about what to produce, how to produce, how much to produce, and (except for the firm in perfect competition) how to price the output. In general, we believe that competition between firms promotes efficiency. We assume that the closer we come to the model of perfect competition (absence of monopoly, internalization of externalities, good information, easy mobility of resources, and the like) the more efficiently the economy will operate.

There also exists in the United States an intense competition over the very different matter of *where* to produce. In this competition, states and municipalities compete for firms with as much intensity as firms compete for customers. One obvious question to consider about interplace as opposed to interfirm competition is whether it, too, performs a useful economic function.

Virtually every candidate for governor and the majority of candidates for mayor, town supervisor, and county executive make economic development a part—often a very central part—of their campaigns. There are well over 15,000 local and state economic development agencies in the United States with an average staff size of perhaps five or six.[1] In the competion between places there are two primary weapons—information and subsidies.

The sales side of the competition occurs because the market for industrial and commercial buildings and sites is, in one key respect, very far from perfect. In the perfect market there is perfect information. Here there is no room for the salesperson, because in the face of perfect knowledge he or she can neither inform nor deceive. But for the firm contemplating a multiplicity of possible locations the costs of information gathering may be very high. Consider the case of a firm that sells to a national market. It has decided to open a branch plant in the northeastern United States—somewhere north of the Mason-Dixon line and east of the Mississippi River. There are hundreds of different cities or counties in which it might locate. And there are thousands of sites on which it might build or thousands of existing industrial buildings that it might buy or rent. For each location there are a myriad of factors to consider including the cost, quality, and availability of labor, environmental rules, land use controls and costs, utility costs, construction costs, and so on. To assemble all the data needed to make the optimal decision is no small task. Economic development agencies are thus, to a very considerable degree, sales organizations.

Economic development organizations and the places that they represent are also big users of subsidies to entice firms. The largest subsidy packages can run into the $100 million-plus range. When Sears, Roebuck & Co. decided that it was unhappy with the Chicago location of its distribution center, economic development agencies from many parts of the United States began plying it with offers. Ultimately, the State of Illinois subsidized Sears' move from Chicago to the Chicago suburb of Hoffman Estates at a cost of about $178 million, about $30,000 for each of the 6,000 jobs at stake. There was no net job gain to the state, but rather a large expenditure to avert a job loss. In the late 1980s, New York City provided Chase Manhattan Bank with a subsidy package of $235 million to remain and expand in Manhattan.[2] The largest offer of which the writer is aware was a $427 million package that the State of Colorado offered to United Airlines for a billion dollar aircraft repair facility to be located at Denver.[3] Despite the offer, United Airlines located in Indianapolis, which put up a $235 million package. In the spring of 1994 the state of Virginia, under newly elected Governor Allen, whose campaign involved major promises about job creation, put together a $163 million package in an unsuccessful campaign to induce the Disney corporation to develop an American history theme park west of Washington, DC, in Virginia's Prince William County.[4] The dollars-per-job figure quoted above for Sears is not unusual. In the 1980s, B. Milward and H. H. Newman, surveying subsidy packages for automotive plants, primarily U.S. branches of Japanese firms, found a per-job range from $11,000 for Nissan in Smyrna, Tennessee to $50,588 for Fuji-Isuzu in Lafayette, Indiana.[5] Much higher figures appear from time to time. In the 1990s a subsidy package for Mercedes Benz in Vance, Alabama totaled $253 million for 1,500 jobs, or about $167,000 per job.

How much is spent on interplace economic competition by the various levels of government is not known with any degree of precision. Direct grants and expenditures, low-interest loans, and tax abatements occur in staggering profusion. Then there are the costs of the 15,000-plus economic development agencies, subsequently referred to as transactions costs. A very conservative estimate by the author placed the total at over $10 billion a year.[6] The actual figure may be as high as $30 billion.[7] There is no central registry for such expenditures and the fact that they come from both the tax and tax expenditure side of the budget makes precise estimation difficult.[8]

MOTIVATIONS FOR INTERPLACE COMPETITION

The two major motivations for states and localities are labor market and tax considerations. Economic growth tightens the state or the local labor market. In our federal system, in which subnational governments have substantial autonomy and are not simply administrative arms of the national government, citizens expect subnational governments to do what they can about local labor markets. Whether or not voters think the mayor and city council have done well in the competition for jobs may determine whether or not they are reelected.

The tax motivation is also easily understood. Bringing in new economic activity provides new sources of property taxes, sales taxes, and other revenues. Of course, the new activity also brings new expenditure needs. If the local administration is fortunate, the revenue gains will exceed the new expenditure needs. For many municipalities the ideal development from a purely fiscal perspective would be employment growth that was unaccompanied by any population growth. As noted in Chapter 11, many suburban communities attempt to achieve this effect through their land use controls. For the local elected official squeezed between the need to provide public services and the public's resistance to further tax increases, economic growth to broaden the tax base is a way out. But what if the economic growth brings as much in new expenses as it does in new revenues? Here we note the principle of rational ignorance. Calculating the real fiscal impact of new development is a somewhat arcane matter and most citizens will not be intimately acquainted with the art of fiscal impact analysis.[9] Nor, if they are the rational beings that we postulate, will it be worth their while to take the time to learn that much about it. But the appearance of government playing the helpful role of easing the citizens' tax burden does offer a substantial political payoff.

There are other motivations behind intermunicipal economic competition as well. In general, economic growth is good for many local businessmen because it means more customers, more transactions, more commissions, and the like. It is clearly good for property owners because it increases the demand for sites and structures and thus puts upward pressure on prices and rents. Therefore, economic development programs have many allies within the business community. Organized labor is another major source of support because of the job creation.

While interplace competition is a game for state and local governments, the federal government is an indirect player through the mechanism of grants and tax expenditures. Federal tax expenditures for Industrial Revenue Bonds (IRBs), a widely used local economic development financing incentive, were estimated at about $1.68 billion in 1992 by the Office of Management and Budget (OMB).[10] Federal Community Development (CD) funds and grants from the Economic Development Administration (EDA), and the Appalachian Regional Commission (ARC) are also used by states and localities to offer economic development subsidies. In the past, funds from the Department of Housing and Urban Development (HUD) under the Urban Development Action Grant (UDAG) program were used to help municipalities compete with each other. Farmers Home Administration funds support local economic development efforts in rural areas. Model Cities and Urban Renewal funds were used to support local economic development efforts, and so on.

The primary federal motivation, as made clear both in legislation itself and also in the supporting regulations, was to attack structural unemployment and poverty.[11] Federal strategy was to encourage the flow of capital into distressed areas in the hope that the resulting increase in the demand for labor would directly reduce structural unemployment and, by tightening the local labor market, indirectly reduce poverty. In general, eligibility for federal aid to local economic development was determined by need. If the place did not show sufficiently high unemployment and poverty figures it was not eligible for aid. Among those places that were eligible, most federal programs awarded aid on a competitive basis.[12] As noted, the basic mechanism of federal aid to support local economic development efforts was to lower the cost of capital investment in the aided jurisdiction—in effect, tilting the playing field toward that place. For example, a typical EDA-supported project might be the municipally owned industrial park for whose development EDA would pay half the costs, thus enabling the municipality to place industrial sites on the market at below a private developer's cost. The UDAG program provided funds for cities to clear land and do site improvements, permitting the city to offer commercial sites at a fraction of cost.[13]

Clearly, local and federal goals differ in a key way. The federal goal is to channel investment toward needy places and, by indirection, to needy people. But the local goal is to bring in jobs and taxable economic activity regardless of whether the locality is poor or wealthy and regardless of whether or not it has a serious structural unemployment problem. Almost any municipality has some unemployed persons even if its unemployment figure is below average and all its personal income statistics are above average. Even if it had no unemployed people at all, most residents would be pleased if economic growth tightened up the labor market and put upward pressure on wages. Then, too, there is almost no municipality, no matter how prosperous, that cannot use a larger tax base. From the municipal or state view the effects of its economic development efforts upon other jurisdictions have no bearing. In the language of game theory, the question of whether interplace economic competition is, in total, a negative sum, zero sum, or positive sum game is not germane.[14]

The federal presence in local economic development can be traced back at least as far as the Urban Renewal program that began with the Housing Act of 1949. It increased in the Kennedy years with the creation of the Area Redevelopment Administration (ARA) in 1971 and probably peaked in the Carter period. It began to decline in the Reagan period for two reasons. First, large budget deficits put pressure on Congress to cut budgets wherever it could and local economic development was one area that could be cut. Second, the idea of using the public purse to rechannel the flow of capital was at ideological variance with the Reagan administration's commitment to the free market. Similar comments can be made about the Bush administration. While the Clinton administration is probably not opposed in principle to a federal presence in local economic development, its priorities are elsewhere, notably health care and welfare reform. Clinton's Secretary of Labor Robert Reich is a believer in "industrial policy," but his focus is on training and on aiding industrial sectors with growth potential. He does not appear to have a geographical focus.

At present, interplace economic competition is primarily a game played with local and state resources. During the 1980s the game, judging by the growth in the number of agencies and the size of the subsidy packages involved, intensified and at present shows no signs of diminishing. To the extent that efforts by one jurisdiction evoke compensating efforts by other jurisdictions, it has a built-in positive feedback property with no clearly visible upper limit.

Given that interplace economic competition involves large sums of money, is a major preoccupation of local and state government, and seems here to stay, we might ask the obvious question: Is it useful? That question can be broken into the two questions that occupy the rest of this chapter. Does it increase aggregate economic efficiency and does it produce an increase in equity?

CAN INTERPLACE COMPETITION INCREASE ECONOMIC EFFICIENCY?

From a national perspective, does intermunicipal economic competition serve a useful purpose? Or does it, at the expense of substantial transactions costs, simply shuffle economic activity from one municipality or state to another?

Intermunicipal competition could be said to increase economic efficiency if it accomplished any or all of the following.

1. Increased the efficiency with which the factors of production are utilized.
2. Caused some negative externalities associated with economic growth or change to be reduced or positive externalities to be increased. Note: This point could be considered a subset of item 1, but for purposes of easy discussion we enumerate it separately here.
3. Caused the total amount of resources utilized to be increased.

We will consider these three points in order.

Efficient Utilization of Resources

In the neoclassical view, resources are allocated efficiently if each factor of production is employed up to the point that its marginal revenue product and its cost are equal. This situation is Pareto optimal because there can be no reallocation that does not make some party worse off. Obviously, this perfect adjustment at the margin is only an ideal, for many reasons noted in the first part of the book. But it can be a useful measuring rod. We can look at policies or events and ask whether they tend to move economic activity closer to or further away from this ideal of equilibration at the margin.

In general, subsidization by places to effect the *where* of economic decision making will reduce the chances of efficient adjustment at the margin. The firm, after considering the costs of all of the factors of production, decides to build its plant in location A. But at the last minute it receives an offer of a below-cost industrial site and generous tax breaks from municipality B. It redoes its calculations and builds in community B instead. Clearly, as was its intent, community B distorts the market in such a way as to change the firm's behavior. A priori, this is an efficiency-reducing act. The true costs of operating from community B are higher than from community A. But the firm moves there because the costs that it must pay are lower. What is now rational behavior for the firm is irrational when viewed from a society-wide point of view. One can state the effect of the subsidy in simple marginal terms. If industrial sites in a given town are available at below cost because of subsidies then they will be overconsumed. At the margin, a dollar spent on industrial sites in the town will produce less than a dollar of marginal revenue product. The reason that the dollar will be spent is that the firm does not bear the full burden of the expenditure.

One can also state the problem in nonmarginal terms. Left to their own devices, firms will locate in whatever is the most profitable place. If the output of the firm will be the same in various locations then it will settle in the lowest-cost location. This is economically efficient. If the costs the firm faces are distorted by a variety of subsidies then it will not locate where its real production costs are lowest. The very point of the subsidy is to create an artificial least-cost location.

Subsidies and Externalities

In principle, subsidies might enhance economic efficiency if they reduced negative externalities or enhanced positive externalities.[15] Suppose that economic growth will visit some positive externalities on town A and some negative externalities on town B. Perhaps some economic growth in town A will expand the town's population and economic base so that various public services can be delivered with greater economy of scale. But in town B the congestion effects of further economic growth will increase the unit cost of delivering public services. In that case, overall economic efficiency might be enhanced if town A offered some subsidies for economic development and town B refrained from doing so, or, even used its tax and regulatory powers to discourage further economic growth. We thus have the notion that the differential subsidization of economic activity by places might be efficiency-enhancing through its effects on place-related externalities. While it makes sense in theory, is it a realistic expectation in practice?

For subsidies to be administered such that negative externalities were reduced and positive externalities enhanced would require a considerable degree of governmental finesse. A national government that could act with great wisdom and could ignore the importunings of state and local governments might, indeed, be able to do the sort of fine-tuning just described. A national pattern of business subsidies and taxes might allow the nation to internalize the externalities associated with economic growth. But this scenario postulates a government with great wisdom and the ability to hew to that wisdom regardless of political pressures. It also postulates a unitary government, not a federal system in which states and substate governments have substantial degrees of autonomy.

At the local and state level the political forces militating against the sort of all-encompassing rationality just described will be powerful. Citizens expect their governments to do something about the state of the local economy. But they will be rationally ignorant about the nuances and trade-offs of the process. The local official who wants to be reelected must aggressively court economic growth and, equally important, be seen to be doing so. To lose a firm to another jurisdiction without having made a strong effort to retain it opens the elected official up to a variety of charges, beginning with "Why didn't you . . ." that are not easily answered. When Governor Thompson of Illinois spent $178 million to encourage Sears to remain in the state he had little political choice, regardless of what he thought about the economic wisdom of the offer. Had he refused to offer and Sears then moved out of state it would have been a political disaster for him. Had he made a smaller offer, say $100 million, that had not been sufficient, he also would have suffered politically. If he had to err, it would be better to err on the side of too much than too little.

Difficulty in accurately calibrating the size of the subsidy also makes it difficult to obtain optimum results with subsidization. From the donor's point of view an optimal subsidy must be the smallest possible sum necessary to induce the desired action. But this condition is very difficult to achieve. The firm seeking subsidies or being courted by various jurisdictions knows its own finances intimately, its own decision criteria, and the details of every offer that it has received. But the municipality(s) offering the subsidies must guess at all of these matters. In the event that the firm does disclose something about an offer by another municipality, the officials of the other municipality have no way to know whether the disclosure is complete or accurate. In short, in the bargaining situation the firm has an enormous advantage. It holds its cards close to its chest. The municipality, as a public body, must play with its cards face up on the table. If the municipality subsidizes frequently it will almost inevitably oversubsidize in some cases. Sometimes it will provide a pure windfall by subsidizing an action that would have occurred in the absence of any subsidy.

Increasing Total Resource Use

It has been argued that subsidizing economic activity in lagging areas might, by bringing structurally unemployed people into the labor force, expand the total supply of labor. Several decades ago John Moes made an ingenious argument to the effect that subsidizing economic growth in lagging regions could expand total employment by serving as a substitute for downward flexibility in wages. To cast Moes's argument in contemporary terms, assume that town X has a serious structural unemployment problem. Acme Widget Corp. considers locating there but decides that the marginal revenue product of the workers it would employ in the plant it could build there will be $4.00 per hour. It knows there are people there who would be willing to work for $4.00 or less. But it cannot hire them at $4.00 or less because the legal minimum wage is $4.25. Thus, it does not build a plant there. People who might have been employed at $4.00 are now unemployed at $0.00. If the town could subsidize Acme Widget to the extent of at least $0.25 per worker hour, some people whose marginal revenue product is now $0.00 could be put to work at a marginal revenue product of $4.00 and the total output of the economy would be enhanced.[16]

The Moes view that economic development assistance may compensate for lack of downward flexibility in wages is of arguable theoretical merit. Consider the case of the town that subsidizes Acme Widget. Its subsidy has put some otherwise unemployable people to work. But their output fills some of the demand for widgets. In addition, the taxes necessary to provide the subsidy take some money away from consumers and thus reduce aggregate demand. Those two effects will tend to reduce employment elsewhere. Therefore, the total effect upon employment nationally is not so clear and the Moes argument takes us into a fairly murky area of macroeconomic theory. But his argument leaves us believing it theoretically possible that a carefully administered subsidy policy might have a positive macroeconomic effect.

There is now, however, a very strong practical argument against his view. At the time that Moes made his argument economic development programs were largely a southern phenomenon. By and large they were used by lagging, low-wage, labor surplus areas in an attempt to catch up with the more prosperous Northeast and North Central portions of the United States. That lent a certain persuasiveness to his argument. Today the economic development game is played by all states and by virtually all large and most small municipalities. It is not a matter of poor places playing the game while wealthy places are passive. A poor town in Mississippi or Arkansas may use subsidies to lure a firm away from a prosperous town in Connecticut. But the reverse may also occur.

OTHER CONSIDERATIONS REGARDING EFFICIENCY

Can one not regard all of the subsidies offered to firms by the myriad of economic development agencies as just a general subsidy to capital formation? Obviously, one can. If one believes that the United States taxes capital investment too heavily relative to other activities, then the net effect of all the subsidies is to help redress this imbalance. In that sense, the net effect of the competition may be to enhance macroeconomic performance. But one must admit that if some stimulus to capital formation is advisable, delivering it through the mechanism of an intermunicipal bidding contest is hardly efficient. Simple across-the-board adjustments in, say, the capital gains tax or the corporate income tax would operate with much greater marginal efficiency than the present process that delivers deep subsidies to some firms and no subsidies to other firms on a basis that has very little if anything to do with the performance of the firm. They would also operate with much smaller transactions costs.

DOES INTERMUNICIPAL COMPETITION PROMOTE EQUITY?

Equity is an overused word in the social science and policy literature, perhaps because of its imprecision. Let us say here that what we mean by it is simply greater equality of personal and household income. To conclude that intermunicipal competition taken as a whole increases income equality, one would have to accept *both* of the following propositions: (1) the net effect of the competition is to cause more capital to be invested in poorer places than would otherwise be the case, and (2) when capital is invested in poorer places it produces some income-equalizing effect when viewed from a national perspective.

How the competition shifts the geographical distribution of capital investment is simply not known. Finding out would require disentangling the net effects of all of the economic development activity from all of the larger forces that affect where capital is invested. This is no easy task. The writer suspects that one effect of the competition is to accelerate the movement of capital out of large cities simply because large cities make good targets. It makes sense for the economic development agency of a nonmetropolitan city or county, say, to make a trip to New York or Chicago to try to talk a few firms into moving because there are many firms in such a small area. It is less likely that economic developers from New York or Chicago would roam the hinterlands calling upon firms in scattered locations, simply because the logistics would be so much more difficult. And, judging from the writer's contacts with economic development personnel, the above is exactly what happens. But that is no more than a priori reasoning supported by a very limited amount of anecdotal evidence. We simply do not know the answer to the question that point 1 raises.

It seems reasonable to believe that point 2 is correct. But it is far from certain. The tightening of the labor market should elevate wages and reduce unemployment, and some of the resulting gains should appear low down in the income distribution. But how much of the total gain appears low down in the income distribution is uncertain.[17] Gains also accrue to proprietors, property owners, stockholders, executives, higher-paid workers, and so on. In many cases new jobs will be taken not by the unemployed heads of poor households but by people who become the second wage earners in nonpoor or even very prosperous households. (Note the similarity to arguments made in the chapter on the minimum wage.) A complete accounting would also have to take into consideration the effects upon the poor in the place from which the firm comes. If a firm moves from a wealthy municipality to a poor municipality that may still result in some low-income people in the wealthy municipality losing their jobs. One should not confuse the wealth or poverty of places with that of people. The gains at the bottom of the income distribution are also diluted by migration. When capital investment creates new jobs it tends to promote in-migration. The urban and regional economist Wilbur Thompson observed some years ago:

Relocating manufacturers contend that they do not have to depend on workers already in town. They simply announce in, say, the Baltimore newspapers that they are headed for, say, Lynchburg, and the native sons return with Northern-acquired skills. . . . In fact, the hard corollary to this easy mobility is that local growth does not really lick the unemployment problem—all it does, in the long run, is enlarge the local labor force. Since it is the returning skilled workers who win away most of the new jobs, the town just gets bigger, still struggling with its chronic unemployment problem—its "unemployables."[18]

Thus, perhaps ironically, the more perfect the labor market is, that is, the more mobile labor is, the more difficult it is for a local government to do anything about wages and unemployment rates within its borders. To the extent that mobility defeats the labor market intentions of local economic development programs, the income redistributing effects of such programs are weakened. The above is not to say that local economic growth does not deliver some gains low down on the income scale, but only to say that it is probably a very inefficient way of doing so.

If we combine the uncertainty regarding point 1 with the relative weakness of the redistributional effect in point 2 it would appear that the national level equity effects of the interplace competition are, at best, not very large.

WHY DOES THE COMPETITION PERSIST?

If we are correct so far, intermunicipal economic competition probably does not contribute to aggregate economy efficiency and, more likely, detracts from it. It may produce some equity gains but this is not certain. In fact, if it turns out that more prosperous places more often defeat less prosperous places in the competition, it may even produce some equity losses. Then, too, it is doubtful that most state and municipal officials are really happy about playing the game—though they are happy when they win. No doubt Governor Thompson of Illinois could have found other uses for the $178 million that the state spent to keep Sears from leaving. The same could be said for New York's then Mayor Koch and the $235 million in tax breaks and other assistance offered to Chase Manhattan. But neither had much choice. To a substantial degree the interplace competition for firms tends to reverse the normal flow of business taxes. Rather than taxing firms, local and state governments find themselves drawing on other revenues to subsidize them. No sensible mayor or governor will be pleased about that.

The obvious explanation for the competition's persistence and growth is institutional. There are, according to the Bureau of the Census, about 80,000 "minor civil divisions" within the United States. There is simply no way that all of these jurisdictions can enter into an enforceable agreement to stop the practice any more than the nations of the world have so far been able to enter into effective, enforceable disarmament agreements.

The situation resembles the "prisoner's dilemma," an element of game theory discussed in many economics textbooks.[19] Without describing the prisoner's dilemma in detail, its central idea is the situation in which what is rational behavior for the individuals involved produces an irrational or suboptimal result. The suboptimal result is achieved because the mechanism by which behavior could be coordinated to produce the collectively optimal result does not exist. In the case of the prisoners, they are interrogated in isolation from each other and each betrays the other for fear of what the other may do. Cartels with a dozen or two members, or sometimes even fewer, founder over the willingness of their members to make side agreements that violate their own pledges to their fellow cartel members. Witness OPEC's past troubles in keeping its own members in line.

Alternatively, one might explain the collective suboptimality in terms of externalities. Each state or locality that enters the competition imposes costs upon other states and localities. If economic development officials in Atlanta made generous offers to Sears to relocate its distribution center to Atlanta, they did so in a calculus limited to what was good for Atlanta. The job losses that they would have imposed on Illinois had they been successful were not part of that calculus. Then, too, the fact that their offer forced Illinois to raise its offer was not part of their calculus. Their unsuccessful offer cost them nothing beyond the transactions costs of making it, but may have cost Illinois many millions.

NOTES

1. John M. Levy, *Economic Development Programs for Cities, Counties and Towns,* 2d ed. (New York: Praeger, 1990), p. 1.
2. R. Guskind, "The Giveaway Game Continues," *Planning* (February 1990), pp. 4–8.
3. J. Castro, "Come on Down, Fast," *Time,* May 27, 1991, pp. 38–42.
4. Lon Wagner, "Incentives Are the Ground Rules That Run This Game," *The Roanoke Times,* July 10, 1994, p. 1.
5. B. Milward and H. H. Newman, "State Incentive Packages and the Industrial Location Decision." *Economic Development Quarterly* (August 1989), pp. 203–22.
6. Levy, *Economic Development for Cities, Counties and Towns.*
7. Guskind, "The Giveaway Game Continues."
8. There is also a cost assignment problem. The roads that were built as part of a subsidy package to a particular firm will also carry traffic that has no connection with that firm. The sewer line extension done on behalf of a particular industrial or commercial development will also provide a connection for other users, and so on.
9. For an introductory presentation of fiscal impact analysis, see Robert W. Burchell, David Listokin, and William R. Dolphin, *The New Practitioner's Guide to Fiscal Impact Analysis* (New Brunswick, NJ: Center for Urban Public Policy Research, Rutgers University, 1985).
10. *Statistical Abstract of the United States,* 112th ed. (1992), table 497. In the

preceding several years the figures were higher because the marginal tax brackets on personal income were higher. For example, the 1989 figure was $2.6 billion.

11. Structural unemployment refers to longtime unemployment that persists through the business cycle, as distinguished from cyclical unemployment. It can be said to stem from either a geographical mismatch or a skills/demand mismatch.

12. The only major exception to this was the Community Development (CD) program that provided assistance on a formula basis.

13. As it happens, many cities thought that hotels and convention centers would be good generators of business activity in general and a large portion of all UDAG funding was used to prepare sites for these. Numerous Marriotts and other chain hotels have been built on UDAG sites. The fact that so much federal money was used to subsidize developments by successful corporations was one fact that ultimately brought about the termination of the program during the Bush administration.

14. In a zero sum game, winnings equal losses. An example would be an informal poker game. Betting at the race track is a negative sum game because the track takes a cut before it distributes the winnings. Playing the stock market when the market is rising is a positive sum game in that gains exceed losses.

15. This possibility is discussed in Dick Netzer, "An Evaluation of Interjurisdictional Competition Through Economic Development Incentives," in *Competition among States and Local Governments,* Daphne A. Kenyon and John Kincaid, eds. (Washington, DC: The Urban Institute, 1991).

16. John E. Moes, "The Subsidization of Industry by Local Communities in the South," *Southern Economic Journal* 28, no. 2 (October 1961), pp. 187–93. See also commentary on the Moes article in the October 1962 issue.

17. For studies of the distribution of the gains from local economic growth, see Timothy J. Bartik, *Who Benefits from State and Local Economic Development Policies?* (Kalamazoo, MI: W.E. Upjohn Institute for Employment Research, 1991). Bartik's book does not deal with the effects of one state or locality's economic development efforts upon other states and localities.

18. Wilbur Thompson, "Economic Processes and Employment Problems in Declining Metropolitan Areas," in George Sternlieb and James W. Hughes, eds., *Post Industrial America: Metropolitan Decline and Inter-Regional Job Shifts* (New Brunswick, NJ: Center for Urban Public Policy Research, Rutgers University, 1975).

19. See, for example, Miltiades Chacholiades, *Microeconomics* (New York: Macmillan Publishing Co., 1986), pp. 342–44.

CHAPTER 15

The Economics of Health Risk Analysis

Bradley K. Townsend

This chapter focuses on how welfare economics can be systematically used to analyze and develop environmental regulations to improve public health and safety. The first section discusses the fundamentals of how cost-benefit analysis can be used in conjunction with risk analysis to determine whether society's scarce resources are used efficiently to reduce risk. The second section explores the adverse consequences of not using such analysis with special reference to present federal regulations and policies.

THE FUNDAMENTALS OF REGULATING RISK

At work or play we are surrounded by both natural and man-made hazards posing various levels of risk. Toxic chemicals, exposure to ultraviolet radiation, or an automobile trip, present risks. Some risks are involuntary but others are not. Should I travel to work by car or bicycle? Bicycling is good for my heart and lungs and causes no pollution, but increases the likelihood of a fatal accident. A car would be safer, but taking a bus is safest. When purchasing a new car, do I choose airbags, which increase the car's price, but reduce the risk of fatality should an accident occur? As individuals we cannot avoid balancing reduction in risk against the cost of reducing risk.

Just as scarcity and risk–dollar trade-offs force individuals to decide which risks to bear, government policy makers are similarly constrained. Only limited resources can be devoted to any risk-reducing policy. Hypothetically, Congress could pass legislation to prevent all 94,500 accidental deaths that occur in the United States every year. The costs would average $55 million per life saved, and consume the entire U.S. Gross National

Product. Even then, society would be left with 9 million disabling injuries.[1] In short, life involves many risks that cannot be eliminated, or whose elimination would be too costly.

Risk-reducing policies quickly reach the point of diminishing marginal returns. Ultimately, the policy exacts huge expense in order to save precious few lives. Ninety-eight percent of a toxic air contaminant may be removed from industrial emissions at a low cost and a high payoff in risk reduction. Removing the next percent may be very costly with little risk reduction, and removing the last percent may be infeasible, requiring the plant to cease production. Policy makers confront the question: At what point do the gains from pollution control no longer outweigh further expenditures? Without the adequate analytical techniques, policy makers cannot make rational decisions.

Unfortunately, the realities of risk–dollar trade-offs are easily ignored and are often not explicitly considered in policy making. Thus, regulations are often ineffective, costly, and clearly suboptimal.

WEALTH AND HEALTH

In the worst cases, regulations may actually increase the very risks that they are intended to reduce. For example, heavy regulatory expenditures reduce the general standard of living. Thus, less money is available for spending on safer consumer goods such as automobiles with airbags, better medical care, or more nutritious food. This phenomenon, termed the "income effect," is not insignificant and is now cited in a growing body of literature. A leading authority, the late Aaron Wildavsky of the University of California at Berkeley, expressed it as "wealthier is healthier." In the same light, Dr. Peter Huber of the Manhattan Institute has observed that

[F]or a forty-five-year-old man working in a typical manufacturing job, a fifteen percent increase in income has about the same risk-reducing value as eliminating *all* hazards—every one of them—from his work place.[2]

High-cost regulations may also divert resources from other abatement activities that more efficiently reduce risk per dollar of expenditure. In addition to the effects of reduced income and opportunity cost, unintended or "indirect" health risks may arise during the construction or operation of equipment required by a regulation (such as hazardous waste incinerators, which may release otherwise confined pollutants over a wide area).

SOME POLITICAL REALITIES OF ENVIRONMENTAL REGULATION

If environmental legislation and policy were made by risk analysts steeped in microeconomic theory and benefit-cost analysis, environmental risk and the costs of risk reduction would be balanced at the margin. To the extent that our technical knowledge would permit, the last dollar spent on risk reduction would reduce risk by one dollar's worth. Alas, not all politicians and administrators are as conversant with the wisdom of Pareto optimality as the microeconomist might wish.

Congress has traditionally been hesitant to draft laws that require agencies to balance health outcomes and expenditures. Often Congress gives only vague, generalized guidelines that may be interpreted as being incompatible with economic analysis. In some cases such balancing is expressly prohibited. Laws may also attempt to achieve a zero risk standard. Although well-intentioned, these laws do not recognize the limits that scarcity places on government's ability to reduce risk.[3] Despite unrealistic congressional mandates or court interpretations, a certain level of minimal (or de minimus) risk must be tolerated to reap the benefits (including health-improving benefits) of a strong, growing economy.

Consider the situation with airborne particulates. A growing body of scientific evidence suggests that airborne particulates at concentrations found in many U.S urban areas produce a wide range of adverse health effects, including early mortality.[4] The evidence also suggests that inhalation of particulates at even very low concentrations may have detrimental health effects for at least some sensitive population groups. If this is correct, a policy problem exists.

The Clean Air Act of 1970 stipulates that pollutant emissions should be set at a level that provides "an adequate margin of safety" to protect human health. Arguably, the only level of emissions truly adequate to meet this mandate of safety would be zero. But a zero emission standard is a technical impossibility for many industries, such as electrical power generation or iron production. Perhaps a more realistic policy would use both risk and cost evaluation in order to design policies that achieve an efficient balance between risk and cost. The first step toward regulatory efficiency begins with toxicology, statistics, and data analysis to estimate the level of risk—a process known as risk analysis.

RISK ANALYSIS

Risk analysis performed thoroughly can make a major contribution to efficient regulatory policy by distinguishing the truly dangerous from the essentially benign.[5] Such analyses identify the risks from hazardous substances and from other risks, such as traffic accidents, in order to quantify the magnitude and uncertainty of those risks.

Not all risks and costs can be estimated with precision. The number of U.S. traffic fatalities that occurred in a specific year is a concrete estimate. Less concrete are estimates for environmental risks, such as cancer risk from secondary tobacco smoke or occupational exposure to benzene. Epidemiological data from exposed human populations is often poor or may be unavailable, requiring the use of tests on sensitive laboratory animals (usually rats or mice) subjected to high exposures over their short life spans. Though not flawless or without potential bias, these data still yield general estimates sufficient to quantify the relative risk when placed against other risks. Once the risks have been quantified risk management is used to decide upon which risks to focus.

As discussed in Chapter 9, cost-benefit analysis is relatively uncomplicated when a market exists for the costs and benefits to be quantified. Information on prices and quantities consumed defines a demand curve to determine the willingness to pay or accept compensation for the respective benefits and costs. Benefits to human health are more difficult to quantify because they are not traded on the open market. Asking an individual how much his or her life is worth yields little guidance, since very few people would directly trade their lives for any amount of money. Economists use two basic approaches to place a monetary value on a life saved.[6] The first approach involves determining consumers' willingness to spend to avoid risks, such as the added safety benefits from purchasing a new, safer car.

The second approach involves estimating the "risk premium," or dollar value of accepting additional occupational risk compared to safer jobs, holding other variables constant. Worker decisions are used to infer the value that those individuals place on accepting risk in exchange for additional compensation. One dramatic example was in the aftermath of the Persian Gulf War. Daring fire fighters risked their lives to earn over $500,000 per year to cap Kuwaiti oil field wildfires.

It is true that factors other than risk-compensation trade-offs play in worker or consumer choices to accept jobs or purchase safer products. Consequently, serious pitfalls exist in attempting to arrive at accurate values for life savings. Aside from uncertainties in quantifying benefits, critics charge that cost-benefit analysis is immoral because converting lives saved to dollars attempts to quantify something of inestimable worth which "cheapens a [life's] value."[7] Nonetheless, the necessity for assigning values to human life cannot be avoided. Imperfect as the above techniques are, they appear to be the best available.

THE PUBLIC CHOICE PERSPECTIVE

From a Public Choice perspective, economic tools play an important role in risk regulation because these tools act as checks and balances to help offset public and private lobbying interests. Rent-seeking behavior by firms and citizens, vote-seeking behavior by politicians, and career-enhancing behavior by bureaucrats may skew policies to their own benefit, irrespective of the general welfare.

Government efforts to regulate efficiently will be complicated by inevitable conflicts among opposing interest groups. Industries tend to argue that a regulation is too strict. Environmentalists demand that the same regulation be made more strict. Risk regulation can shield firms from competition by smaller, upstart rivals. Thus, well-established firms often lobby for regulations with which smaller firms will have difficulty complying. For example, in connection with the 1977 Clean Air Act Amendments, old, well-established industrial states in the midwest lobbied hard against allowing younger rivals in western states to meet emission standards by simply switching from high sulfur to low sulfur coal (which was most economically efficient for western states), instead of installing expensive control equipment. Other companies press for environmental regulation that will create markets for their products.

The situation is complicated by "rational ignorance," for the majority of voters and politicians are not likely to have invested the effort to become entirely comfortable with terms like "nanograms" and "picocuries" or the finer points of multivariate analysis. The combination of technical ignorance and strong emotions is likely to produce policy debates and political contests characterized by more heat than light.

U.S. Supreme Court Justice Stephen Breyer discusses what he terms bureaucratic "tunnel vision" as a serious problem in risk regulation today. This occurs when well-intentioned and competent regulators with narrow agendas to protect the environment and human health pursue a single goal without regard to the economic consequences.[8] Another influence, perhaps unique to risk regulation, is how perceived crises tend to drive legislation in this area.

CRISES-OF-THE-DAY POLICY MAKING

William Reilly, the former administrator of the Environmental Protection Agency and a leading proponent of economic analysis in risk management, has observed that "policy driven by 'crises and alarms' often leads to inefficient outcomes." Reilly has been highly critical of laws to combat environmental problems, constructed without reference to other environmental problems or laws. As Reilly observes: "No law has ever directed that [the EPA] seek out the best opportunities to reduce environmental risks in toto; nor that we employ the most efficient, cost-effective means of addressing them."[9]

The use of cost-benefit analysis in risk management would stem from a simple premise: In regulating health and safety risks, government policies should maximize net benefits, promulgating only those regulations whose benefits to society outweigh their costs. Although this sounds like simple common sense, the history of health and safety regulation in the United States paints a different picture. Significant strides have been made in rem-

Figure 15.1

Risk Estimates from Asbestos Exposure in Schools Compared to Other Common Risks

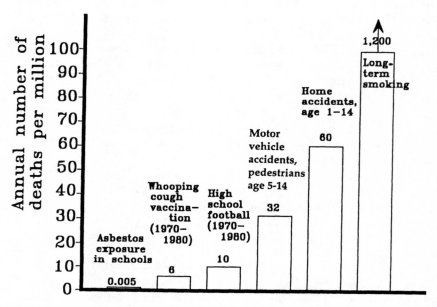

edying the worst pollution problems, but many recent health and safety regulations have been very costly with precious few benefits. Consider the case of asbestos exposure in schools.

Significant funds are being spent to remedy what experts consider minimal health risk in attempts to remove asbestos from public schools as required by the Federal Asbestos Emergency Response Act of 1986. While evidence shows that occupational exposure to certain types of asbestos can create significant risks, the type of asbestos commonly occurring in public schools, left in place and undisturbed, poses very little risk. The risks are very small relative to other common risks, many of which go unregulated, as shown in Figure 15.1.

The annual risk of death in schools from asbestos exposure is very low, less than one in ten million. However, removal costs for asbestos will be about $100 billion over a 40-year period with approximately ten lives saved per year for 40 years. This is equivalent to approximately $250 million per statistical life saved,[10] far more than the example discussed earlier in which $55 million dollars per life saved would be necessary to prevent all accidental deaths in the United States. Aside from being costly, asbestos removal increases air concentrations of asbestos dust, exposing removal workers to high concentrations. Experts believe that high concentrations produced from removal create risks greater than the original risks if the asbestos were simply left in place.

THE COSTS OF POLLUTION CONTROL REGULATION

The United States spent over $115 billion in 1990 for pollution control, more than any other nation. Even as a percentage of GNP, U.S. spending for pollution control is among the highest worldwide. By the year 2000, aggregate pollution control costs are projected to be over $185 billion per year, or 2.8 percent of the U.S economy.[11] While these amounts are not necessarily excessive, the essential question arises whether they are being spent as effectively as possible, and if some of these expenditures could be used in other ways that would provide more health protective benefit.

The cost of individual regulations issued during the 1980s was far higher per unit of safety than earlier regulations. Before 1985, only two regulations exceeded a cost of $100 million per death averted. After 1985 at least eight regulations have been enacted that exceed $100 million per life saved. Although relatively low in total costs, EPA's rule regulating wood preservatives costs at least $5 trillion dollars per life saved and is estimated to avert only one case of cancer every 2.9 million years.[12]

Such wide disparities do not imply large-scale environmental deregulation. Perhaps a more realistic approach would simply be to give proposed environmental policies the same level of scrutiny to which other legislative proposals are typically subjected.

Importantly, significant gains in life savings are available in areas of unfunded (or underfunded) public health interventions. For example, the cost to save a life during neonatal intensive care averages only $26,000, and breast cancer screening is typically very cost-effective when compared to environmental interventions. The Harvard School of Public Health has complied data showing that medical interventions on average yield a median cost per life year saved, in 1991 dollars, of approximately $15,000.[13] In comparison, consumer product safety regulation averaged $42,000 per life year saved, and occupational exposure intervention costs $324,000 per life year saved. The median environmental regulation came to $579,000 per year per life saved. Clearly, at this time medical interventions are more cost-effective.

Even if one accepts that resources might be better allocated to medical interventions, it might be argued that because large corporate polluters are bearing the brunt of the environmental control costs, the level of controls should still be ratcheted up, even for very costly regulations. However, this would be a naive assumption. As Paul Portney, of Resources for the Future, a renowned environmental think-tank, observes:

There are no disembodied corporate entities into whose deep pockets we can reach for pollution control spending without at the same time imposing losses on ourselves or our fellow citizens. This is because corporations are merely legal creations, the financial returns to which all accrue to individuals in one capacity or another.

Thus if corporations spend more for pollution control, these costs may be passed on to others in the form of higher product prices.[14]

As noted earlier in this chapter, higher product prices (or lowered wages) would affect consumers' ability to purchase safer products, or spending on medical care. Thus, the optimal level of pollution control is that point which balances direct health benefits of reducing a particular risk against the generalized health disbenefits of lowered real incomes.

An example of this phenomenon was pointed out by the Office of Management and Budget (OMB) in 1990 in response to a 1990 Occupational Safety and Health Administration (OSHA) imposed standard for benzene that had estimated costs in the hundreds of millions of dollars for each premature death avoided. The OMB argued that OHSA had failed to examine the effect that the cost of compliance would have on overall economic activity and therefore on employment. OMB concluded that the cost of compliance with regulation would force employers to lower their workers' salaries or, worse, to cut their jobs, thereby causing adverse health effects that were on balance higher than the small health improvement resulting from the benzene regulation. In fact, OMB calculated the regulation would cause 22 deaths, 8 to 13 *more* than it would avert.

THE PROBLEM OF COMPETING RISKS

In short, reducing risk is not riskless. For example, nitrites may cause cancer but they preserve foods and reduce the incidence of botulism. As Wildavsky has noted, controlling one risk often means that another risk may unexpectedly arise.[15]

In 1989 the National Highway Traffic Safety Authority made Corporate Average Fuel Economy (CAFE) standards very stringent, despite evidence showing that such standards encouraged car manufacturers to market smaller, less crash-worthy cars that would cost hundreds of lives per year. According to the judge who heard the case, there was a failure to consider important trade-offs between lives and fuel economy.[16]

Consider current proposals to save energy by enhancing vehicle fuel efficiency. These proposals will result in lighter weight vehicles, which offer their occupants less crash protection. Thus, additional deaths or serious injuries among motorists will result. John Graham of the Harvard University School of Public Health estimates that current proposals to raise car fuel economy requirements to 40 miles per gallon from 27 miles per gallon will nullify all of the safety gains from airbag technology.[17]

ARE NONGOVERNMENTAL ALTERNATIVES A SOLUTION?

Given the less than optimal quality of public risk management policy, one might consider turning to the prospects for private solutions. The common law tort system and private insurance are two other ways to lower overall risk. However, both common law solutions and private insurance are limited in that they may compensate victims only after harm has arisen and are not calculated to lead to optimal levels of risk reduction based on data gathered before harm occurs.

Under common law, any citizen has a right to be compensated for damages to his property. If a neighboring chemical plant damages an adjacent property or health, the property owner has a right to take that plant to court, to hold the owners liable, and obtain compensation or other redress. In reality, however, property rights may be ill-defined. There may be many polluters and it may be difficult to establish the particular cause of the damage. Then, too, litigation is expensive and its outcome often uncertain. Thus, although effective in theory, a purely common law approach would be subject to major market failure. Government regulation is therefore unavoidable. Unfortunately, like market failure, government failure in risk regulation is common.

The 1992 Economic Report to the President succinctly noted the dilemma of government and of private means of dealing with risk: "Any proposal to regulate the market should be tempered by an understanding that regulation can be at least as imperfect as the market it is trying to improve." Understanding these imperfections, both in the public and private spheres, can lead to better decision making and a cleaner, healthier, and safer environment for all of us.

NOTES

1. Kip W. Viscusi, "Pricing Environmental Risks," Center for the Study of American Business, Publication no. 112, June 1992.

2. P. Huber, "Safety and the Second Best: The Hazards of Public Risk Management in the Courts," *Columbia Law Review 277*, 1985.

3. One of the best-known zero-risk rules is the Delaney Amendment, which prohibits any food additive shown to be carcinogenic. Although it has not been strictly enforced, this no-risk standard, if applied strictly, would prohibit even highly beneficial food preservatives because the preservative posed some minute risk of carcinogenicity. See Food Additives (Delaney) Amendment of 1958, 21 U.S.C. sec. 348 (c) (3) (A) (1982).

4. S. K. Friedlander and M. Lippman, "Revising the Particulate Ambient Air Quality Standard," *Environmental Science and Technology* 28, no. 3 (1994), pp. 148A–150B. See also J. Schwartz, "Total Suspended Particulate Matter and Daily Mortality in Cincinnati, Ohio," *Environmental Health Perspectives* 102, no. 2 (February 1994), pp. 186–89.

5. For a compilation of different perspectives on risk analysis, see Thomas A. Burke and Nga L. Tran et al., eds., *Regulating Risk* (Washington, DC: National Safety Council, Life Sciences Institute, 1993). Also see "Risk," *Daedalus: Journal of the American Academy of Arts and Sciences* 119, no. 4 (Fall 1990).

6. For methodological explanation of calculating cost per life saved, see Thomas H. Tietenberg, *Environmental and Natural Resource Economics* (New York: HarperCollins Publishers, 1992), pp. 80–85.

7. Stephen Kelman, "Cost-Benefit Analysis: An Ethical Critique," Washington, DC: The American Enterprise Institute for Public Policy Research, from *Regulation* 5, no. 1 (January/February 1981), pp. 33–40.

8. Stephen Breyer, *Breaking the Vicious Circle: Toward Effective Risk Regulation* (Cambridge, MA: Harvard University Press, 1993).

9. William Reilly, "Risky Business: Life, Death, Pollution, and the Global Environment," lecture delivered at Stanford University, January 12, 1994.

10. See B. T. Mossman et al., "Asbestos: Scientific Developments and Implications for Public Policy," *Science* (January 1990).

11. United States Environmental Protection Agency, *Environmental Investment: The Cost of A Clean Environment*, EPA-230-12-90-084.

12. *Economic Report of the President* (Washington, DC: United States Government Printing Office, 1992), p. 183.

13. Tammy Tengs and Joseph Pliskin et al., "A Comparison of the Cost-Effectiveness of Interventions to Prevent Premature Death," unpublished paper presented at the 11th annual meeting of the Society for Medical Decision Making, Center for Risk Analysis, Harvard School of Public Health, October 1993.

14. Paul Portney, "EPA and the Evolution of Federal Regulation," in Paul Portney, ed., *Public Policies for Environmental Protection*, p. 15.

15. Aaron Wildavsky, "No Risk Is the Highest Risk of All," in Theodore Glickman and M. Gough, eds., *Readings in Risk, Resources for the Future* (Baltimore: n.p., 1990), pp. 190–91.

16. *Competitive Enterprise Inst. v. NHTSA*, 956 F. 2d 321, 327 (D.C. Cir 1992). See also Robert W. Crandall and John D. Graham, "The Effect of Fuel Economy Standards on Automobile Safety," *Journal of Law and Economics* 32, no. 97 (1989).

17. John K. Graham, "Regulation: A Risky Business," *Wall Street Journal*, May 18, 1994, p. A10.

Bibliography

Aaron, Henry. *Who Pays the Property Tax*. Washington, DC: The Brookings Institution, 1975.

Alonso, William. "Urban Zero Population Growth." *Daedalus* (Fall 1973).

Asch, Peter. *Industrial Organization and Antitrust Policy*. New York: John Wiley & Sons, 1983.

Auletta, Ken. *The Streets Were Paved with Gold*. New York: Random House, 1979.

Baker, Samuel H., and Elliot, Catherine S., eds. *Readings in Public Sector Economics*. Lexington, MA: D.C. Heath and Co., 1990.

Barrett, Nancy Smith. *The Theory of Microeconomic Policy*. Lexington, MA: D.C. Heath & Co., 1974.

Bartik, Timothy J. *Who Benefits from State and Local Economic Development Policies?* Kalamazoo, MI: W.E. Upjohn Institute for Employment Research, 1991.

Baumol, William J., and Oates, Wallace E. *The Theory of Environmental Policy*. Englewood Cliffs, NJ: Prentice-Hall, 1975.

Bezdek, Roger H., and Jones, Jonathan D. "Federal Categorical Grants-in-Aid and State-Local Expenditures." *Public Finance* 43, no. 1 (1988).

Bork, Robert. *The Tempting of America*. New York: Macmillian, Inc., 1990.

Brennan, Geoffrey, and Buchanan, James. *The Reason of Rules*. Cambridge: Cambridge University Press, 1985.

Breyer, Stephen. *Breaking the Vicious Circle: Toward Effective Risk Regulation*. Cambridge, MA: Harvard University Press, 1993.

Brown, Charles, Gilroy, Curtis, and Kohen, Andrew. "The Effect of the Minimum Wage on Employment and Unemployment." *Journal of Economic Literature* (June 1982), pp. 487–528.

Browning, Edgar K., and Browning, Jacquelene M. *Microeconomic Theory and Applications*. Boston: Little, Brown & Co., 1983.

Buchanan, James M. *Constitutional Economics.* Oxford: Basil Blackwell, 1991.

Buck, Peter L., ed. *Modern Land Use Control.* The Practicing Law Institute, 1978.

Burchell, Robert W., Listokin, David, and Dolphin, William R. *The New Practitioner's Guide to Fiscal Impact Analysis.* Rutgers, NJ: Center for Urban Policy Research, 1985.

Burke, Thomas A., and Tran, Nga L., eds. *Regulating Risk.* Washington, DC: National Safety Council, Life Sciences Institute, 1993.

Burmaster, David E., and Harris, Robert H. "The Magnitude of Compounding Conservatisms in Superfund Risk Assessment." *Risk Analysis* (April 1993), pp. 135–40.

Card, David. "Do Minimum Wages Reduce Employment: A Case Study of California," and "Using Regional Variation in Wages to Measure the Effects of the Federal Minimum Wage." Both appear in *Industrial and Labor Relations Review* (October 1992).

Castro, J. "Come on Down, Fast." *Time,* May 27, 1991, pp. 38–42.

Chacholiades, Miltiades. *Microeconomics.* New York: Macmillan Publishing Co., 1986.

Chamberlin, Edward H. *The Theory of Monopolistic Competition.* Cambridge, MA: Harvard University Press, 1933.

Chinitz, Benjamin. "Growth Management: Good for the Town, Bad for the Nation?" *Journal of the American Planning Association* 51, no. 1 (Winter 1990), pp. 3–8.

Coase, Ronald H. "The Problem of Social Cost." *Journal of Law and Economics* (October 1960), pp. 1–44.

Corcoran, Edith. "Anatomy of a Deal: Microsoft's Settlement." *Washington Post,* July 18, 1994.

Crandall, Robert W., and Graham, John D. "The Effect of Fuel Economy Standards on Automobile Safety." *Journal of Law and Economics* 32, no. 97 (1989).

Davis, Devra Lee, and Mandula, Barbara. "Airborne Asbestos and Public Health." *Annual Review of Public Health,* 1985.

De Mandeville, Bernard. *The Fable of the Bees: or Private Vices, Publick Benefits,* with commentary by F. B. Kaye. London: Oxford University Press, 1957.

Dockery, D. W. et al. "An Association Between Air Pollution and Mortality in Six U.S. Cities." *New England Journal of Medicine* 329 (December 9, 1993).

Downs, Anthony. *An Economic Theory of Democracy.* New York: Harper, 1957.

———. *Residential Rent Controls: An Evaluation.* Washington, DC: The Urban Land Institute, 1988.

Dupuit, J. "On The Measurement of the Utility of Public Works," translated in *International Economic Papers,* no. 2 (1952), pp. 83–110.

Economic Report of the President. Washington, DC: U.S. Government Printing Office, 1992.

Environmental Quality: Annual Report of the Council on Environmental Quality. Washington, DC: U.S. Government Printing Office, 1971–1994.

Etzioni, Amitai. *The Moral Dimension: Toward a New Economics.* New York: The Free Press, Macmillan, 1988.

Field, Brian G. "Road Pricing in Practice." *Transportation Journal* (Fall 1992).

Fischel, William. *The Economics of Zoning Laws: A Property Rights Approach to Zoning.* Baltimore: The Johns Hopkins University Press, 1985.

Fischel, William. "Introduction: Maxims for Research on Land Use Controls." *Land Economics* 66, no. 3 (August 1990).

Fischel, William. "The Property Rights Approach to Zoning." *Land Economics* 54, no. 1 (February 1978), p. 64.

Fisher, Ronald C. *State and Local Public Finance.* Glenview, IL: Scott, Foresman, 1988.

Frankel, Glenn. "Thatcher's Replacement Completes Policy Reversal by Dumping Poll Tax." *Washington Post,* March 25, 1991.

Friedlander, S. K., and Lippman, M. "Revising the Particulate Ambient Air Quality Standard." *Environmental Science and Technology* 28, no. 3 (1994), pp. 148A–150B.

Friedman, Milton. *Capitalism and Freedom.* Chicago: University of Chicago Press, 1962.

Graham, John K. "Regulation: A Risky Business." *Wall Street Journal,* May 18, 1994, p. A10.

Gramlich, Edward M. *A Guide to Benefit-Cost Analysis.* 2d. ed. Englewood Cliffs, NJ: Prentice-Hall, 1990.

Greenhouse, Steven. "Labor Official Retreats on Higher Minimum Wage." *New York Times,* October 30, 1993.

Guskind, R. "The Giveaway Game Continues." *Planning* (February 1990), pp. 4–8.

Gwartney, James, and Wagner, Richard E. "The Public Choice Revolution." *The Intercollegiate Review* (Spring 1988), pp. 17–26.

Hagman, Donald G., and Misczynski, Dean J., eds. *Windfalls for Wipeouts: Land Value Capture and Compensation.* Chicago: American Society of Planning Officials, 1978.

Hahn, Robert W. and Hird, John A. "The Costs and Benefits of Regulation: Review and Synthesis." *Yale Journal on Regulation* (Winter 1991).

Heller, Walter W. et al. *Revenue Sharing and the City.* Baltimore: Johns Hopkins University Press, 1968.

Hewlitt, Sylvia Ann. *When the Bough Breaks: The Cost of Neglecting Our Children.* New York: Basic Books, 1991.

Hicks, John R. "The Foundations of Welfare Economics." *Economic Journal* 49 (December 1939), pp. 696–712.

————. *Value and Capital: An Inquiry into Some Fundamental Principles of Economics.* London: Oxford Press, Clarendon Press, 1939.

Hobbes, Thomas. *Leviathan: or the Matter, Forme and Power of a Commonwealth Ecclesiastical and Civil,* edited by Michael Oakeshott. Oxford: Basil Blacksford, 1946.

Hochschild, Jennifer L. *What's Fair? American Beliefs about Distributive Justice.* Cambridge, MA: Harvard University Press, 1981.

Hoerner, Andrew J. "The Infancy and Early Childhood of Pollution Taxes." *Tax Notes,* November 12, 1992, pp. 855–58.

Huber, P. "Safety and the Second Best: The Hazards of Public Risk Management in the Courts." *Columbia Law Review* 227 (1985).

Johnson, William R., and Browning, Edgar K. "The Distributional and Efficiency Effects of Increasing the Minimum Wage: A Simulation." *American Economic Review* (March 1983), pp. 204–11.

Kaldor, Nicholas. "Welfare Propositions in Economics and Interpersonal Comparisons of Utility." *Economic Journal* 49 (September 1939), pp. 549–52.

Kelman, Stephen. "Cost-Benefit Analysis: An Ethical Critique." Washington, DC: The American Enterprise Institute for Public Policy Research, from *Regulation 5*, no. 1 (January/February 1981), pp. 33–40.

———. " 'Public Choice' or Public Spirit," in Samuel H. Baker and Catherine S. Elliot, eds., *Readings in Public Sector Economics*. Lexington, MA: D.C. Heath & Co., 1990, pp. 74–86.

Keynes, John Maynard. *The General Theory of Employment, Interest and Money*. New York: Harcourt, Brace and World, 1964. First published in 1936.

Landsberg, Steven E. *Price Theory and Applications*. 2d ed. New York: The Dryden Press, 1992.

Lange, Oskar. *On the Economic Theory of Socialism*. Minneapolis: University of Minnesota Press, 1938.

Levy, Frank, and Michel, Richard C. *The Economic Future of American Families: Income and Wealth Trends*. Washington, DC: The Urban Institute, 1991.

Levy, John M. *Contemporary Urban Planning*. 3d ed. Englewood Cliffs, NJ: Prentice-Hall, 1994.

———. *Economic Development Programs for Cities, Countries and Towns*. 2d ed. New York: Praeger, 1991.

———. "The U.S. Experience with Local Economic Development." *Environment and Planning* C 10 (1992), pp. 51–60.

Lutter, Randall, and Morral, John F. III. "Health Health Analysis: A New Way to Evaluate Health and Safety Regulations." *Journal of Risk and Uncertainty* (January 1994), pp. 43–66.

Lux, Kenneth. *Adam Smith's Mistake: How a Moral Philosopher Invented Economics and Ended Morality*. Boston: Shambala, 1990.

Mandelker, Daniel R. *Land Use Law*. Charlottesville, VA: The Michie Co., 1982.

Marks, Denton. "On Resolving the Dilemma of Rent Control." *Urban Studies* 28, no. 3 (1991), pp. 415–31.

McCarthy, Patrick S., and Tay, Richard. "Pricing Road Congestion: Recent Evidence from Singapore." *Policy Studies Journal* (Summer 1993).

McKinley, James C., Jr. "Council Vote Lifts Control on Luxury Units in Future." *New York Times*, March 22, 1994, p. B3.

Milward, B., and Newman, H. H. "State Incentive Packages and the Industrial Location Decision." *Economic Development Quarterly* (August 1989).

Mishan, E. J. *Cost Benefit Analysis*. New York: Praeger, 1976.

Moes, John E. "The Subsidization of Industry by Local Communities in the South." *Southern Economic Journal* 28, no. 2 (October 1961), pp. 187–93.

Moore, Michael J. and Vicusi, Kip W. "Doubling the Estimated Value of Life: Results Using New Occupational Fatality Data." *Journal of Policy Analysis and Management* 7, no. 3 (1988).

Mossman, B. T. et al. "Asbestos: Scientific Developments and Implications for Public Policy." *Science* (January 1990).

Musgrave, Richard A., and Musgrave, Peggy B. *Public Finance in Theory and Practice*. New York: McGraw-Hill Book Co., 1984 and earlier editions.

Netzer, Dick. *The Economics of the Property Tax*. Washington, DC: The Brookings Institution, 1957.

————. "An Evaluation of Interjurisdictional Competition Through Economic Development Incentives," in Daphne A. Kenyon and John Kincaid, eds., *Competition Among States and Local Governments*. Washington, DC: The Urban Institute, 1991.

Nicholson, Walter. *Microeconomic Theory*. 2d ed. Hinsdale, IL: Dryden Press, 1978.

Orshansky, Mollie. "Counting the Poor: Another Look at the Poverty Profile." *Social Security Bulletin* (January 1965).

Oser, Alan S. "Altering the Rules on Who May Take Over Apartments." *New York Times*, Real Estate Section, January 16, 1994.

Pechman, Joseph. *Federal Tax Policy*. Washington, DC: The Brookings Institution, 1987.

Pollakowski, Henry O., and Wachter, Susan M. "The Effects of Land Use Constraints on Housing Prices." *Land Economics* 66, no. 3 (August 1990), pp. 315–24.

Portney, Paul. "EPA and the Evolution of Federal Regulation," in Paul Portney, ed., *Public Policies for Environmental Protection*. N.p., n.d.

Posner, Richard. *The Economics of Justice*. Cambridge, MA: Harvard University Press, 1981.

Rawls, John. *A Theory of Justice*. Cambridge, MA: Harvard University Press, 1971. December 15, 1994.

Reilly, William. "Risky Business: Life, Death, Pollution, and the Global Environment." Lecture delivered at Stanford University, January 12, 1994.

Rhoades, Stephen E. *The Economist's View of the World: Governments, Markets and Public Policy*. New York: Cambridge University Press, 1985.

Riding, Alan. "Jubilant French Students Celebrate Wage Victory." *New York Times*, April 1 1994, p. A3(N).

"Risk." *Daedalus: Journal of the American Academy of Arts and Sciences* 119, no. 4 (Fall 1990).

Schwartz, J. "Total Suspended Particulate Matter and Daily Mortality in Cincinnati, Ohio." *Environmental Health Perspectives* 102, no. 2 (February 1994), pp. 186–89.

Shaman, Diana. "Apartment Succession Rule at Issue." *New York Times*, Real Estate Section, November 12, 1993.

Siegan, Bernard H. *Land Use Without Zoning*. Lexington, MA: Lexington Books, 1972.

Smith, Adam. *The Wealth of Nations*. New York: Random House, 1965.

Smith, Lawrence B., and Tomlinson, Peter. "Rent Controls in Ontario: Roofs or Ceilings." *American Real Estate and Urban Economics Journal* 9, no. 2 (Summer 1981).

Smith, Vernon. *Papers in Experimental Economics*. New York: Cambridge University Press, 1991.

So, Frank, and Getzels, Judith, eds. *The Practice of Local Government Planning*. Washington, DC: International City Management Association, 1988.

Sternlieb, George, and Hughes, James W., eds. *Post Industrial America: Metropolitan Decline and Inter-Regional Job Shifts*. New Brunswick, NJ: Rutgers University, Center for Urban Public Policy Research, 1975.

Sternleib, George, and Sagalyn, Lynne B. *Zoning and Housing Costs*. New Brunswick, NJ: Center for Urban Public Policy Research, Rutgers University, 1972.

Stewart, Alan. "How Judge Greene's Recent Decision Changes Business Telecommunications." *Communications News* (November 1991).

Surrey, Stanley S. *Pathways to Tax Reform: The Concept of Tax Expenditures.* Cambridge, MA: Harvard University Press, 1973.

Tawney, R. H. *Religion and the Rise of Capitalism.* London: John Murray, 1994.

Tengs, Tammy, and Pliskin, Joseph et al. "A Comparison of the Cost-Effectiveness of Interventions to Prevent Premature Death." Unpublished paper presented at the 11th annual meeting of the Society for Medical Decision Making, Center for Risk Analysis, Harvard School of Public Health, October 1993.

Thompson, Wilbur. "Economic Processes and Employment Problems in Declining Metropolitan Areas," in George Sternlieb and James W. Hughes, eds., *Post Industrial America: Metropolitan Decline and Inter-Regional Job Shifts.* New Brunswick, NJ: Center for Urban Public Policy Research, Rutgers University, 1975.

Thurow, Lester. "Cash Versus In-Kind Transfers." *American Economic Review* (May 1974), pp. 190–95.

Tiebout, Charles. "A Pure Theory of Local Expenditures." *Journal of Political Economy* 64 (October 1956).

Tietenburg, Thomas H. *Environmental and Natural Resource Economics.* New York: HarperCollins Publishers, Inc., 1992.

U.S. Department of Commerce, Bureau of the Census. *Statistical Abstract of the United States, 112th ed.* Washington, DC: U.S. Government Printing Office, 1992.

U.S. Department of Commerce, Bureau of the Census. *Statistical Abstract of the United States, 113th ed.* Washington, DC: U.S. Government Printing Office, 1993.

U.S. Environmental Protection Agency. *Environmental Investment: The Cost of a Clean Environment.* EPA-230-12-90-084.

Vicusi, Kip W. "Pricing Environmental Risks." Center for the Study of American Business, Publication no. 112, June 1992.

Wagner, Lon. "Incentives Are the Ground Rules That Run This Game." *The Roanoke Times,* July 10, 1994, p. 1.

Wagner, Richard. *To Promote the General Welfare: Market Processes vs. Political Processes.* San Francisco: Pacific Research Institute for Public Policy, 1989.

Weber, Max. *The Protestant Ethic and the Spirit of Capitalism.* New York: Scribner, 1958.

Wicksteed, Phillip H. *The Commonsense of Political Economy,* reprinted by Augustus M. Kelly, New York, 1967.

Wildavsky, Aarron. "No Risk Is the Highest Risk of All," in Theodore Glickman and M. Gough, eds., *Readings in Risk, Resources for the Future.* Baltimore: n.p., 1990, pp. 190–91.

Index

About the Author

JOHN M. LEVY is a Professor in the Urban Affairs and Planning Program at Virginia Polytechnic Institute and State University (Virginia Tech). Prior to becoming an academician, he worked for a decade in urban planning and local economic development. He is the author of *Urban and Metropolitan Economics* (1985), *Economic Development Programs for Cities, Counties, and Towns* (Praeger, 1990) and *Contemporary Urban Planning* (1988, 1991, 1994).